cf. article
re Mex.
children
162

role of substance abuse
minimized?
ignored? 71, 88

Lives on the Edge

medical
model
155
103, 149
deficit - 105, 124
? devi. - 112
? approp.

role of fed. gov.

parens patriae - 197, 99, 107, 120

critiqued -
ironically, invoked - 179, 181

min. wage 180, 94

concepts of
"democracy"? -
179
"enfranchisement" - ?
177

"universal" ?
169

95 - Charles Murray
new bk.: genetic
justif.'s for poverty;
cause w/in indiv.
(cf. failure in schools);
pathological / medical
model
meritocracy

Lives on the Edge

Single Mothers and their Children in the Other America

Valerie Polakow

THE UNIVERSITY OF CHICAGO PRESS
Chicago & London

[handwritten annotations:]

Canteen mark candy

margins of society & society is "range of vision;" "ragged edge of nothing" [destitution]

67, 82, 95
73, 82
75, 92, 134
101, 133, 34
135, 140, 141, 146
148, 150, 152
162, 163
164, 165
, 72

56
59 - 60
90
97
100, 103, 121, 124, 130, 146, 149, 150, 151, 152, 153, 154, 156, 157, 158, 161, 164, 165, 166, 167

"turn us like tired children to the arms of divine Love."

177
178
181

The University of Chicago Press, Chicago 60637
The University of Chicago Press, Ltd., London
© 1993 by The University of Chicago
All rights reserved. Published 1993
Paperback edition 1994
Printed in the United States of America
02 01 00 99 98 97 96 95 94   3 4 5 6

ISBN (cloth): 0-226-67183-6
ISBN (paperback): 0-226-67184-4

Part of chapter 2 appeared as "Deconstructing the Discourse of Care: Young
Children in the Shadows of Democracy," © 1992 by The University of Chicago,
in *Reconceptualizing the Early Childhood Curriculum*, edited by Shirley A. Kessler
and Beth Blue Swadener (New York: Teachers College Press, 1992).

Library of Congress Cataloging-in-Publication Data

Polakow, Valerie.
    Lives on the edge: single mothers and their children in the other America /
Valerie Polakow.
        p.   cm.
    Includes bibliographical references and index.
    1. Single mothers—United States.   2. Poor women—United States.
    3. Poor children—United States.   I. Title.
    HQ759.45.P66   1993
    306.85′6′0973—dc20
                                                                    92–21977
                                                                    CIP

♾ The paper used in this publication meets the minimum requirements of the
American National Standard for Information Sciences—Permanence of Paper for
Printed Library Materials, ANSI Z39.48-1984.

In memory of my parents Archie and Golda Polakow

CONTENTS

ACKNOWLEDGMENTS

THIS BOOK IS A TRIBUTE to the women and the children whose lives are chronicled here, and whose voices echo through this book and throughout history. There are many others I wish to thank who have supported and encouraged the telling of this story. My research assistant, Josh Cohen, spent a critical year "in the field" with me, conducting interviews and observations as well as researching library sources; and the first class of graduate students who participated in my 1989 seminar, "Women and Children in Poverty," provided a stimulating forum for many dialogues. In addition, two of my graduate students, Alice Kopek and Sharryl Sullivan, assisted me in gathering material for some of the portraits in Part Three. My sons Shael and Sasha have been enthusiastically involved in seeing this book to a successful conclusion. Shael has scrupulously prepared the index and has offered challenging feedback and valuable suggestions for change. Sasha has been my most meticulous proofreader, assisted me in the early transcribing of tapes, and with his marvelous sense of humor kept me going through the final hectic weeks. Ton Beekman has contributed in significant ways to this book from its inception, and I am particularly appreciative of his scholarly critique and assistance in the chapters dealing with the history of childhood and the family. Begoña Garcia's ongoing assistance and her wealth of multicultural insights, have been both professionally and personally meaningful. Jerry Weiser has participated in every phase of this book; our continuing dialogues, his support, insights, incisive critique, and depth of commitment to the entire project have been invaluable to me. Finally, I am extremely grateful for the round-the-clock computer expertise of Erdwing Coronado and the fine research skills of my graduate assistant, Annette Zetterholm, who prepared the bibliographical notes. I also wish to acknowledge the timely financial support of a Spring-Summer Research Award from the Graduate School at Eastern Michigan University, which provided me with four months of uninterrupted time to complete the writing of this book.

"She was brought here last night," replied the old woman, "by the overseer's order. She was found lying in the street. She had walked some distance, for her shoes were worn to pieces; but where she came from, or where she was going to, nobody knows."

The surgeon leaned over the body and raised the left hand. "The old story," he said, shaking his head: "no wedding-ring, I see. Ah! Good night!"

The medical gentleman walked away to dinner; and the nurse, having once more applied herself to the green bottle, sat down on a low chair before the fire, and proceeded to dress the infant.

What an excellent example of the power of dress young Oliver Twist was! Wrapped in the blanket which had hitherto formed his only covering, he might have been the child of a nobleman or a beggar; it would have been hard for the haughtiest stranger to have assigned him his proper station in society. But now that he was enveloped in the old calico robes which had grown yellow in the same service, he was badged and ticketed, and fell into his place at once a parish child—the orphan of a workhouse—the humble half starved drudge—to be cuffed and buffeted through the world—despised by all and pitied by none.

Charles Dickens
Oliver Twist

THIS BOOK IS ABOUT "the old story" revisited, and it is the telling of a modern story: a story in which the central characters—poor women and their children—have their exits and their entrances in much the same way, in the shadows, on the edges. While Dickens has recreated the world of pauper children in nineteenth-century England in literary fiction, it is a strand from the tapestry of his social realism—an unfolding story of gender, class and state, decisively intersecting at the moment of Oliver's birth—that threads through the cloth of Oliver, his dead mother, and all to come. One hundred and fifty progressive years later, in the United States, we too can witness destitution if we choose to see it. The language of democracy muffles the voices of poor women and their children that echo in the invisibility of the spaces *we* have constructed for *them*. In 1991, over thirteen million children were born into and lived in poverty, but we, like the "medical gentleman" before us, "walk away to dinner."

> *We had no place to go—it was summer—school was out and DSS gave us*
> *this voucher for a motel, and you're only meant to stay there for thirty days,*
> *but there was no housing for us so they extended it. We lived for sixty-nine*
> *days in that motel—DSS put us there—they said there was nothing else . . .*
> *There were rats and roaches. I called the health department and told them*
> *but they never came . . . Outside they were dealing drugs and there were*
> *prostitutes walking up and down . . . My children just lost their personali-*
> *ties—my eight-year-old stopped eating.*

Christy's struggle and sense of desperation is an increasingly common experience among poor, single mothers, part of the feminized poor whose children are increasingly becoming members of a new infantilization-of-poverty trend, where both mothers and children stand alone on the margins of democracy—dispossessed citizens with few opportunities to build a viable future.

> *Seven-year-old Heather was easy to identify as a "problem" second grader*
> *as she sat at her desk pushed out in the hallway. The children passing by told*
> *me that they were not allowed to speak to her; neither was she allowed to*
> *speak to anyone. She could not go to recess, nor eat lunch with the others in*
> *the cafeteria anymore. The teacher, Mrs. Mack, came outside: "This child*
> *just does not know the difference between right and wrong—she absolutely*

does not belong in a normal classroom with normal children." Heather, now being sent to the principal's office, awkwardly slips in her flip-flops three sizes too big for her as she walks down the corridor in the middle of a snowy December, dressed in a summer blouse several sizes too small and a long flimsy skirt. What had Heather done? "I've given up on this child—she's socially dysfunctional—three times now we've caught her stealing free lunch and storing it in her desk to take home!"

Heather's school crime was indeed noteworthy. The child of a single mother, she lived with her sister and mother in a trailer park. They all appeared chronically hungry, particularly when food stamps ran out before the end of the month. Apparently Heather had been caught stealing extra free lunch on three Fridays, knowing that she and her sister would have to wait until Monday for their next free meals.

What do childhood and motherhood mean to citizens of the other America? What do they mean to those living in the America of privilege, who make policies about the *other* motherhood and the *other* childhood?[1] What are the prevailing historical and cultural images of childhood, the myths of motherhood and of the family, and, most significantly, the place of private wealth and public responsibility? In attempting to decode these meanings, visible and invisible, and to prise apart the assumptions and taken-for-granted practices upon which our own definitions of identity and responsibility rest, we begin to see how our ways of seeing and thinking about the family and child development go to the heart of our own anthropology of self. To construct a language of women and children in poverty is to speak a shadow language of patriarchy and domestic ideology, of power and control and privilege, which embeds histories of discrimination.

The profoundly unequal and undemocratic landscape that the feminization and growing infantilization of poverty have created in the United States has given rise to another discourse—a discourse of otherness. *Those living out there in the unnamed landscapes, are placeless, inhabiting other lifeworlds.* Out of this landscape of otherness we have constituted a discourse of concealment that fails to name the full face of poverty, that allows the horrors of public indifference to make possible a "social asphyxia" described by Victor Hugo in 1862, in his preface to *Les Misérables,* as "the ruin of woman by starvation, and the atrophy of childhood by physical and spiritual night." Poverty has always been with us in the West and the New World. The difference in 1991 is that western Europe has largely eradicated the destitution of single mothers and their children; the United States has not.

Poverty, as Michael Katz points out, "no longer is natural; it is a social product." In a wealthy, powerful, industrialized society, which generates surpluses, "poverty becomes not the product of scarcity, but of political economy.[2] Yet poverty has been artfully reconfigured as a social/cultural/ psychological pathology, corroborated by a public educational discourse of deficiency and remediation. It is otherness that is at risk, reframed as an individual or minority problem in need of redress. The renaming and the redefining of the worlds of those who are destitute permit public denial of our social responsibility for poor mothers and their children. For if Dostoyevsky is right and each of us is responsible for everything and to every human being,[3] where are our commitments to the existential futures of children as we approach the twenty-first century?

This question forms the backdrop to my book, as I attempt to unpack the multiple layers of historical and contemporary images, to deconstruct the discourses and practices that have imperiled so many lives and continue to do so. Since this book addresses the lives of single mothers and their children, it reveals only part of the "social asphyxia" that continues to stain so many lives of color, of single men, of married couples, of the aged. But slices of life must be looked at in microscopic ways to illuminate the existential experiences of dailiness—the patterns that are present, the "nuts and bolts" of suffering and survival. I have chosen to tell the story of one vulnerable and growing group of people, for I too am a mother. I have been profoundly affected by the experience of researching and writing this book, realizing how little existential distance separates my life as a mother from that of the mothers and children whose lives are chronicled here. Yet the geography of privilege is all-encompassing—and living on the side of privilege in the first America puts one in a world apart from the grim contingency of life on the edges in the other America.

In the following chapters I explore the texture of life of poor mothers and their children, first by grounding the present situation historically and pointing to the early ascription of deviant, *other* status that emerges against the horizon of "normalized" motherhood and family images. The dominant images are Western in origin and Eurocentric in tradition. I begin by tracing that monocultural history which until now has dominated public sensibilities and public policies. To explore what we have made of childhood history and what we continue to make of childhood's future is also to look with clear eyes at a swelling tide of homelessness and poverty, of abandonment and abuse at the cusp of the twenty-first century. This necessitates decoding our own myths of democracy and enlightened progress as one out of four infants, one out of five children, and one out of two single mothers[4] already live in destitution, and as thousands more stand on the edge of a landscape that condemns them, like young Oliver Twist, to their "proper station" in society; for in making them *other,* we too have badged and ticketed them.

In portraying daily existence, both of the past and of the present, stained with injustice and constrained by the inequities of gender, class, and color, I attempt to challenge the enduring legacy of these images. I have written this book with the hope of helping to build a different set of images—images that might lead us to a different way of seeing, to a different praxis. As Toni Morrison reminds us in *The Bluest Eye,* "there is really nothing more to say—except why. But since why is difficult to handle, one must take refuge in how."[5]

Part
One

IN THE FOLLOWING TWO CHAPTERS the historical images of childhood and the family are discussed as they have developed in western Europe, including Britain, and in North America. The prevailing historical constructs of bourgeois motherhood and the family, as well as the romantic conceptions of childhood are explored in order to understand the historical place occupied by single mothers and their children—a zone of deviance and moral suspicion. Deconstructing the myths of childhood, of the family, and of motherhood leads us to the ideology of care and the far-reaching implications this ideology has wielded for all women, though it is poor, single mothers who have suffered the most pernicious public-policy consequences. Childhood too emerges as a historical space, stained by abuse and power and muted by regulation. Children of all classes suffered; yet poor children, caught in the intersecting webs of scarcity and hunger, of immigration, of rapid urbanization and industrialization, became early victims of the state.

Childhood Revisited

One day a serf boy, a little child of eight, threw a stone in play and hurt the paw of the general's favourite hound. "Why is my favourite dog lame?" He is told that the boy threw a stone that hurt the dog's paw. "So you did it." The general looked the child up and down. "Take him." He was taken—taken from his mother and kept shut up all night. Early that morning the general comes out on horseback, with the hounds, his dependents, dog-boys, and huntsmen, all mounted around him in full hunting parade. The servants are summoned for their edification, and in front of them all stands the mother of the child. The child is brought from the lock-up. It's a gloomy cold, foggy autumn day, a capital day for hunting. The general orders the child to be undressed; the child is stripped naked. He shivers, numb with terror, not daring to cry . . . "Make him run," commands the general. "Run! Run!" shout the dog-boys. The boy runs . . . "At him!" yells the general, and he sets the whole pack of hounds on the child.

> Fyodor Dostoyevsky
> *The Brothers Karamazov*

DOSTOYEVSKY CHRONICLES THE SUFFERING of children—both of the poor and the privileged—as Ivan Karamazov questions the absurdity of a universe in which children are the victims of adult power and brutality, of the ideals of a civilization run amok. "And if the sufferings of children go to swell the sum of sufferings which was necessary to pay for truth, then I protest that the truth is not worth such a price," he tells his brother Alyosha.[1] But childhood has always been a historical space of suffering and abuse, and the formation of an obedient and docile child has taken many forms. The body of the child has become the site where the most intimate social practices have been linked to the apparatus of parental and state power.[2] The poorer the child, the more dramatic that child's vulnerability.

Lloyd DeMause has argued that "the history of childhood is a nightmare from which we have only recently begun to awaken," and that the further back in history we delve, the worse the levels of abandonment, brutality, abuse, and terror.[3] Boswell's panoramic study of the abandonment of children from late antiquity to the Renaissance reveals how widespread the practice was among parents of all social classes. It was the poor who were driven to abandon their infants most frequently, for many were illegitimate, and during the medieval period, infant deformity—a particular cause for abandonment—was viewed by the church as a visible consequence of parental incontinence.[4] While our ways of seeing childhood have changed—from its apparent placelessness in the medieval consciousness, to a Puritan and, later, Evangelical "break the will if you would not damn the child" orientation, to a seemingly progressive management-and-compliance perspective in the twentieth century—the conquest of the body and the domestication of the mind have remained dominant themes in the developing concept of childhood. Childhood, however, is not and never has been a timeless developmental essence that stands above history and class and culture and religion; rather it is a social product, rooted in diverse ways of seeing self, family, motherhood and fatherhood, and one's place in the social order.

In trying to trace the historical sensibilities of parents and other adults toward children, we return to the question of the meaning of childhood. What images of childhood prevailed in centuries past? Was there an idea of childhood as a distinctive phase of development? Philippe Ariès's seminal work *Centuries of Childhood* takes a sociohistorical view of both childhood and family life, as Ariès questions the notion of any constructed social space for childhood in the medieval world.[5] Drawing on demographic evidence, he argues that high infant mortality rates deadened parental sensibilities toward their children, leaving children vulnerable to abandonment. Ariès claims that there was no distinctive "idea" of childhood. Early infancy was recognized, only to be followed by a period of miniature adulthood, in which adults and children shared the same world—a world in which sexual play with young children was common, documented particularly among the nobility. As late as the seventeenth century, a distinctive terrain of psychological and developmental space had not yet been charted. J. H. Plumb supports this view, seeing children as "victims of time," of place, of the brutality and indifference that characterized human relations in the premodern world.[6] Prior to the Enlightenment, which marked a shift in such sensibilities, it was rare to see children depicted as children in either literature or art.

In the premodern world, both the young and adults tended to live without privacy, without personal space.[7] People lived before the eyes of others, in boundaryless public spaces. Most peasant households in the Middle Ages shared not only the same room, but also the same large, makeshift bed, to which visiting strangers would be invited.[8] Even in the houses of the nobility, and later of the rich merchants, where diverse members of the household were accommodated, private space as a demarcation of the boundaries between self and other did not exist. People ate, slept, labored, and danced in general-purpose rooms. As Ariès writes, "It is easy to imagine the promiscuity which reigned in those rooms where nobody could be alone . . . , where several couples and several groups of boys and girls slept together (not to speak of the servants, of whom at least some must have slept beside their masters, setting up beds which were still collapsible in the room . . .)."[9] Robert Darnton, too, describes how "whole families crowded into one or two beds and surrounded themselves with livestock to keep warm."[10] Martine Segalen points out that adults and children shared a common world and that because there was no distinctive spatial demarcation of the self, there was also no distinctive social space for childhood in either the medieval or the Renaissance periods.[11]

Both women and children were properties of men. Under a patriarchal structure in which fathers and husbands maintained exclusive economic and legal authority, the nonboundary spatial configurations symbolized ownership of the body space of both children and their mothers. The lives of numerous female saints illustrate their choice of virginity as an act of freedom—an escape from male control of the body.[12] St. Augustine, one of the most authoritative of medieval theologians, claimed that "the innocence of children is in the helplessness of their bodies, rather than any quality of soul."[13] He demanded the suppression of concupiscence, thereby justifying brutal punishment of the body of the child. "If left to do what he [the child] wants," St. Augustine maintained, "there is no crime he will not plunge into."[14]

The conquest and subjection of the body of the child have formed part of what Alice Miller describes as a "poisonous pedagogy" that masquerades under the guise of "For your own good." Physical abuse is steeped in a long history of legitimated power and control through the subjugation of the body—forms of "biopower," which Foucault argues are part of a disciplinary technology of regulation aimed at creating "docile bodies."[16] Sulzer, an eighteenth-century German pedagogue, put it this way: "One of the advantages of these early years is that then force and compulsion can be used. Over the years, children forget everything that happened to them in early childhood. If their wills can be broken at this time, they will never remember afterwards that they had a will."[17] This legacy of a "poisonous pedagogy," which can be traced to the Puritans in colonial America, later found strong support in the Evangelical movement. Susanna Wesley, stern mother of John (the leader of the Evangelical Revival and founder of the Methodist Church), advised him to "break the will, if you would not damn the child . . . make him do as he is bid, if you whip him ten times running to effect it."[18] John and Elizabeth Newson argue that the Evangelical movement, despite its minority status, cast a moral net over pedagogy; conquering the will of children as early as possible was deemed a necessary foundation for a religious education.[19] This deity-centered pedagogy saw the subjugation of the body as the pathway to the proper formation of mind.

While the discourse changed in the early part of the twentieth century to one of development and compliance, the conquest of the body and the domestication of the mind have remained critical pedagogical imperatives for a child's early years. Thus, although the construction of childhood has taken many forms, the body of the child has remained the site of subjugation,[20] where the most invasive practices have become linked to parental, pedagogical, and state power, concealing and legitimating continuing violence against the young. And in the microworld of the child, Dostoyevsky continues to remind us, benevolence and malevolence rest in the power structure of the adult world. "I've collected a great, great deal about Russian children," Ivan tells his brother Alyosha. "You see, I must repeat again, it is a peculiar characteristic of many people, this love of torturing children, and children only. To all other types of humanity these torturers behave mildly and benevolently, like cultivated and humane Europeans; but they are very fond of tormenting children, even fond of children themselves in that sense."[21]

As we turn toward the twentieth century, we do not witness a progressive humanization in attitudes toward children, as anticipated by DeMause.[22] Current statistics indicate that both sexual and physical abuse are widespread experiences of childhood; it is reported that 22 percent of American adults have been victims of child sexual abuse.[23] Yet the taboo on probing interfamily abuse and violence is strong. Questions about the physical punishment of children are not often asked, Philip Greven points out, for it is a legitimated and rationalized violence which in turn "reveals the power of the taboo against our acknowledgment of the childhood sufferings experienced by so many people, generation after generation." In exploring what he terms the apocalyptic impulse in American Protestantism, Greven questions the impact of physical punishment on both private and public aspects of American culture. He suggests that "physical punishment of children appears to be one of the subjects in America that are still profoundly disturbing, because they are too deeply rooted in our individual and our collective psyches to be confronted directly."[24] Physical punishment is still widely used as a legitimate form of parental discipline and is permitted within public schools in many states as an acceptable method of control. It is estimated that every year twenty thousand children receive injuries from corporal punishment in school that are serious enough to require medical attention.[25] Yet assaults on children are determined abusive only when severe bodily harm results.

The construct of childhood and the disciplinary technology that have prevailed from medieval to modern times reveal patterns of power, control, brutality, and indifference to the sensibilities of children despite a growing discourse about childhood as a separate state to be nurtured. Clearly, childhood for some *has* been a pleasant idyll, a playful and joyous landscape painted on a Dylan Thomas canvas, "green and carefree famous among the barns/About the happy yard and singing as the farm was home,"[26] where parents cherished their children and where to grow up was an invitation to self-formation, to begin, in Merleau-Ponty's words, "a new personal history."[27] But the invitation to self-formation, to the discovery of an open future, was not granted to many children in ages past, nor in our time. There have of course been competing discourses in our Western history that have urged a pedagogy of compassion and gentleness, such as we see in a Tolstoy or a Froebel; but as we begin to deconstruct the central themes of childhood history, we find not light but pervasive shade. The progressivist myth of childhood improving with each successive century is disputed by historians such as J. H. Plumb and John Demos; and in particular by Philip Greven, who demonstrates how the discourse of concealment has operated with such efficiency and continued the ongoing assault on young lives. Educational and theological discourses too have played a vital role in eclipsing patterns of abuse. We must confront the knowledge revealed by a deconstructed childhood in order to see how easily brutality toward children has been rationalized. Powerlessness and silence are willing collaborators with those who exploit the vulnerable and voiceless among us.

While the dark side of childhood remains dark for all children who have endured the violence of a poisonous pedagogy—poor and privileged alike—it is the experiences of children who have lived on the edges of the dark side that are the focus of this discussion. Their young lives have been largely eclipsed in the pages of development and the romantic, post-Rousseau images of the discovery of childhood, as a separate state to be nurtured and tended, a garden of blossoming growth. Those romantic sensibilities have avoided the scorched ground on which poor children lived out a stunted *other* childhood, bounded by the horizons of class and ousted from the garden of privilege.

The Other Childhood: Child Labor in Britain and America

"It is good when it happens," say the children,
   "that we die before our time" . . .

"For oh," say the children, "we are weary,
   And we cannot run or leap;
If we cared for any meadows, it were merely
   to drop down in them and sleep.
Our knees tremble sorely in the stooping,
   We fall upon our faces, trying to go;
And underneath our heavy eyelids drooping
   The reddest flower would look as pale as snow
      For, all day, we drag our burden tiring
      Through the coal-dark, underground;
Or, all day, we drive the wheels of iron
   In the factories, round and round."

Elizabeth Barrett Browning
The Cry of the Children

Child labor is an enduring symbol of the harshness and brutality of the Industrial Revolution; from Elizabeth Barrett Browning's impassioned "Cry of the Children" to Engels's *Childhood in the Potteries,* in which he reports, "Many of the children are pale. Their eyes are inflamed and they often go blind for weeks at a time. They suffer also from violent nausea, vomiting, coughs, colds and rheumatism."[28]

In 1835, fifty-six thousand children under the age of thirteen were employed in British textile factories. If we add to that the thousands of thirteen- and fourteen-year-olds, we see that children accounted for over 20 percent of the work force in the textile factories. Several thousand more children labored in workshops and in the metal, machinery, and pottery industries.[29] Paul Mantoux shows that child labor in England was an integral part of the British economy, for which the early lives of poor children were sacrificed. Since adult male workers found the discipline of the textile factory intolerable, women and children had to be hired to fill the labor pool. Many of the children, eagerly supplied by parishes, were pauper apprentices; sometimes their only payment was food or lodging.

> Regular bargains, beneficial to both parties if not to the children, who were dealt with as mere merchandise, were entered into between the spinners on the one hand and the Poor Law authorities on the other. Lots of fifty, eighty or a hundred children were supplied and sent like cattle to the factory, where they remained imprisoned for many years to come. Certain parishes drove even better bargains and stipulated that the buyer should take idiots in the proportion of one to every twenty children sent.[30]

These pauper children—among the weavers in the North and the Southwest of England, children as young as four years old were sent to work as soon as they were deemed capable of obedience and attention—were bound over as apprentices for at least seven years and often until they were twenty-one. Their small sizes and their delicate fingers were well suited for certain processes. As Mantoux notes, "their weakness made them docile, and they were more easily reduced to a state of passive obedience than grown men." They were also cheap; their wage varied between a third and a sixth of an adult wage. Accidents at the factories were common and discipline was brutal; children were whipped, many so exhausted that they would fall asleep at the machines, and the "tale never ended of fingers cut off and limbs crushed in the wheels."[31]

While the opposition to child labor that emerged in England appeared to focus on children's well-being, it frequently was part of a discourse that involved either the "social question" of a large population of "morally unfit" pauper children or the economic necessity for children in the labor force, particularly the textile industry under early industrial capitalism. The factory movement, for example, campaigned not so much against child labor as for its regulation, and this formed part of a general effort by primarily adult male workers to secure better wages and working hours. It was the Romantics—Wordsworth, Coleridge and others—who saw in industrialization the blight of civilization, and promoted an idyll of a playful childhood in the English country air, such as we read in Wordsworth's *The Prelude* (book 1):

> Oh, many a time have I, a five year's child,
> In a small mill-race severed from his stream,
> Made one long bathing of a summer day;
> Basked in the sun, and plunged and basked again . . .

This idyllic vision influenced the Tory humanitarians and philanthropists, who diluted the idyll considerably for its pauper recipients. One of the leading philanthropists of the day, the Earl of Shaftesbury, an active and influential campaigner on the duty of English society to its children, was at the same time one of the driving forces behind Britain's shameful child migrant system in which destitute children, some as young as four years old, were shipped out as indentured servants to the Colonies.[32] This system was rationalized as a healthy farm life in the countryside of Canada for urban paupers! While basking and bathing were reserved for the children of the professional classes and the landed gentry, it was decided that pauper children deserved to labor in healthier surroundings, even if shipped thousands of miles away, all alone at the youngest of ages, to escape the moral depravity of urban blight.

When we examine the treatment of children during the industrial revolution, we are confronted once again with a generalized indifference toward the suffering of the working poor. Children were a visible feature of the "social asphyxiation" of poverty and its central victims under industrial capitalism. If not condemned to the world of the factory or the workhouse, poor children, illegitimate children, urchins or "street arabs," and children from "morally depraved" families were all prime candidates for export to the colonies. "I conceive that London has become too full of children," proclaimed R. J. Chambers, a metropolitan magistrate in 1826. "There has been a great increase of juvenile offences . . . I therefore suggest emigration as a remedy."[33]

In the eighteenth century, child migration was also tied to the exportation of convicted felons, and under common law an offender as young as seven years old could be prosecuted. Britain began shipping its poor children to America in 1618—the first group of orphans and urchins arrived in Richmond, Virginia, in that year—and later exports went to Canada, Australia, and other outposts of the Empire. Between 1800 and 1850, five hundred to one thousand children a year were shipped overseas, primarily to Australia. When the gold rush began in the 1860s, Canada became a favored site. Ironically, the era of the child-savers also began during this period. The philanthropists who were outspoken in their criticism of child labor were also empire builders, and as they turned to Canada between 1870 and 1925, another hundred thousand children were sent over.[34]

In colonial America, industrial child labor began in the late eighteenth century. Two systems were developed for the recruitment of children to the factory. Samuel Slater's model, following the English plan, employed the entire family; every member above the age of seven worked from sunrise to sunset six days a week. In the other model, the parents remained on the farm while the laboring children were boarded out. This practice became common after the 1820s in Maine, Massachusetts, and New Hampshire, where large textile factories employed older girls. The employment of children in factories redefined child labor in North America in terms of the sanctity of work and the fear of "the idle." In the factories, children were a distinct and classified labor force. New machinery estimated and measured their efficiency. We read how John Baxter advertised his machines with six spindles as being easily turned by "children of from five to ten years of age," whereas the twelve-spindle machine would require "girls from ten to twenty." While minimal protection laws existed regarding indentured child apprentices and servants, factory owners were under no obligation to teach a child laborer a trade or to provide general education. In the late 1700s the contribution of little children to the American economy was celebrated as the nation's leaders "struggled to secure national protection for infant industries, but did not find it necessary to protect the 'little fingers' that worked them."[35]

The abuse of children, whether in factories or as indentured servants, was a common feature of poor children's lives during both the colonial and industrial periods of America. Not only were slave children sold, but so, too, were indentured servant children, as we see in the advertisements of the time:[36]

> Bargains, black and white.
> (*Boston Evening Post,* October 21, 1751.)

and

> To be sold by Thomas Overrend, at the
> Drawbridge, Two white Boys and a Negro Lad;
> all about fourteen Years of Age. Also very
> good Lime juice, by the Hogshead or Gallon.
> (*Pennsylvania Gazette,* April 3, 1760.)

The language of such advertisements fashions such a clear portrait of the "commoditization" of both pauper and slave children; their bodies compete with lime juice as their race and class strip them of their humanity.

And what of the slave children, who shared with their parents the brutality of the slave ships and the degradation of the plantations? Due to plantation owners' practice of selling slave mothers "with their increase," young children under the age of ten generally remained with their mothers and accompanied them to the field, or were taken care of by older female slaves; on the large plantations they often lived with both parents in a slave household unit.[37] Parents and children, however, were frequently separated when estates were divided among heirs, or when slave traders purchased and sold slaves on their river journeys. One such harrowing story is recounted by William Wells Brown, a slave assistant to a slave trader:

> He bought a number of slaves as he passed the different farms and villages . . . he purchased a woman who had a child in her arms, appearing to be four or five weeks old . . . Soon after we left St Charles, the young child grew very cross, and kept up a noise during the greater part of the day. Mr Walker complained of its crying several times, and told the mother to stop the child's d—d noise, or he would. The woman tried to keep the child from crying but could not. We put up at night with an acquaintance of Mr Walker, and in the morning, just as we were about to start, the child again commenced crying. Walker stepped up to her, and told her to give the child to him. The mother tremblingly obeyed. He took the child by one arm, as you would a cat by the leg, walked into the house, and said to the lady, "Madam, I will make you a present of this little nigger; it keeps such a noise that I can't bear it." "Thank you, sir," said the lady. The mother as soon as she saw that her child was to be left, ran up to Mr Walker, and falling upon her knees begged him to let her have her child; she clung around his legs, and cried, "Oh, my child! my child! master, do let me have my child! oh, do, do, do. I will stop its crying if you will only let me have it again." When I saw this woman crying for her child so piteously, a shudder,—a feeling akin to horror, shot through my frame.[38]

In this story, much is told and much is not told about the worlds of slaves and their masters in the early 1800s. The brutal indifference to the life of the child, the desperation and powerlessness of the mother, the power structure that legitimated such a tearing apart of infant from mother, and the acquiescence of the white woman, also probably a mother, in the acceptance of a seized and stolen child. What life lay in store for that black slave baby in the new house? Who would rear him? When would he begin his slave childhood in the house? How was he viewed? As a bedraggled animal? A human child? What were the differential sensibilities that the white mother would exercise in terms of her own babies and this cast-off child?

These narratives of the lifeworlds of children speak not only to their experiences but, more significantly, to the way in which an Anglo-American attitude of indifference toward the lives of pauper, poor, and slave children characterized the eighteenth and nineteenth centuries. These attitudes, as

I will argue throughout the book, continue in our time. The callous indifference that eroded countless children's lives coexisted with the romantic vision of childhood that increasingly came to dominate middle-class sensibilities. In order to explore this further, it is instructive to glance across the Continent, through the windows of nineteenth-century France, brimming with postrevolutionary fervor, sparkling with the enlightened romanticism of Rousseau's images of childhood. Once again the childhood of "the noble savage" is far removed from the grim realities of a destitute childhood.

France's Social Question and the Discarding of the Young

Five years old! It will be said that's hard to believe, but it's true; social suffering can begin at any age . . . Cosette was made to run errands, sweep the rooms, the yard, the street, wash the dishes, and even carry heavy loads. The Thenardiers felt doubly authorized to treat her this way, as the mother, who still remained at Montreuil-sur-mer, began to be remiss in her payments. Some months remained due.

Had this mother returned to Montfermeil at the end of these three years, she would not have known her child. Cosette, so fresh and pretty when she came to that house, was now thin and pale. She had a peculiarly restless air. A sneak! said the Thenardiers.

Injustice had made her sullen, and misery had made her ugly. Only her eyes remained beautiful, and they were painful to look at, because, large as they were, they seemed to increase the sadness.

It was harrowing to see the poor child, in winter, not yet six years old, shivering under the tatters of what was once a calico dress, sweeping the street before daylight with an enormous broom in her little red hands and tears in her large eyes.

In the neighborhood she was called the Lark. People like figurative names and were happy to give a nickname to this child, no larger than a bird, trembling, frightened, and shivering, first to wake every morning in the house and the village, always in the street or in the fields before dawn.

Except that the poor lark never sang.

Victor Hugo
Les Misérables

In her illuminating study of abandoned children in nineteenth-century France, Rachel Fuchs argues that the widespread abandonment of infants and young children was part of the very fabric of the culture and the corresponding lifestyles of the poor and destitute. For mothers it was "a radical solution to the social psychological, and above all economic pressures the woman faced . . . They abandoned the baby, because to keep the infant meant loss of job, income and even life for them and the child."[39] We read in Hugo's *Les Misérables* how Fantine is forced to abandon her little daughter Cosette in this way.

Abandonment constituted part of the "social question" that preoccupied France as late as the eighteenth and nineteenth centuries; for the rising tide of destitute abandoned children threatened the state as they grew up to form the "dangerous classes." The desperate conditions of poor mothers and their children illuminate not only state policies toward children but also "nineteenth-century French attitudes toward unwed mothers, illegitimate children, working class and middle class families, and the peasantry."[40] Social economists saw all forms of deviance as having their origins in the poor and uneducated population. H. A. Fregier, in 1840, contended that "the poor and vicious classes always have been and always will be the most fertile crucible for all categories of wrongdoers; it is these classes that we designate more specifically as the dangerous classes."[41]

The late eighteenth century saw a rise in population and growing rates of illegitimacy, so starvation threatened both the rural and the urban poor and abandonment became a problem of enormous magnitude. Hence France began to develop a state policy for receiving and maintaining destitute and unwanted children. Influenced by the secular reformers, a national, secular, state-supported form of public assistance was initiated. The constitution of 1791 proclaimed that the task of the nation was to raise abandoned children and to make useful citizens by training them for the military, for agriculture, and for populating the colonies. Prostitution and vagabondage were the vices most feared by the authorities. Because abandoned children were believed to "carry the most dangerous instincts in their hearts," France's public policy for children developed two strategies: the first institutionalized abandonment through the notorious "tour," and the second disposed of disposable children through the wetnurse institution.[42]

The "tour"—a revolving cylindrical box in which mothers placed their babies—was built into the walls of hospices and foundling hospitals, a stark symbol of anonymity. It was stipulated by decree in 1811 that each hospice should have one. The cradle swiveled so that the mother who deposited the baby from the street could not be seen on the inside, and a bell would be sounded to announce that a baby had been dropped. Thus "the tour was deaf, dumb and blind. The total anonymity of the mother and baby was assured, unless the mother or her messenger put some identifying tag or note on the infant."[43] This anonymity was believed necessary to avoid abortion and infanticide, but it was controversial since many authorities believed it encouraged immorality and irresponsibility on the part of destitute women. The tour, in essence, centralized child abandonment. It regulated the process by which the state took control of pauper children and fashioned them into useful capital for the state. When its controversial practice was discontinued, French child policy continued to permit the "displacement" of babies to the countryside.

In 1780, one year after the French Revolution, Lieutenant Lenoir noted that of the twenty-one thousand babies born in Paris that year, nineteen thousand were sent away to wetnurses outside the city. The institutionalization of the wetnurses, women exploited by their own grinding poverty and, in turn, often abusive to their charges, created a new structure for abandonment, not restricted to destitute babies. The use of wetnurses was a routine practice among all social classes. The more privileged the child, the better-quality milk and care received, and the more hygienic the wetnurses. The babies of the working poor who survived the rigors of the trip to the countryside (5–15 percent died en route) were "packed like sardines, with hardly any protection, while the unfortunate nurses were obliged to follow them on foot. Exposed to the cold or heat, to the wind and rain, they received only the milk heated by the fatigue and hunger of the nurses."[44]

Police reports of the time document frequent accidents—babies lost in falls off carts, crushed under wheels—and a general indifference to their young lives on the part of the transportation agents, the middlemen, and even the pauper women barely able to survive themselves. Elizabeth Badinter cites numerous reports from the Paris and Lyons records which describe agents losing count of their charges, drivers falling asleep, nameless infants misplaced and never found. Physicians reporting the health problems of these infants regularly accused the wetnurses of laziness, ignorance, sin, and uncleanliness. Only one such physician, Jean-Emanuel Gilibert, pointed to the deplorable conditions of the wetnurses themselves, whom he described as "women dulled by extreme poverty, living in hovels." Many of these destitute single women suffered from smallpox, were covered with scars, and had either lost their own babies or had abandoned them in order to secure a livelihood as a wetnurse. The typical rural wetnurse was forced by circumstance to work all day in the fields, while the child was "left to himself, drowning in his own excrement, bound like a criminal, devoured by mosquitoes."[45]

Thus were poor women and poor babies locked together in a doomed embrace; for the wetnurses, standing at the cusp of a system of discarded children, were themselves the victimized agents of indifference and abandonment. The poorer the natural mother, the more likely her baby would fall victim to abject poverty in the hovel of another wetnurse. Once again, the full horror of young lives in poverty emerges, this time not through the brutality of child labor and indentured servitude, but in the destitution of a discarded infancy. As Fuchs shows us, the way in which a state cares for the young is an essential clue to understanding the fabric of the society itself. Brief snapshots of historical policies toward poor children reveal their existential placelessness, part of a wider, all-encompassing net that trapped the poor in misery and degradation.[46] As we have seen, Britain in the seventeenth century developed an ingenious child-labor system for the Empire, shipping off its surplus pauper children and street urchins to the distant colonies. Colonial America instituted not only the brutality of slavery but child labor and indentured child servitude as well. Nineteenth-century France institutionalized state abandonment of the destitute infants who carried the "dangerous instincts in their hearts." And where were the mothers of these children as they were sent to the colonies, to distant countrysides, to the textile mills, to the streets? Like Oliver's mother, like Cosette's mother, like the little serf boy's mother forced to watch the hunt of her child, like the slave infant's mother whose child was ripped from her breast, poor and destitute mothers have been participants in and witnesses to the discarding or destruction of their own children. What do care and motherhood mean in such a context? As we unveil the forms of life that characterized the dailiness of poverty, mothering emerges as a set of practices shaped both by economic conditions and state policies.[47] Attitudes toward childhood and the family emerge that are tinted by the lens of class, colored by the prism of race and gender, and, above all, dulled by the haziness of a history that has concealed rather than revealed the eroded texts of children's lives.

But children's lives have always been inextricably entwined with their mothers' lives; both women and children have shared in different ways the fate of the voiceless. We also need to look at the social spaces in which women and children have been placed; regulated by patriarchal authority, by religion, and by the state, their lives have been lived under surveillance, submission, and often the contestation of power. When mothers are deserted, mistreated, or made destitute, so too are their children. Such mothers constitute the gray zone, against which the twilight of the moral order fades; for moral and physical poverty are seen as interchangeable. In more modern terminology, single-parent families are "broken" families, deviant, dysfunctional, forming part of a pervasive social pathology, evaluated against a norm of the two-parent companionate family. But is that norm part of an enduring myth that serves to legitimate the patriarchal power structure of family and state, against which single mothers have been juxtaposed, judged, and condemned? Historically, single mothers have been made incomplete mothers as they have failed to fulfill the obligations of a wife, of a "normalized" family life, and of a "proper" motherhood.

2

Motherhood and the Ideology of Care

Woman was made specially to please man; if the latter must please her in turn, it is a less direct necessity; his merit consists in his strength, he pleases by that fact alone. This is not the law of love, I grant; but it is the law of nature, which is antecedent even to love. If woman is formed to please and to live in subjection, she must render herself agreeable to man instead of provoking his wrath; her strength lies in her charms . . . She is the bond which connects the children with their father; she alone can make him love them and inspire him with confidence to call them his own. What tenderness and care must she not exert to preserve unity in the family!

Jean-Jacques Rousseau
Emile

THE LAW OF NATURE AND THE IDEOLOGY OF CARE; his and hers; the public space and the private domestic sphere; the stable enduring family with tender mother at center stage; she, the mainstay of civilization, the nestmaker, the bearer of the burden of the inner world. Have we yet separated the idea of family from patriarchy? For if women and children are still "formed to please," what landscape do incomplete mothers occupy—those who have transgressed the laws of nature and of public morality?

The family, like childhood, has never been a stable structure, an unchanging essence, but rather is a social construct which, like childhood, has undergone dramatic historical shifts, even if our "metanarratives" persist to unusually strong degrees, in maintaining stable enduring images of the natural order of things.[1] During the past three centuries American families have experienced a series of far-reaching "domestic revolutions" that have fundamentally transformed family structure and organization, demographic characteristics and emotional dynamics. The claim that the family as a social institution has been most resistant to change, "an island of stability in a sea of social, political, and economic change," is, as Steven Mintz and Susan Kellogg remind us, "largely an illusion."[2] While families have changed in profound ways, particular myths of *the family* and consequently of motherhood have endured, myths that have placed mother in a specific domestic and social space in relation to husband, children, and the state. It is these myths of "normalized motherhood" that are unpacked in this chapter, because in order to understand the social space in which poor, single mothers have been placed, it is necessary to trace the contours of a "normalized" motherhood against which "deviant" mothers are measured.

The Eurocentric Family Legacy

Family, as both a theological and secular construct, has been produced and reproduced throughout our Western history by theologians, social scientists and the state as a monolithic, homogeneous, natural form of life. Unmodified dogmas have thus been created, such as the assumed historical durability of emotional bonding within families, even though "in our peasant predecessors, . . . family membership was evanescent, familial relationships brief, intermittent and presumably unstable."[3] Furthermore, as Michael Mitterauer and Reinhard Sieder point out, in central Europe the concept of family as a unit of husband, wife, and children did not even exist as a single expression in the German language before the eighteenth century. The term *Paterfamilias* (father of the family) expresses not a genealogical bond but a structure of authority in which the male head was given title to his wife, his children, his servants, and their children. In short, throughout the Middle Ages into early modern times "family" largely meant patriarchy, with western Europe (a little earlier than central Europe) shifting to the concept of a nuclear unit during the Enlightenment.[4]

Even as the modern concept of the nuclear family emerged, however, it was limited and class specific; for only those who owned their own houses—such as the nobility, the burghers, and the rich peasants—were permitted to have families. Families were not an entitlement for university lecturers, journeymen, servants, apprentices, farmhands, or other landless peasants. Hence the legal structure of the family, tied to land ownership and inheritance through the father, led to late marriages of short duration, illegitimate births, and high infant mortality, which in turn contributed to rampant mobility, urban disorder, and destitution as large numbers of propertyless men and women flocked to the growing cities or took to the woods. The instability of the family and of a godless spiritual order contributed to the disaffection of the Puritans, who in their escape to the New World sought to reestablish a godly family in the New World.[5]

The New World Family as a Little Commonwealth

The Puritan family was organized as a nuclear unit, "a little common-wealth,"[6] in which fathers as masters owned the property and represented the household in politics. Each household received one vote cast by father; a wife was permitted to represent the household only if widowed or in her husband's absence. Both church and legal doctrine made it the duty of wives, children and servants to submit to father's authority.

Patriarchal control within the Puritan family rested on transfer of both landed property and craft skills. Thus children were kept economically dependent for years and were forced to submit to paternal authority out of deference and fear of failure to acquire an inheritance. In the colonies of Massachusetts, New Hampshire, and Connecticut, children were subject to the death penalty if they cursed or hit their fathers. A Puritan wife was to submit to the authority of her husband. She was considered a helpmeet, not an equal, and should submit to his demands with "a noble and generous fear, which proceeds from love"; for her role was to "guid the house &c. not guid the Husband." In cases where Puritan fathers failed to govern their own children, Puritan law permitted their removal and placement with another master in order to "force them to submit unto government." Women who refused to obey their husbands were also subject to harsh punishments. Two hundred and seventy eight women were brought to court in New England for heaping abuse on their husbands and were punished by fines and whippings.[7]

The "better whipt than damned" view of childrearing expressed by Cotton Mather, a famous Puritan preacher of the seventeenth century,[8] encapsulated the belief in infant depravity and original sin. To break the will of the child early through repeated beatings and moral reprimands ensured later obedience and subjection not only of one's own children but of indentured servant children and other family members. While a form of the nuclear family existed in Puritan times, in reality the Puritan household was hardly a nuclear enclave; rather it was peopled by other children and household members. The widespread custom of putting children out as apprentices or servants or to attend school meant that most children in Puritan America left home for long periods of time before reaching adolescence. And while wetnursing was less widespread in America than in France, many Puritan colonists who became wealthy fostered out their newborn infants to wetnurses, thus enabling mother to devote more time to the household economy.

Although the formal structure of the patriarchal Puritan family emphasized moral and spiritual values, marriages were primarily economic arrangements to which the woman brought both dowry and services, and children performed essential productive functions. Physical abuse toward children was defined as moral training and shadowed the power structure that inhered in the marriage, which promoted obedience and submission to male authority. To be an obdurate child or an arrogant wife threatened that structure; and to engage in an illicit relationship, as did Nathaniel Hawthorne's Hester Prynne in *The Scarlet Letter*, transgressed the moral boundaries of the "little commonwealth." Neither Hester nor her young daughter Pearl qualified as a family; husbandless and fatherless, they were outcasts in the wilderness of the single-mother family terrain.

A cursory look beyond New England reveals that the Chesapeake colonies of the seventeenth century were populated primarily by young male indentured servants, taken from their mothers as young children, sent over as child migrants, and bound to their masters for long periods of service.[9] As plantation houses grew and African slaves were forcibly sold to serve as a labor pool, slave society developed with its distinctive African-American family and kinship networks.[10] As in the story told by William Wells Brown, cited in chapter 1, many slave mothers had their children ripped from their breasts to become child slaves to white families. Thus family forms and motherhood, circumscribed by economy, power, and privilege, differed vastly in experience in colonial America. Among Native Americans, from the Pueblo to the Cheyenne, both matrilineal and partilineal family structures existed, expressing further diversity and cultural forms.[11] While early American family forms varied widely, however, a uniform *image* of family has dominated historical sensibilities and public memory. This monolithic image is traceable to the patriarchal structure of the Puritans and the nineteenth-century ideal of the "democratic" family, which Tocqueville discovered on his voyage to the New World. It is a pervasive and obstinate image.

When we examine the impact of this image on early industrial capitalism, we see the change from a society based on a familial domestic economy in which women shared in economic production, to an industrial one in which the family unit no longer formed the basis for the organization of labor and production. The social forms of the family during industrialization underwent dramatic shifts. As the separation of the workplace from the dwelling place became institutionalized, a sentimental rather than a productive image was ascribed to the family. Demos sees nineteenth-century America as being the period in which the construct of family acquired an extremely sharp image as a separation of spheres was introduced—the dangerous outside world of commerce, and the home as refuge and haven.[12]

When Tocqueville visited the United States in the 1830s, he found this new form of family already in existence—the "democratic" family characterized by a marriage that emphasized companionship and a specialization of roles with father as breadwinner and mother as gentle household monarch devoting herself to domesticity and the new concepts of childrearing. During this period a new recognition of childhood as a distinctive phase of life also emerged. From the late eighteenth to the late nineteenth century we view the development of the "new mother" and the "cult of womanhood" inextricably tied to the image of family as haven, nestled within a golden past. In order to examine this ideal more closely we must look beyond the American horizon and across the Atlantic to trace its origins in the writings of Rousseau and other European pedagogues.

A Second French Window—Bourgeois Motherhood

We now take a second look through the windows of eighteenth- and nineteenth-century France, but this time we glance not at poor and desperate mothers but at bourgeois motherhood. Just as mothering emerged as a set of practices shaped by circumstances for the most destitute of women, so too was middle class mothering invented and shaped by the prevailing social constructs of the time. As Badinter points out, maternal love mythologized as a biological female instinct has never been an unquestionable constant. Rather it is another metanarrative, which, when decoded, reveals its historical fragility. In fact, while destitute mothers were abandoning their babies to the tour or shipping them off to the rural hovels of their destitute sisters, bourgeois mothers were experiencing their children as both an annoyance and a hindrance. Breastfeeding was perceived as "a ridiculous and disgusting habit," and women of rank were supported by doctors in choosing social obligations over care, for "nothing was less fashionable than to seem to love one's children too much and to give up one's precious time for them."[13] This refusal to nurse on the part of bourgeois women, who modeled themselves on the aristocracy, was part of a widespread class practice. Putting their children out to wetnurse enabled educated bourgeois women to pursue both social and intellectual activities. Freed from the burden of children, many women hastened to follow the lead of the nobility in emancipating themselves from domestic life. In a

see Emma Bovary

society of both wealth and privilege, it was common for mothers as well as fathers to lose all interest in their children's well-being. Four years was the average stay with the wetnurse. Badinter cites numerous cases of maternal neglect on the part of influential families: Mme Talleyrand, for example, for four years made no contact with her baby son, who lived with his wetnurse on the outskirts of Paris, and she was therefore unaware of a crippling accident which left him with a clubfoot.[14]

If mother love is a gendered destiny, how do we explain these apparent norms of indifference among the most privileged of French mothers? Furthermore, how do we explain the sudden change from an indifferent motherhood to the all-absorbing mother love that suffused bourgeois notions of family on the eve of the French Revolution? Badinter argues that it was the male invention of motherhood—propelled by Rousseau's "emancipatory" views on love, male companionate control over the marriage, and domesticity—that shaped the "new mother" among the bourgeoisie. In a society where women, even after the revolution, were effectively denied a civic and political voice, effacement in the public realm led to a search for interior visibility; hence the sentimental nest was born as woman became the "holy domestic monarch."[15]

whose?

In Rousseau's *Emile*, Sophie is raised to fulfill the desires of Emile and to form his children; and mother gains status and power within the domestic sphere, becoming the approved ally of the physician. Rousseau's image of the (male) child as "noble savage," as a free, developing self, offered on the one hand a passionate defense of the right of the child to a natural and spontaneous childhood. On the other hand, girls were not considered noble savages, but rather were destined to be tamed creatures, receiving an education for domestication, not freedom. "Woman is formed to please and live in subjection," declared Rousseau.[16] Mother's task was to guide children by love and tenderness toward their different inclinations, and to protect them against the unnatural, corrupting forces of the time.

In this way, mother love as instinct was elevated to the status of a natural law. Biology became destiny, and mother alone became responsible for the interior health of husband and children, ultimately cradling the crucible of the state. Physicians and public officials increasingly opposed the abandonment of bourgeois children to wetnurses and servants. As industrialization proceeded, many of the poor and destitute rushed to the cities. This flight of the poor was believed responsible for saturating the cities and creating disaffection in the countryside, increasing the number of illegitimate babies left to the care of the state. A paradoxical situation arose, argues Jacques Donzelot, that created differential contours: a bad *public* economy forced poor mothers to abandon their children, desert the countryside, and burden the state with abandoned babies; similarly, a bad *private* economy caused the educated and the wealthy to entrust the upbringing and early education of their children to the corruption of the servants. This situation created the conditions for "the policing of families" through various technologies of power based on tutelage and surveillance of the poor; and a contractual set of constraints for the bourgeoisie using the emergent institutions of pediatrics and pedagogy as a regulatory mechanism.[17] Thus, mother as bourgeois monarch became a central force in bringing her children—snatched from the clutches of the servants and their misdeeds—back to the family. Allied with the physician, she became the central actress in the avant-garde social theater of the new motherhood, where "between Versailles and Paris, an entire group of women decided to raise their children 'à la Jean-Jacques.' "[18]

And what of poor mothers? How did they fare backstage, behind the scenes of an enveloping play of a bourgeois pedagogy of love? These mothers, along with all others who shared the world of poverty, formed part of the rationale for a new consolidation of state technology during the nineteenth century. Donzelot describes this process as a regulation of all forms of life of the poor, "to diminish the social cost of their reproduction and obtain an optimum number of workers at minimum public expense: in short what is customarily termed philanthropy."[19] Women also became the privileged instruments for civilizing the poor. Maternal and financial subsidies dependent on a marriage contract were introduced; aid was given to mothers if they stayed home to nurse their babies, with medical and welfare workers assigned to investigate their situations and to distinguish between the moral needy and the "depraved." Relief had to serve the purposes of the state, and mothers were charged with responsibility for restoring family life to the poor, which, it was believed, would serve to civilize the masses. As we read in the 1847 *Annales de la charité*, "The task at hand is not only a social necessity and a highly moral endeavor; it is also an excellent piece of business, an obvious and immense saving for the state, the departments and the municipalities."[20]

Donzelot's critique of philanthropy and the biopower of the state though well formulated as a poststructuralist argument, lacks context—the existential tissue of poor women's lives. For while their lives were certainly subject to increased state surveillance and regulation, their destitution was alleviated in part by subsidies, their children were sometimes able to remain with them, and state aid did give them some power in relation to their men in the form of a required marriage contract. As Linda Gordon has argued, social welfare intervention was a regulatory form of control, but it also gave poor women forms of access to regulatory power over men who abused them and abandoned their families.[21] Hence, welfare was a double-edged sword, both in nineteenth-century France and in the United States. When poor women and children lack access to power within a patriarchal family structure, regulatory welfare agencies can penalize them for deviant mothering practices; but these same agencies have been used by women to enlist state aid in freeing them from patriarchal domination and abuse. In France, a poor mother could engineer destitution strategies so as to become the paid wetnurse of her own children, recalling the biblical story of Moses in the bulrushes.

Whatever contours of family we choose to trace, whether in Europe or America, the lives of the poor or the privileged, the public or the private sphere, we return to a central ideology of care which burdens women with "the terrifying assignment"[22] of a mother-child couplet. Mother stands at the center of the private sphere of family and, contingent upon her class and place in the social realm, moves in spreading circles of powerlessness and simultaneous domestic responsibility. As we watch this ideology of care developing in the nineteenth and early twentieth centuries, we also view the increasing placelessness of women in the public sphere, a placelessness now scientifically rationalized in the language of a psychology of mothering. It is this discourse that needs to be decoded as we approach the end of the twentieth century; for it has had a far-reaching impact on public policy for women and their children.

The Cult of American Motherhood and the Ideology of Care

A System of laws must be established, which sustain certain relations and dependencies in social and civil life . . . These must be the magistrate and the subject, one of whom is superior, and the other the inferior. There must be the relation of husband and wife, parent and child, teacher and pupil, employer and employed, each involving the relative duties of subordination. The superior, in certain particulars, is to direct, and the inferior to yield obedience. Society could never go forward, harmoniously, nor could any craft or profession be successfully pursued, unless these superior and subordinate relations be instituted and sustained.

Thus Catharine Beecher, one of the early domestic feminists, attempted to develop an ideal and practice of domesticity that emphasized the moral superiority of womanhood, elevating motherhood to a glorious temple of self-sacrifice "whose summit shall pierce the skies, whose splendor shall beam on all lands."[23]

This ideal of domesticity and the separation of spheres was embraced by the domestic feminists of whom Catharine Beecher was a leading exponent. Female submission and withdrawal from the closed public space was necessary to create a domestic sphere under women's control. Beecher consistently argued that women should neither compete with men nor vote, for female power lay in the domestic world. Woman, with her superior capacity for self-sacrifice, was eminently suited to the lofty calling of wife and mother. Such was the moral philosophy of domesticity that Beecher espoused and promoted. It was a cult of "true womanhood" that dominated the sensibilities of the middle class, in much the same way that the cult of the new mother dominated the sensibilities of the French bourgeoisie in the nineteenth century. Barbara Welter comments, "It was a fearful obligation, a solemn responsibility, which the nineteenth century American woman had—to uphold the pillars of the temple with her frail white hand."[24]

Her frail white hand also upheld the virtues of piety and chastity; religion and church work were supported as they were viewed as enhancing the ever widening circle of domesticity. Catharine Beecher, as the daughter of a renowned Evangelical preacher, actively used her church connections to disseminate her domestic feminism. The "true woman" was also above the baser passions of lust and sexuality to which her fallen sisters had succumbed. Control of one's sexual appetites was an integral part of Victorian ideology, for "the *best* mothers, wives, and managers of households know little or nothing of sexual indulgence. Love of home, children, and domestic duties are the only passions they feel."[25]

In the discourse of the mid-nineteenth century, the "true woman" emerged as desexualized, uninterested in intellectual pursuits, imbued with piety, and devoted to home and hearth. In this she was supported by medical, educational, and popular advice literature of the time, all of which stressed the "naturalness" of her condition and constructed the female sphere as irrational and emotional, psychologically primed for motherhood and childrearing.

Motherhood and Pedagogy

As we saw in France, Rousseau's conception of the "new mother" promoted motherhood as a natural destiny to guide and train children according to their natural developmental inclinations. Mother was also the child's first essential teacher and the centerpiece of the family morality. J. H. Pestalozzi in his late eighteenth-century novel *Leonard and Gertrude,* presents Gertrude as the ideal mother-teacher.[26] It is through her "mother's heart," for which there is no substitute, that she is called upon to set up a village school founded on the principles of harmony that echo domestic life, of which the pious, gentle, and sacrificing Gertrude is such a shining examplar. Friedrich Froebel, developing the founding principles of the kindergarten in the 1830s and 1840s, rests his earliest phases of pedagogy on the "natural mother," who instinctively guides the child to a developing selfhood with gentleness and compassion. While mother's natural instinct is vital, it is not sufficient, for the natural mother can also be trained "to awaken and develop, to quicken all the powers and natural gifts of the child" through conscious activity.[27] Froebel emphasizes the need to educate the child's religious feelings, believing them to be the germ of the intellect and will, which emerge in the union with a righteous mother and teacher.

This legacy of a mother-centered pedagogy was elevated into a national ideology by Beecher during the mid-nineteenth century in the United States. She urged that the nation fortify itself through the devout efforts of "the Christian female teacher."[28] The developing pedagogy of compassion and moral training thus coincided with domestic feminism, which attempted to legitimate a separate domestic sphere for women, where mother-as-teacher was a natural coupling. Both Froebel and Pestalozzi are quoted at length in the numerous mothercraft manuals that proliferated in the late nineteenth century in this country. One such manual, by the Women's Temperance Society, quotes Froebel approvingly in describing "mother-love [as] being the centre and pivot on which all turns" and "one of the strongest instincts of human nature."[29]

Thus we return once again to the natural law of mother love as instinct, not as a relationship of choice and commitment; and we have arrived full circle into the arms of biology as destiny. It is mother, complete or incomplete, who now is destined to be judged on the innate qualities of her natural reproductive fate; a mother who fails defies the natural inclinations of her sex, subverts the God-given order of the family; for "she will live for others . . . and not for herself . . . She must love and give birth, that is her sacred duty."[30] It is mother alone who also bears responsibility for the flowering or deformation of her offspring, or, in the language of the twentieth century, for the health or pathology of her child.

The elevation of woman to the pedestal of "domestic monarch" led once again to different outcomes for women of different classes. The well-to-do became childsavers and the protectors of the family; and poor mothers became eligible either for salvation or for damnation, often benefiting from progressive reforms such as child custody laws and mothers' pensions. If poor and single, however, they suffered for their moral improprieties, often losing their children to childsaving agencies, which many mothers ironically labeled "The Cruelty."[31] Single mothers could not conform to the norms of domesticity, since many worked long hours outside the home, leaving their children home alone or roaming the streets. Their domesticity was always suspect because they were paupers, dependent on charity and the state rather than on their husbands for economic support; hence, "failing domesticity, they by definition failed at proper femininity and mothering"[32] as they failed to abide by the norms of a complete family in the mirror of their middle-class sisters.

The moral reform movements of the child-saving era (1875–1910) initiated a consciousness of children's rights, child labor laws, and the rehabilitation of the family as central to social reform. A developmental perspective on childhood emerged that was integrally tied to motherhood. "His life has become an autonomous world set within that of maternity," wrote Isabel Simarel in 1916.[33] Leading reformers of the childhood advocacy movement, such as Robert Hunter, Florence Kelley, and John Spargo, argued that a specially nurtured childhood was in the interests of national self-preservation and the formation of orderly citizens.[34] The reformers focused on destitute, abused, neglected, and delinquent children from poor and immigrant families, which, as noted earlier, led the philanthropists and child-savers to impose a separate world of childhood on poor children, and an ideology of family and motherhood on poor women, of whom the most desperate were those living in large urban industrial centers.[35] While the dominant ideals of domestic feminism flourished during this period, a small and influential countertradition was represented by the social and material feminists, who challenged the split between domestic and public life and the cult of motherhood.

Social and Material Feminism

We have so arranged life, that a man may have a home and family, love, companionship, domesticity, and fatherhood, yet, remain an active citizen of age and country. We have so arranged life, on the other hand, that a woman must "choose"; must either live alone, unloved, uncompanied, uncared for, homeless, childless, with her work in the world for sole consolation; or give up all world-service for the joys of love, motherhood, and domestic service.[36]

A little more than half a century separated Charlotte Perkins Gilman's tract of social feminism, cited above, from that of her aunt and early role model, Catharine Beecher. Yet Perkins Gilman and others challenged the whole notion of "women's sphere" and "women's work" specifically in regard to the physical separation of the household from the workplace and the creation of two parallel economies. These material feminists, in demanding a "grand domestic revolution" in women's material conditions, focused on the housework and housing needs of women, arguing that the redesign of households and neighborhoods was central to the question of equality.[37] Interestingly, they saw this as more important than winning the right to enter the world of male suffrage; for the right to vote for men as the sole occupiers of public office would guarantee women neither economic justice nor freedom from the drudgery of housework. The feminist critiques ranged from Melusina Fay Pierce's denouncement of the educated woman's "costly and unnatural sacrifice . . . to the dusty drudgery of house ordering,"[38] to the free love utopian socialist experiments modeled on Fourier's *Familistère* at Guise, which Marie Howland attempted to replicate in the United States. Together with Robert Owen, Howland worked to design and build kitchenless houses with cooperative housekeeping and developmental child care, embodying remarkably progressive educational ideals—specially designed children's spaces with child care arrangements to suit the needs of working mothers. Howland argued that economic independence for women was vital and that "the freeing of woman from the household treadmill must be effected before she can cultivate the powers so vitally needed in the regeneration of her race."[39]

But it was Perkins Gilman who in her public lectures, writings, and utopian fiction most widely disseminated the themes of women's oppression by integrating social feminism with the thinking of the suffragettes and the politics of space. In her *Women and Economics* she envisioned an egalitarian socialist infrastructure, where women, having economic independence, could enjoy a family life in cooperative, kitchenless housing and thus experience both motherhood and paid employment in a public world.[40] The key theme of the diverse thinkers of the "grand domestic revolution" was that a reorganization of labor and the spatial environment would end the exploitation of women and free them to enter the market economy on an equal basis with men. Spatial analysis became the key to the transformation of the domestic sphere, which, the material feminists still argued, should be placed under women's control, thereby linking their campaigns for social equality, economic justice, and urban reform. The bourgeois Victorian home represented, in spatial form, the patriarchal hier-

archies of public man at work and domestic mother at home—the woman
cradling the underlife that propelled her man to face the world outside. As
Foucault would argue almost a century later in *Discipline and Punish*,
understanding the politics of space is the key to the technology of power.

Despite the vigorous campaigning of the material feminists and their
attempt to advance alternative images of the family, it was the domestic
feminists who held sway, supported by public sensibilities about the proper
role of wife and mother. While family historians have generally described
the changes in family structure during the late nineteenth and early twentieth centuries as heralding the rise of the democratic family, the use of the
term "democratic" actually conceals clear hierarchies of class and gender.
In reality, the rise of the democratic, companionate family corresponded to
an emergent middle-class structure of power relations where, in Catharine
Beecher's words, "it is needful that certain relations be sustained, which
involve the duties of subordination."[41] The image of home as nest and shelter from the aggressive materialistic forces of the marketplace and public
life transformed the family into a private refuge for its members of privilege.

The material feminists, who battled for almost sixty years to push
through their program of domestic transformation and economic autonomy, thus failed to achieve their goals. They were barraged by attacks from
corporations, trade unions (who were campaigning for men to receive a
"family" wage, thereby excluding women), and, later, public red-baiting.
Their platform for the redesign of urban households and neighborhoods
suffered a severe setback during and after the Great Depression. Hoover's
National Conference on Home Building and Home Ownership in 1931
supported home ownership for men of "sound character and industrious
habits," implying woman's role was that of domestic manager. Banks, builders, and developers all promoted the single-family suburban home on its
own lot, with father as breadwinner and mother as full-time domestic
housewife. The term "housewife" is in itself evocative of the assumed union
between woman and house—effectively accentuating her removal from
the public sphere and fencing her, together with her children, within the
nuclear yard complete with attached garage. While it was gender that
united women under the common umbrella of a patriarchal social and economic structure which denied them equal access to public and civic life
(and, for those who labored outside the home, to "man-sized" wages), it
was class that determined the degree of women's destitution or desperate
survival under industrial capitalism. For the poor, whose family structure
was destined to failure and incompleteness, the privileged ideal of family

was ominously present, ever hovering as unreachable. This very unreacha-
bility legitimated public surveillance and state regulation over those family
members whose lives deviated from the ideal.

Attachment and the Ideology of Care

If we analyze the growth of developmental theory during the early part of
the twentieth century we see that the "cult of child psychology" followed
closely on the high heels of the "cult of womanhood." Placing the changes
in childrearing practices over the past two centuries in historical and an-
thropological perspective, John and Elizabeth Newson point out that a self-
conscious preoccupation with the *psychological* consequences of childrearing is distinctive to the twentieth century.[42] In the ephemeral landscape of
the psychological, attachment theory begins to loom larger than life on the
horizons of motherhood.

If we trace the growth of a psychology of childhood, and the particular
construction of motherhood in this century, we see the deity-centered
pedagogy of the nineteenth century (largely influenced by the Evangelical
movement in Britain and the United States), shift to the developmental
and medical morality of the twentieth, in which the science of childrearing
emerges with mother as primary research assistant to the physician and
psychologist. The image of mother as exclusive developer of her child's
psyche complements mother as builder of the "glorious temple" of womanhood. The psychological and medical evidence for woman's biological
destiny gains credibility as the influence of Freud enters the sentimental nest. Once again we return to Europe, but this time our gaze turns to
Vienna.

Sigmund Freud's patriarchal image of the family wove a tapestry of a
desexualized woman, forever fated to suffer through her Electra complex,
yet a vital force for the psychosexual development of her child's healthy
ego. Infant-mother bonding, systematically addressed by Freud in his later
life, is given serious attention in *Inhibitions, Symptoms and Anxiety*. Here,
as in his other writings about anxiety, Freud dwells on "the peculiar painfulness" of the separation of child from mother.[43]

The theme of infant-mother bonding continues to echo through the
later discourse of attachment theory. For Anna Freud, for René Spitz, and
for John Bowlby,[44] the normal development of object relations through the
healthy formation of the ego was crucial. Object relations theory, in turn, is
rooted in fixed images of a patriarchal Victorian family, typical of Freud's
milieu in late nineteenth-century Vienna. While Freud was clearly icono-

clastic and revolutionary in his theories of psychosexual development and
the pathologies resulting from sexual repression, his model of the family
remained both bourgeois and conventional. Perhaps that is why he re-
versed his seduction theory and committed what Jeffrey Masson has
termed the "assault on truth,"[45] for if hysterical women were made so by
actual early child sexual molestation rather than their own fantasies, the
edifice of family as normalized domestic haven and the carefully staged
structures of psychosexual development were threatened with collapse.

Data on child sexual abuse indicate that perhaps one in four American
girls and one in seven American boys will encounter an experience of sexual abuse prior to their eighteenth birthday.[46] Freud's Vienna was, in all
probability, not markedly different. "The world of 1899, however," as Larry
Wolff shows in his study of child abuse in Vienna, "barely recognized the
concept of child abuse, and a powerful Victorian sentimental ideal of the
loving family made it hard to believe that parents brutalized their children."[47] Thus we return once again to images of family, of domesticity, of
motherhood, which, when prised apart, often reveal the silence of distorted
relations. This too, is our developmental-theory heritage: a complicit participation in concealment and the renaming of forms of pathology as normality.

Helene Deutsch, a student of Freud's, argued persuasively in the
1940s to a ready academic and lay American public for the necessary sublimation of woman's aspirations and desires as necessary for healthy female
development culminating in the experience of motherhood. She describes
motherhood as "the expression not only of a biologic process, but also of a
psychologic unity"; and in analyzing "maternal instinct" and "maternal
love" as "differentiated ingredients of motherliness as a whole," Deutsch
argues for both an instinctual and a psychological gender-specific sphere.[48]
Not only does woman-as-mother bear the "terrifying assignment" of private
and personal responsibility for her child's future health or pathology, but
woman is developmentally disabled if she fails to sublimate and invest herself totally in her biological destiny.[49]

Deutsch, writing about female sublimation from a psychoanalytic, developmental perspective, echoes Catharine Beecher, who, a century earlier, defined a "prosperous domestic state" as "the peculiar responsibilities
of American Women,"[50] which would ensure the continuing development
of the democratic state.

While Erik H. Erikson expanded the deterministic psychosexual markers of development within a broader and more diverse cultural framework,
he too founded his psychosocial stages on the resolution of developmental

crises initiated by the fundamental trust-versus-mistrust duality, where mother as attachment persona was central.[51] In the burgeoning cult of motherhood discourse, however, it was Bowlby's widely read studies of infant attachment and loss that shaped much of post–World War II thinking in this area. Bowlby theorized that the mental health of both mothers and children was based on a stable, intimate relationship, buttressed by a joint dependency on husband and father.

> Just as the baby needs to feel that he belongs to his mother, the mother needs to feel that she belongs to her child and it is only when she has the satisfaction of this feeling that it is easy for her to devote herself to him. The provision of constant attention day and night, seven days a week and 365 in the year, is possible only for a woman who derives profound satisfaction from seeing her child grow from babyhood, through the many phases of childhood, to become an independent man or woman, and knows it is her care which has made this possible.[52]

In this way, Bowlby portrays mother-child attachment in suffocating images of reciprocal development, in which bonding is recast as mother bondage. Mental health can only be assured by exclusive maternal care conducted within a nuclear family structure in which the strict division of male/female roles forms part of the natural order. Other family forms and child care settings become potential landscapes of pathology. Bowlby also cautions against any form of institutional care arguing that even "bad homes" are better than good institutions.[53] Mary Ainsworth's studies, following in the tradition of Bowlby, elevated attachment behavior to a functional scientific model of healthy infant adaptation, where under controlled laboratory conditions she conducted her famous stranger-situation experiments, measuring the degree of attachment to mother.[54] This experiment with its findings of separation anxiety augmented the ahistorical and often hysterical assumptions about the "natural laws" of attachment. In contrast, Nancy Chodorow, adopting a feminist-revisionist psychoanalytic perspective, has argued that mothering and the reproduction of mothering is a product neither of biology nor of intentional role training, but rather a product of "social structurally induced psychological processes," which constitute personality and sex differences in early childhood.[55] Hence children reach adulthood with distinctive, gendered conceptions of identity and definitions of mothering and fathering. It is woman, then, who must reproduce attachment as a social form, and woman-as-mother who finds her identity in such psychological formation and incorporation. While at all times some mothers, both privileged and poor, have wanted and loved their children, the construct of mother love as biological, instinctive, or innate has served to legitimate particular conceptions of womanhood and motherhood as subordinate. Such conceptions cast sweeping shadows over public and private landscapes in which family texts are written.

It is interesting to recall the political conditions in the United States in the mid-twentieth century, when the construct of child-inextricably-tied-to-mother gained such dominance and was illuminated in the silhouettes of suburbia. In the late 1940s and early 1950s, attachment, mother-child bonding, and the Norman Rockwell vision of Middle America's home and hearth were being promoted. Yet between 1942 and 1945, during World War II, 4.7 million women had entered the workforce for the first time (many of them married and over the age of thirty-five), with 3.5 million of these taking jobs they would not normally have taken and being paid "man-sized wages."[56] In 1942, $4,000,000 in federal funds had gone to local communities to assist in the building of child care centers to house the young children of working mothers. But in 1945 the women were sent home, displaced by returning veterans, and in 1946 federal child care funds were terminated and 100,000 children were threatened with eviction as child care centers were forced to close.[57] The G.I. bill with low-cost mortgages for the single-family home, and the Highway Act of 1944, contributed to the swell of suburbia and domestic isolation of which Levittown, built in 1946, is but one visible symbol.

Economic strategies to keep women out of the workplace, buttressed by the developmental/attachment arguments for the healthy growth of children, placed pathology in the laps of insufficiently bonded infants and insufficiently identified and sublimated mothers; once again the mother-child couplet was at center stage. The exclusion of women from public space returns us to the *home* as a domestic site of confinement, the boundary of private and public space, the concrete site of woman's inner space, the terrain for her production of a well-developed child. It was here that the private space between mother-and-child also became the object of the scientific gaze, and here too that the child became the product/object of mother's labor—a double internment. As woman's placelessness in public life was sealed by domestic ideology, so too were the practices of family life.

Behind Closed Doors—the Other Face of the Family

While the image of family as "haven in a heartless world" has been so central to our cultural consciousness, the patterns of family life that lie behind closed doors, fenced facades, and manicured lawns, and also behind peeling lead paint and roach-infested tenements, are often sites of abuse and fear, of violence and humiliation. These are patterns of family as hell, sites in which hidden abuse and violence are the countertext to attachment and bonding and nurturance.[58] Linda Gordon's historical study of family violence demonstrates how the definitions of abuse have shifted in accordance with changing class constructs of male-female relations and images of childhood and childrearing. Gordon argues that family violence must always be located within the power relations of the family, and that public anxieties expressed about the decline of the family often mask socially conservative fears about the increasing autonomy of women and children, which in turn corresponds to a decline in male control of the family.[59] Family violence—a silent and concealed landscape of many women and children's lives—emerges as the other face of the family.[60] This other face of family life—child abuse, incest, wife-beating, marital rape—has been concealed for centuries, and its visibility has varied along class and ethnic lines. The legitimation of intrusion through surveillance of and intervention into the private territory of the individual family bears a direct relation to the class status of its members and their distance from the institutional norms of the society.[61] While abuse and violence occur across all socioeconomic lines, their visibility in terms of public consciousness resides in the poor and in the perceived dysfunctionality of their family structures.

Women as mothers have occupied multiple and diverse worlds, from sentimental nests to the most destitute of hovels. Families have been both sites of nurturance and sites of violence, yet abuse has generally been concealed in complicit images of the stable, enduring family. The ideology of care has placed mother at the center of an unfolding drama of a "normalized" motherhood, the product of natural law, biological fate, and a gendered psychological determinism. These images are not plural but monolithic. Fathers have hardly featured in the long history of the discourse of care. Such a persistent and obdurate imaging of the past has eclipsed the existential experiences of family and motherhood, a complex layering of diverse and complicated worlds of pain that stand in the shadows of our ideologies.

One of the most pernicious outcomes of such concealment is the treatment of the family as an isolated private unit that survives or sinks by its own resources and fitness—a kind of family Darwinism—where the prevailing power structure legitimizes married women as mothers. When the structure fails, women fail, thereby justifying the indifference of the state to the lives of those who cannot conform to such norms by virtue of their poverty, their lifestyle, or their race. It is at these intersecting contours that the ideology of care begins to corrode. In short, the ideology of mother care and *attachment* has effectively served to conceal and rationalize a public policy of *detachment*. It is the specter of *otherness* that we see in the current welfare policies that assault poor mothers and their children. In the following pages, we begin to uncover the policies of otherness before listening to the voices of those we have made other.

Part
Two

PART TWO OPENS WITH AN INTRODUCTION to "the other motherhood," to the landscape of single mothers and their children who have lived and continue to live in poverty. The way in which poverty discourse about single mothers and their children is woven through the flimsy threads of public policy is traced in chapter 3. History speaks with a cold voice as poverty statistics continue to frame the contingency of poor mothers' lives, and poverty forms the objective contour against which the horizons of daily life coalesce. The feminization of poverty—women and their children on welfare—creates bureaucratic categories on the one hand and, on the other, stories of lives on the edge. In chapters 4 and 5, mothers from diverse worlds tell their stories.

In listening to these stories, one sees not only desperation but also, how interventions that *are* supportive can make possible the beginnings of a viable, if still contingent life. All the stories that are documented here are drawn from oral interviews with women resident in Michigan between 1989 and 1991 (see Appendix), but all names, places, and other identifying characteristics have been changed to protect confidentiality. While the lives of these women have been scarred by their struggles to survive with their young children their stories are ones of resilience, not defeat. For every voice that emerges tenacious, fighting, and angry in these pages, there are countless other silent voices, lost, unheard of; stories untold; lives lived out on the invisible contours. Why choose mothers of resilience rather than mothers of defeat? Partly because the horrors of public policy indifference are thrown into relief against these narratives of endurance and survival. As one young teenage mother tells, "I can become what statistics has designed for me to be—a nothing—or I can make statistics a lie."

As we listen to these mothers talk, the echoes of their voices bounce back and forth between the spaces of other mothers' lives scattered across the country, for the "other motherhood" has a shared existential text—the distinctive suffering of young children.

41

The Other Motherhood:
The Landscape of Single
Mothers in Poverty

When Americans talk about poverty, some things remain unsaid. Mainstream discourse about poverty, whether liberal or conservative, largely stays silent about politics, power, and equality. But poverty, after all, is about distribution; it results because some people receive a great deal less than others.

>   Michael Katz
>   *The Undeserving Poor*

"Since Thou my God and Father doest claim me as Thine own, I richly shall inherit all good from Thee alone."

Unpacking Poverty Discourse

THE WAY IN WHICH WE CHOOSE to talk about poverty—as a social problem, an urgent issue in need of attention, a dilemma, a menace, a threat to the society, a cost to the taxpayer, or, as one of my colleagues once stated, just "another variable of development"—creates a noise, followed by echoes that locate the invisible lives of poor women and their children. They, living out there in the unnamed landscapes, periodically swell into visibility as the poverty *issue* is targeted for public attention by competing political agendas. Poverty talk,[1] however, is always a discourse about *them.* As they get closer and their proximity makes us uncomfortable, we clamor for laws to contain them, to regulate their space in relation to ours, to keep the most destitute and homeless away from our homes, our walking and jogging routes, our subway stations, our parking lots, our libraries. When we turn and look at *their children,* we feel concern about this future citizenry, this growing young population "at risk," whom we call "at risk" less out of outrage and compassion than because their condition threatens our security and comfort, our children, our schools, our neighborhoods, our property values. Their *otherness* places *us* "at risk"; yet it is we who have named them. We have both invented and named poverty. *?*

Calling poverty a "disease" implies a fatalistic perspective: poverty hits those who are less healthy than us; the unchecked virus that afflicts them must be contained, and it may be possible to effect a cure if they take the

hereditary?

43

medicine we have prescribed for them. Or there is the "poverty as enemy" talk, necessitating a war on poverty, which, we are now told, has been fought and lost at taxpayer expense. Another discourse entangles poverty with immorality and depravity and draws the boundaries of poverty in family pathology. Still another creates a geography of poverty as an embedded culture from which there is no psychological exit. But, there is one common theme that unites the different forms of poverty discourse—the silence about class, about a political economy that creates poverty by its very economic structure. For as Michel Foucault has pointed out, poverty is always an essential ingredient of wealth.[2] Yet the language of poverty continues to contaminate our sensibilities, to frame our ways of seeing and not seeing. Why, we might ask, is it so difficult to see that children do not catch poverty but are made poor by state neglect; that single mothers need not be destined to fall into poverty but are made poor by a state-constructed policy. A different set of policies and a different kind of discourse can change lives.

Poverty is neither natural nor necessary in a wealthy, postindustrial state that generates not scarcity but surpluses. As Michael Katz argues in *The Undeserving Poor,* "descriptions of the demography, behavior, or beliefs of subpopulations cannot explain the patterned inequalities evident in every era of American history. These result from styles of dominance, the way power is exercised, and the politics of distribution."[3] When we question what Katz terms the "supply-side view of poverty," we begin to decode the assumptions and taken-for-granted definitions of needs and entitlements, of private and public responsibility, as well as the politics of language, where "needs talk" becomes "a medium for the making and contesting of political claims."[4]

One telling example of the framing of "needs talk" is the use and multiple meanings of the term "poverty line." What exactly does the line refer to? Depending on the way we define the level of poverty, we can either incorporate or sweep away thousands of poor people as part of our public poverty discourse. In the United States, during the War on Poverty in the mid-1960s, the poverty standard adopted was calculated on the Orshansky Index, which assumed that low-income families spent roughly a third of their income on food; on the basis of what was considered a minimally adequate diet according to the Economy Food Plan of the Department of Agriculture, the figure was multiplied by 3 and adjusted for family size. It should be noted that this standard was designed for "temporary or emergency use when funds are low," and the Department of Agriculture itself estimated that only 10 percent of people on the plan could manage to eat an adequate diet.[5] In addition, Mollie Orshansky, who had developed this index as a research tool in the Social Security Administration Office, pointed out that, at best, it was a crude criterion of income adequacy. Yet, the Office of Economic Opportunity adopted Orshansky's Index as a standard while using the estimates of the Department of Agriculture Food Plan, which were originally 25 percent lower than the low-cost plan devised by Orshansky! In addition, Orshansky points out that if the Census Bureau had revised the poverty line in 1975 to account for changed nutrition and consumption practices, the number of poor people would have increased by between 10 and 13 million!

Since the inception of the poverty index, successive critics from within the federal government, as well as public policy advocates and academics, have consistently charged that the official index is too low. Despite small-scale revisions since the 1960s, the standard remains largely unchanged. It is adjusted each year for overall inflation as measured by the Consumer Price Index, but it remains an arbitrary standard applied to annual income, irrespective of regional differences, relative housing costs, the variability of benefits from state to state, and changing patterns in the relation of food to income. "The history of the poverty line illustrates the politics of numbers," Katz contends. "Federal administrators have waged a quiet but persistent campaign against increased standards and, at every junction, have chosen the lowest plausible figure. In this way they have both checked the expansion of benefits and minimized the problem of poverty in America."[6]

In contrast, the European Economic Community defines poverty as having an income which is *less than half of the median income* in individual countries. If we used this standard in the United States, the numbers would rise dramatically. In 1990, for example, the poverty line for a family of four was pegged at an income of $12,700 by the federal government, but the estimated median income for a family of four for 1991 is $39,051.[7] When Grubb and Lazerson analyzed the official poverty statistics for the 1970s, they demonstrated how once again using the European standard of less than half of the median income would have raised the official statistics of 15.1 percent of children in poverty to 24.5 percent in 1974![8] Hence our most recent poverty rate for children, 20.6 percent, officially released by the Census Bureau in September 1991, suggests staggeringly higher rates. The language of statistics implies objectivity; yet such objective measures serve to conceal the way poverty statistics are manipulated. Many children are conjured into invisibility as part of an overall policy of minimal or zero support of the "undeserving poor," who are relegated to the outer periphery of the public economy.

Poverty—a Private Affair or a Public Responsibility?

In speaking of poverty, let us never forget that there is a distinction between this and pauperism. The former is an unavoidable evil, to which many are brought from necessity, and in the wise and gracious Providence of God. It is the result, not of our faults, but of our misfortunes . . . Pauperism is the consequence of willful error, of shameful indolence, of vicious habits. It is a misery of human creation, the pernicious work of man, the lamentable consequences of bad principles and morals.

Reverend Charles Burroughs, 1834[9]

Let me repeat it, the causes of poverty are looked for, and found, in him or her who suffers it.

Walter Channing, 1843[10]

Reduction of poverty requires restoration of the moral environment in which the poor live.

George F. Will, 1991[11]

Not much has shifted in our public sensibilities from the religious moralism of the eighteen hundreds pointing to the depravity of the undeserving poor, to contemporary conservative commentaries on the "politics of conduct" of the nonworking poor. Poverty is a private affair—its causes are rooted in failed individuals, failed families, and moral degeneration rather than in a failed public economy and a discriminatory public policy. It is an individual or underclass or ethnic problem in need of redress, not a structural one requiring a fundamental shift in our ways of seeing the politics of distribution.

This perception of poverty as a private affair, argue Grubb and Lazerson, is rooted in a basic nineteenth-century American dilemma—public or private responsibility and the role of the state, "whether poverty should be considered a public problem requiring expanded state involvement, or a private and individual problem for which the state should accept minimal responsibility."[12] As the ideal of family as a domestic island, and the cult of motherhood, emerged during the mid-nineteenth century, the doctrine of *parens patriae* permitted public intervention, when parenting was judged inadequate, by legitimating surveillance and regulation of "defective" families in order to protect children.[13] This intervention targeted poor and vulnerable families, such as those headed by a woman, even though the doctrine legally applied to all families. As public responsibility for children received major attention during the Progressive Era, the assumption that families would remain private persisted, as did the assumption that the economy would remain private. If public money was to be spent, it should always be less than what the individual would gain in the private market. The consequence was that poor families should have poor children, whose lives should have fewer perceived advantages than those of other children. Thus public action becomes "a second-best resort, aiding those who are often considered second-class citizens."[14] This instrumental view of children, which in contemporary form represents a more sophisticated view of the non-deserving poor, also continues to rationalize a minimalist public responsibility where anticipated payoffs are supposed to justify the interventions. The success of both Head Start and High/Scope early intervention programs is demonstrated by their outcomes in terms of later payoffs for society. High/Scope has shown a 7.01 percent rate of return for one year of compensatory preschool,[15] which is widely touted as the rationale for continued funding. It is argued that these results demonstrate among targeted participants, that there is less crime, less drain on state resources, less adolescent pregnancy, and a decreased high school dropout rate.

None of these arguments is premised on compassion for children or concern for their existential well-being. Strangely absent for poor children is the democratic expectation that all young children are entitled to a decent life and to an equal educational opportunity. Rather, because their parents are poor, they too are punished. This construct of poverty as a private affair continues to mask the causes of poverty, which lie in structural inequalities of access and opportunity. In turn this has effectively limited public responsibility which has "reinforced the tendency towards private wealth and public squalor."[16] As long as the notion of poverty as a private affair dominates our public discourse, the dominant focus will be the "politics of conduct" of the poor. This discourse serves to conceal the continuing mean-spirited treatment of poor people and legitimates the minimalist and degrading support policies for single mothers and their children, who suffer the snowball effects of class and race as well as gender discrimination. Their poverty is viewed not as state-constructed but as their due, a condition into which they are born or fall and, most importantly, which they perpetuate. Poverty is regarded as a deserved condition. We see how pervasive the ideology of "blaming the victim" has been,[17] and how it continues when those of us who are both privileged and non-poor attempt to understand the condition of otherness. When otherness is imputed to those with least power—poor women and their children—a viable childhood and motherhood are dramatically eroded. But do incomplete mothers who have made incomplete families deserve decent lives?

Incomplete Mothers

> It's not a long life we live, . . . My kind die early, but the children will be well along, an' all the better when the time comes that they've full sense for not having to know what way the living comes. But let God almighty judge who's to blame most—I that was driven, or them that drove me to the pass I'm in.

Rose Haggerty, 1887[18]

> . . . there are expensive children and cheap children, just as there are expensive women and cheap women.

Marina Warner, 1989[19]

Mothers without husbands are cheap; they deserve less and if deserted, divorced, or unmarried constitute a gray and dubious category of the undeserving poor. While widowhood occurs through a tragedy of fate, the choice to live and bear children without a spouse engenders state suspicion and historically has threatened the moral order, from the Puritan patriarchy of New England to the welfare state with its mothers who "take our hard-earned tax dollars" in the 1990s. Why should we pay for them—they who are the repositories of what the French once termed the "dangerous instincts"? The argument is a historical one, with new forms of modernity—new illustrations for "the old story" of Oliver's mother and all to come. It is not scarlet letters that we now affix to the bosoms of errant women; rather, it is the discourse of "benefits"—food stamps that brand her, visibly humiliate her, in the supermarket, welfare offices that regulate her sexual relationships and judge her mothering as at risk.

In Hawthorne, we see Hester Prynne's disturbance of the moral order etched in sharp relief against the winds of shame in Salem, Mass:

> In this manner, Hester Prynne came to have a part to perform in the world. With her native energy of character, and rare capacity, it could not entirely cast her off, although it had set a mark upon her, more intolerable to a woman's heart than that which branded the brow of Cain. In all her intercourse with society, however, there was nothing that made her feel as if she belonged to it. Every gesture, every word, and even the silence of those with

whom she came in contact, implied, and often expressed, that she was banished, and as much alone as if she inhabited another sphere, or communicated with the common nature by other organs and senses than the rest of humankind.[20]

Hester is otherness incarnate; the starkly visible sinner, the immoral mother, who conceals her reverend lover from the Puritan community, goes to prison with her infant, and is forever branded in her scarlet shame. Even her daughter is potentially tainted by moral contagion. As the Governor attempts to remove the child, the "naughty elf," the "witch-child," so that she can be "disciplined strictly," we watch this condemned and humiliated single mother fight desperately to keep her child:

> "God gave me the child!" cried she. "He gave her, in requital of all things else, which ye had taken from me. She is my happiness!—she is my torture, none the less! Pearl keeps me here in life! Pearl punishes me too! . . . Ye shall not take her! I will die first!"
>
> "My poor woman," said the not unkind old minister, "the child shall be well cared for!—far better than thou canst do it."
>
> "God gave her into my keeping," repeated Hester Prynne, raising her voice almost to a shriek. "I will not give her up!"[21]

And she does not; but many of her less strong and less defiant sisters do, across the divide of centuries, forced by the state to surrender to their particularly female destitution and their own moral ignominy. And so Hester and Pearl begin their isolated existence outside the prison walls; a form of house arrest, the spatialization of power in moral exclusion, a constant reminder to the community of the lot that befalls a fallen woman and her child.

Single mothers have historically occupied the zone of suspicion, the horizon of potential depravity; from the destitute in early nineteenth-century France, who were forced to abandon their babies to the tour or the wetnurse's hovel; to single immigrant and black mothers in industrializing America, who were exhorted to maintain "proper" incomplete families and were faced with the constant specter of neglect charges as "they struggled to meet the contradictory expectations of raising and providing for children in a society organized on the premise of male breadwinning and female domesticity."[22] The poorer and less patriarchal the household, the more imperative the need for state-sanctioned *parens patriae* intervention to judge the moral rectitude of the home and the correct upbringing of the family.

At the turn of the twentieth century in a large urban center such as Boston, 20 percent of families were headed by single mothers. Linda Gordon describes the Progressive Era and its aftermath as the period in which single motherhood was specifically constructed as a clinical problem in the United States. "Their very life style was suspect. Single motherhood and child neglect were mutually and simultaneously constructed as social problems, and many of the defining indices of child neglect, such as a lack of supervision, were essential to the survival of female-headed households."[23] Such mothers could not conform to norms of domesticity. Their children were often dirty, infected with lice and worms, and so were they, because they lived in squalor in overcrowded, seeping tenements. Rapid urbanization, a soaring immigrant population, and wage labor under industrial capitalism had made a minimally tolerable existence impossible. There was little available child care, day nurseries for poor children were rare, and many women worked night jobs while their children were asleep, fearing that discovery might lead to neglect charges.

In reviewing the case records of the Massachusetts Society for the Prevention of Cruelty to Children, Linda Gordon presents clear evidence of the bias that dominated that organization: children from single-mother families were frequently removed by child protectors. Rather than support women's independence from husbands who were abusive, caseworkers would try to force a woman to remain in the marriage, or would remove her children if they were classified as neglected or abused. The most common form of moral neglect was out-of-wedlock relations, which caseworkers presumed led to "low moral standards" in the children and subsequent "vice." Caseworkers frequently concluded that parenting and breadwinning by one person also led to child neglect; therefore it was argued that "single mothers were morally bad, bad for children, bad for society." These case records also reveal the ethnic/racial prejudice of the predominantly white, native-born, Protestant social workers of the time—a prejudice which, coupled with a pervasive bias against poor women, resulted in clinical entries describing clients as "a typical low-grade Italian woman," "primitive," "limited, not nearly as talkative as many of her race," "fairly good for a colored woman," "brassy, indifferent, . . . coarse," "degenerate," "immoral."[24]

How could such single mothers survive? Taking in boarders was frowned upon as leading to immorality, for the single boarding population was predominantly male in large cities such as Boston. Prostitution and bootlegging were lucrative but illegal, although prior to Prohibition many women manufactured and sold home brew. Women were excluded from a "family wage"; meager though that was, the wage was a male domain. While not permitted to enter the economy on equal terms with men, women, when single, were expected to be both provider and nurturer for their children. They could not fulfill either role adequately as their single status condemned them to be incomplete mothers, unable to meet the norms of domesticity expounded by their more privileged sisters. Nor were they able to remove themselves and their children from destitution without help. In both cases their lives were fated to dependency by virtue of their gender and their class, and their plight was frequently exacerbated by their blackness or ethnic immigrant status.

As industrialism proceeded apace and individualism and free-market competition flourished, self-sufficiency formed not only an economic ideal but a moral ethos encoded in the Protestant work ethic. For women, however, as Virginia Shapiro points out, it was not self-sufficiency and rugged individualism that was promoted but rather dependency; dependency on men as breadwinners, while men and children in turn were dependent on women as wives and mothers to create the domestic nest. When the nest fell apart and the family threads began to unravel, or worse, when there was no family structure, women moved from male/husband dependency to becoming wards of the state. The patriarchy circle widened in concentric rings, from marriage to welfare, from private to public control. Throughout, "social policy (has) assumed that women are not autonomous individuals and moral agents, but that they live contingent lives . . . Choice as a moral agent is missing."[25]

Welfare and the Making of Contingency

The gendered nature of the welfare state has often concealed the roots of poverty for women and children. It is an economy of inequitable distribution and production that creates the need for women's welfare programs in the first place.[26] The relationship of women to the welfare state has always been one of contingency and subordination to the ideal of domesticity. Mothers' Pensions, the forerunner of Aid to Families with Dependent Children (AFDC), was expressly designed to keep woman at home when a male breadwinner was absent, thereby defining her dependent status and relegating her to a regulated life. Welfare expenditure funneled to AFDC has not transcended the norm of a stay-at-home, unskilled, untrained mother, to be supported by her husband. But those norms represent an ideology of domesticity and motherhood which are themselves the product of a gendered system. This ideology continues to see women as citizen-mothers, not citizen-workers, thereby perpetuating low-wage temporary employment, low-status pink-collar jobs, and the unavailability of public child care and maternity leave provisions, all of which leave poor single women with few options other than welfare when they have young children.

To pursue this long-standing public perception of women as mothers rather than citizen-workers, let us shift our attention back to France, where, as we have seen, a cult of the "new mother" had dominated bourgeois sensibilities. By the end of the nineteenth century, the French perceived working women quite differently than did the Americans. In France, women were seen as citizen-workers whose necessary participation in the labor force required state policies for their protection in their dual roles of worker and mother. It followed that both working mothers and their babies were entitled to state protection, and while women still lacked political rights, they were accorded civil rights in recognition of their productive and reproductive functions.[27] As France continued to debate its "social question," single mothers, *femmes isolées,* were viewed as the representation of misery, the potential producers of the "dangerous classes"; hence French social policy began to take a radically different turn. Because high infant mortality rates were linked to deprivation of breastfeeding in the first months after birth, paid pre- and postnatal maternity leave was instituted and written into labor legislation at the turn of the century. Factory creches, state-provided child care, and the regulation of hours for women working in factories all served as protective legislation for working women, where state policy recognized and supported women's needs as workers and mothers. Ironically, while such workplace rights were guaranteed, female suffrage was opposed; for France affirmed the social-economic identity of woman as citizen-worker but denied her identity as political actor.

In the United States, however, maternity leave, paid or unpaid, was never entrenched as state policy. In 1916, the American Association for Labor Legislation lobbied to introduce maternity legislation modeled on that of northern Europe; but it was opposed as unnecessary by employers who did not think women should work after marriage.[28] Once again, the implicit moral assumption was that only married women needed consideration and that these were best taken care of by husband-breadwinners; single mothers were excluded from the discourse. Hence the ideology of separate spheres, of dependence and self-sufficiency, of private and public realms, haunted the working women of the first decade of the twentieth

century and continues to do so in the 1990s. The United States stands together with South Africa as the only Western postindustrial society with no
maternity policies for working mothers. American working women thus became "invisible as workers for everyone but those who argued for their
'exceptional' needs. Women's citizenship rights were claimed almost exclusively because of their supposed maternal qualities. Absent was an identity
for working women or for women unencumbered by nurturing responsibilities."[29]

Once again, we return to the question—how did single mothers and
their children survive? Between 1890 and 1910, the proportion of women
in the paid labor force increased from 16 percent to 25.5 percent. While
most married women were expected to give up employment, strong class
and racial differences existed; immigrant women had a 50 percent higher
labor force participation rate than native-born white women, and black
women averaged far higher rates than white women.[30] In 1910, 10.7 percent of *married* women worked in the labor force and here again, more
black women than white women.[31] After 1911, when Mothers' Aid Laws
(mothers' pensions) were introduced, some white "deserving mothers" began to receive minimal public assistance. During this same period, Workmen's Compensation was introduced for working men as an early form of
social insurance. This two-tiered hierarchy of benefit programs enacted for
men and women during the Progressive era illuminates the peculiar status
to which poor women and their children have been relegated since the
inception of the welfare state.

Workmen's Compensation was designed to serve men as a form of social insurance to compensate them and their families for their sacrifice to
industrial labor through disability or death and was premised on a "deserving worker" assumption. Entitlement to a pension was dependent on how
much the worker had earned and how long he had been attached to the
work force. The program was primarily developed for Northern white men
who were employed in heavy industry. Since heavy industry exacted a high
toll of accidents and deaths, public outrage propelled the program as did
comparison with much lower casualties in western Europe, where compensation programs were already in place in many countries in the early nineteen hundreds.

While the Widow's Pension Program was originally designed to assist
widows and their children and to place them in a category above that of the
Poor Law Aid applied to paupers, many settlement house workers and reformers campaigned vigorously for a more inclusive mothers' pension. Be-

tween 1910 and 1920, forty states enacted mothers' pension laws, with the primary purpose of reinforcing home life and officially recognizing that successful domesticity prevented women from being both homemakers and breadwinners. The first mothers' pension law enacted in Illinois included deserted and unmarried mothers, but this inclusion provoked such an outcry that many states restricted aid to widows or wives with disabled husbands. By 1934, only three states had expanded their laws specifically to include unwed mothers, and in eight other states the law was broad enough to include them. Children of divorced mothers could be aided in only twenty-one states, and children of deserted mothers in thirty-six. A central requirement in all states was the "suitable home" provision, which enabled local authorities to keep subsidized mothers under surveillance, regulating their lifestyles and mandating certain family norms. The regulation included the fostering of religion, prohibition of the mother from taking in male boarders, and monitoring of the child's school records.[32] If mother failed, she risked removal of both pension and child. Mothers' pensions, though designed to keep women out of the marketplace and at home, were never sufficient to enable women to maintain viable families. Between 1911, the year pensions were first offered, and 1935, when Aid to Dependent Children (ADC) was instituted, only a small proportion of "deserving" white mothers qualified for pensions. Even so, many lost their children to institutions because they could not support them.[33] In 1931, for example, although a high proportion of female-headed families were black, only 3 percent of pension recipients were black and in Houston, Texas, where blacks made up one-fifth of the population, no black mothers received mothers' pensions.[34]

Workmen's Compensation and mothers' pensions were the first federal benefit programs enacted in the United States (after the Civil War Pensions, which had excluded all but Union men). The former was considered an earned right, the latter a stigmatized handout. Since its inception, welfare for women has been viewed as a favor, as begrudged and limited public assistance to incomplete women and mothers that legitimates the regulation of their suspect lifestyle and the invasion of their privacy, since *we* are giving our money to *them*. On the other hand, social insurance—social security and unemployment compensation—were and continue to be supported by the opponents of welfare. It is no coincidence that historically the primary beneficiaries of welfare have been poor mothers, and the primary beneficiaries of social insurance have been male breadwinners. This two-tiered benefit system has been described by Barbara Nelson as the "two-channel welfare state."[35] Nelson shows how Workmen's Compensation was characterized by a set of decision-making rules and standardized criteria for eligibility which reinforced the social legitimacy of the clients' claims. It served primarily white men, who constituted its working-class leadership. These, in turn, through criteria of eligible labor, excluded both domestic workers and agricultural laborers, who by 1930 made up fully 60 percent of the black labor force. Hence both women and blacks were largely excluded from this primary-sector program. The mothers' pension movement, in contrast, lacked working-class leadership. Instead, philanthropists, educated professional women of the settlement houses, and welfare advocates joined forces to endorse a program for childsaving and family strengthening by supporting the cause of poor, deserving mothers, left destitute as widows or enduring the loss of labor earnings by a disabled breadwinner husband. Only later did deserted and divorced women gain the same entitlements.

One of the key differences in the administration of the two programs was the control of conduct of the beneficiaries. The behavior of the mother was closely monitored and her moral conduct was cause for approval or disapproval of benefits. Not so with Workmen's Compensation; for when the benefits were claimed, the beneficiary had independent control over the resources. The male worker filled out a standardized claim form and underwent a physical examination by a physician. Mothers, on the other hand, needed to pass an examination for moral fitness, which covered sexual behavior, use of alcohol and tobacco, absence of boarders, and suitable housekeeping and childrearing skills. Thus Nelson, in analyzing the creation of a two-channel welfare state that corresponds to the separate spheres of the public and private, argues that "these programs had different ideologies, clienteles, principles of entitlement and administrative styles and they set the tone for the Social Security Act, which in turn greatly reinforced the gender, racial, and class organization of the welfare state."[36]

In 1935, when the Roosevelt administration enacted the Social Security Act, five new federal support programs came into being. They, too, were distinguished by their two-channel orientation. The social insurance programs—unemployment and old age insurance—were designed to prevent poverty on the part of able, attached workers who had actively sustained occupational careers; the benefits were proportionate to the clients' earnings. The deserving beneficiaries had demonstrated a work ethic and attachment to the labor force. In the case of unemployment insurance, benefits were intended to be short-term. The three welfare—or relief—programs were Aid to the Blind, Old Age Assistance, and Aid to Dependent Children. The ADC benefits, according to the *Report of the Commit-*

tee on Economic Security of 1935, were "designed to release from the wage earning role the person whose natural function is to give her children the physical and affectionate guardianship necessary, not alone to keep them from falling into social misfortune, but more affirmatively to rear them into citizens capable of contributing to society."[37] ADC expanded the number of beneficiaries, finally incorporating children of divorced and unmarried mothers, so that the number of families receiving benefits jumped dramatically from 227,000 (receiving mothers' pensions) in 1935 to 527,000 (receiving ADC) in 1937.[38] However, because the "suitable home" provisions, a leftover from the mothers' pension program, were still enforced, many black children and children of unwed mothers continued to be excluded. Race and moral fitness continued to operate as regulatory mechanisms that perpetuated the stigma suffered by single mothers.

After World War II, as we saw earlier, both wives and mothers were evicted from the workplace in unprecedented numbers to make way for returning GI's. The children of wartime working mothers were evicted from their wartime daycare centers, which were forced to close as women and children entered a new, mid-century cult of domesticity. Hence, homemaking and childrearing as natural biological destiny were once again reinforced. The ADC Program was changed to AFDC (Aid to Families with Dependent Children) in 1950, and the custodial parent (mother) also became a recipient of benefits and was required to stay home and rear her children. If she worked, one dollar was deducted from welfare payments for every dollar earned, so that many women ended up poorer if they worked part-time and had to pay work-related expenses such as transportation. Throughout the 1950s and early 1960s, single mothers, while prevented from earning subsistence wages, were also targeted as welfare parasites in need of rehabilitation. Ironically, the public discourse about welfare centered on dependency; yet public policy had made women wards of the state. With punitive restrictions on any economic self-sufficiency, such as the 100 percent "tax" on benefits, they could hardly become independent unless they developed strategies to cheat the system. They were trapped in escalating public accusations: if not parasites, then they were cheats; if not cheats, then welfare queens, producing countless children at taxpayer expense. Through all these charges the belief persisted that women should remain male-dependent and fulfill their domestic responsibilities. The "man in the house" provision permitted welfare funds to be withheld if any able-bodied man, related or not, was found to be cohabiting with the mother, or merely resident in the household. This assumption of male as breadwinner and female as dependent once again reveals the patriarchy of the state.

In 1965, during the War on Poverty, both Medicaid (health care for the poor) and Medicare (health insurance for the aged) were enacted. The food stamp program, initiated under Roosevelt and revived under Kennedy, was expanded, as were housing programs. AFDC benefit levels were increased by 36 percent in the states between 1965 and 1970. Rates of participation in AFDC soared; between 1967 and 1971 the proportion of eligible female-headed families who received benefits increased from approximately 60 percent to 90 percent.[39] The late 1960s have been described by Teresa Amott as a period in which black women, previously closed out of the New Deal programs, gained collective access as the National Welfare Rights Organization (NWRO) pressed federal and state authorities for a living income that would enable mothers and their children to live with dignity.[40]

This period saw the inception of the Head Start Program for poor children, of legal advocacy for the poor and minorities, and of major civil rights legislation, all as part of the Great Society reforms. At the same time, a rehabilitative perception toward the poor was gaining currency—an attempt to transform their attitudes and lifestyles by means of workfare programs, where the poor were expected to work their way off welfare.[41] The Work Incentive Program (WIN) at the end of the 1960s, while giving priority to men in hiring, began to demand that women on welfare should work too, and "employables" were required to register for training and employment programs. In 1971, AFDC regulations began to require for the first time that women with school-age children should seek employment. The dollar reduction for every dollar earned was reduced and the "thirty and one-third rule" instituted: designed to function as an incentive, it allowed recipients to keep the first thirty dollars of monthly earnings and one-third of the remainder. WIN, however, not only proved ineffective in moving women off welfare but served as a source of continuing harassment for single mothers. Since a minimal allowance was given for child care, since child care itself was frequently unavailable or unaffordable, and since most women had access only to low-wage jobs, with no support system when children were ill or not in school, poor mothers found themselves in a no-win situation.

Carol Stack's ethnographic account of women's strategies for survival in "The Flats," a black community in the Midwest, illuminates the emptiness and hopelessness of the job experience for poor black women (and men). It shows how women on welfare develop survival strategies through the security of their kin and friendship networks, in which they must "wager their relationship against the insurmountable forces of poverty and racism."[42] Stack's study, conducted in the late 1960s, is as telling over two decades later; welfare-to-work and training programs still do not provide tickets out of poverty for poor single women, but rather create a pool of temporary "employables" readily absorbed and readily discarded in the service industries. As Piven and Cloward point out, welfare is a form of regulating the poor, and "relief arrangements . . . have a great deal to do with maintaining social and economic inequities."[43]

Between the years 1970 and 1973, the welfare rolls continued to expand dramatically, with the average number of recipients rising by 50 percent. The composition of AFDC families too had changed; they no longer consisted primarily of white widows and wives of disabled husbands, but included increasing numbers of single separated, divorced, or unwed mothers, white and black, who with their children were becoming both destitute and homeless. During this expansion, which took place within the context of other social change movements such as civil rights, more and more women began to see welfare as an entitlement. Welfare rights organizers stressed the feminist perspective inherent in the struggle. As Johnnie Tillman, the first chairwoman of the National Welfare Rights Organization (NWRO), stated: "I'm a woman. I'm a black woman. I'm a poor woman . . . And I'm on welfare. In this country, if you're any one of those things . . . you count less than a human being . . . On AFDC, you're not supposed to have any sex at all. You give up control of your own body. It's a condition of aid . . . *The* man, the welfare system controls your money."[44]

The conservative backlash against women on welfare that followed the War on Poverty was unleashed in the mid 1970s, reaching full force under the Reagan administration, with disastrous consequences for poor women and their children. Between 1973 and 1986, for example, the number on AFDC remained constant at 10.7 million, yet the number in need, predominantly single mothers and young children, rose dramatically. In 1973 nearly 85 percent of eligible children received benefits, but by 1986 the number had dropped to less than 60 percent.[45] Major cuts were instituted when Congress passed the 1981 Omnibus Budget Reconciliation Act (OBRA) soon after Reagan's election and in essence "turned back the clock on welfare policy," eliminating the eligibility of many poor working women and their families. Medicaid, food stamps, child care, school lunch allowances, and prenatal, maternal, and child-health care were cut or drastically reduced for poor working women and their children. One and a half mil-

Joan

lion children were eliminated from the welfare rolls. Deborah Zinn and Rosemary Sarri, investigating the impact of OBRA on poor working mothers in Michigan, present a picture of public policy-induced family destitution and stress, as single mothers were confronted with termination not only of AFDC benefits but of their Medicaid insurance and housing as well.[46] These devastating cuts were rationalized by a discourse of dependence and cheating, reaching ironic pinnacles when poverty was seen as its own cause. We are reminded of Walter Channing's 1843 Address on the Prevention of Pauperism: "The causes of poverty are looked for, and found in him or her who suffers it." Channing's words were to be echoed over a century later in President Reagan's 1986 State of the Union address, in which he blamed "the welfare culture" for "the breakdown of the family . . . , female and child poverty, child abandonment, horrible crimes and deteriorating schools."[47]

The answer, of course, was sought in further regulation and restrictions, rather than in the provision of adequate family support benefits, including a viable minimum wage, child care, and affordable housing. Diana Pearce, revisiting her "feminization of poverty" thesis fifteen years later, in 1990, contends that "welfare is not *for* women."[48] As we approach the twenty-first century, it becomes disturbingly clear that the minimal welfare state, constructed within the political economy of the United States, is integrally implicated in the perpetuation of the feminization and, by extension, the growing "infantilization" of poverty.

Women's Lot: Feminized Poverty and Pink-Collar Contingency

In 1959, 23 percent of poor families were headed by single mothers. By 1989, that number had soared to the current figure of 52 percent. Children who live with their mothers are far more likely to live in poverty: 51 percent of such children were poor in 1989, compared to only 22 percent in single-father-headed families and 10 percent in two-parent families. It is estimated that more than half of all children born today will spend part of their childhood in a single-parent home. A key factor in the poverty of single-mother households is the absence of child support by fathers. In 1988 only 51 percent of single mothers were awarded child support payments, and of that group only 26 percent actually received their full award.[49] Payments are small, often averaging as little as $2100 annually per family.

In 1990, for a family of three, the poverty level was defined as an annual income of less than $10,560; yet at new minimum-wage levels, a single mother working full time will earn under $700 per month, more than 20 percent below the poverty level. Because minimum-wage employment is unlikely to provide health insurance or other benefits, and because child care is unaffordable, the mother is forced to turn to AFDC to receive Medicaid. In 1990, the maximum AFDC benefit for a family of three averaged $367 per month, 55 percent below the poverty line. In five states the maximum AFDC grant for a three-person family was less than $200 per month. Furthermore, AFDC kept pace with inflation in only Maine and California; in the other thirty-seven states the inflation-adjusted value of the maximum AFDC benefit fell by more than 25 percent between 1970 and 1990. In eight states it fell by more than 50 percent. Unaffordable housing costs alone during the eighties have made it virtually impossible for a three-person family on AFDC to secure housing. In thirty-nine states the fair-market rent now exceeds—and in a number of states is two or three times—the amount of the entire maximum grant for a family of three. AFDC criteria have become more stringent, and by 1988 were reaching only 61 percent of eligible poor children in female-headed families. As mentioned earlier, food stamp allowances were cut during the Reagan years, and recent reports from the Food Research and Action Center report that millions of children are currently hungry.[50]

Attempts at welfare reform during the past years have failed to confront the gender base of the welfare system and the issues of private, public, and corporate responsibility. The Family Support Act of 1988, which the states began to implement in 1990, was a small and mean-spirited attempt to reform welfare, but along *workfare* lines.[51] The act, written by Senator Moynihan, passed with bipartisan support on the assumption that paid employment leads women off the welfare rolls. The states are permitted to require mothers of children over one year of age to participate in welfare-to-work programs. Both the training and child care benefits built into the act, however, are woefully inadequate; the latter do not meet the costs of enrolling a child in a quality child care center. States are allowed to receive federal matching funds for child care only at the 75th percentile of the local market rate, condemning the vast majority of young poor children to substandard care. Given the current crisis in child care availability, the Children's Defense Fund estimates that in the majority of states, only a fraction of AFDC children find child care slots. While the Family Support Act does provide federal support for education and training through the new Job Opportunities and Basic Skills Program (JOBS), there is pressure to operate very short-term low-cost programs. As states lay off workers and attempt to trim budgets, such pressures increase, and the first programs targeted are the welfare programs.

The conviction that AFDC women should have to work went counter to a pervasive set of ideological assumptions about domesticity. Yet the assumptions correlative to welfare reform—that women are entitled to public child care, maternity leaves, and child allowances, as is the case in all western European countries—are seldom voiced in American legislatures. The current reform package reflects "a strange and novel combination of conservative motives (tax cutting, hostility to single mothers and to women's sexual and reproductive independence, racism) with an acceptance of women's employment."[52] Both conservative and liberal views are injurious to women, argues Diana Pearce, as both perspectives are grounded *either* in the assumption that women should be male-dependent, *or* in the assumption that women are second-class workers.[53]

Many women are poor for the same reasons men are poor—because they lack education or skills, or live in a poor job area, or are minorities who suffer the long-term continuing effects of discrimination. But women are also poor because they are both nurturers of and providers for their children, and because they are disadvantaged in the labor market.[54] The median income for a woman worker in 1989 was only 68 percent of the median income for a male worker.[55] The average woman college graduate working full time, earned less than the average male high school graduate. Women are far less able to obtain full-time, year-round work. Many mothers who attempt to support their families can find only part-time or seasonal work, and encounter severe child care problems if their children are young. Women often become casual, secondary-sector workers, ineligible for unemployment and health insurance benefits by virtue of their low wages and part-time work. For women, particularly mothers, a job is no certain route out of poverty,[56] precisely because there is no job security and few fringe benefits. In contrast, workers in the primary sector receive higher pay as well as fringe benefits, and if they lose their jobs they are entitled to unemployment compensation. As Pearce points out, disproportionate numbers of women and minorities occupy the secondary sector: 87 percent of the recipients of primary benefits are in white families headed by men or married couples; only 3 percent are headed by black single mothers. The difference in poverty incidence between those who receive social insurance and those who receive welfare is dramatic: only 8 percent of the families of primary-sector beneficiaries as against almost 75 percent of the families of secondary-sector beneficiaries are living in poverty. Women, especially minority women, are disproportionately represented in the latter category. Pearce concludes that "the secondary welfare sector destroys not only one's incentives but also one's prospect of ever working one's way out of poverty." While public myths implicate welfare mothers as nonworkers, Pearce indicates that 90 percent of welfare mothers have worked, many recently, and that they apply for public assistance only when men and the labor market fail to provide income support for family maintenance.[57] The tragedy is that AFDC fails dismally as a back-up support and serves to disempower and humiliate such mothers further, as the welfare bureaucracy creates modern-day paupers of them and their children.

Yet there are stories to be told that float between the coarse pages of welfare statistics, there are voices that speak not a language of otherness, but a language of ours—of mothers and children who confront the dailiness of lives in poverty. It is time to listen to their stories.

Young Mothers' Stories: Being Teenage, Black, and Single

J OEY WELTER WAS SEVENTEEN, an honors student in her senior year of high school, when she became pregnant with twins. She was the oldest of six children, her mother a single parent struggling to support the family. Joey received no help or financial support from her twins' father, whom she had dated for two years prior to the pregnancy. He is currently living in the same part of the state and has another girlfriend. Joey describes the struggles she has experienced over the past three years as a single mother:

I was seventeen when it happened . . . I went to the abortion clinic and then they said I had two on the way and I cried—and I wanted to use my mom's Medicaid and the lady said I couldn't use it—you know they won't pay no more so second semester they put me in the hospital—in January 'cos my water bag had busted so they put me in the hospital and I was there until January 31, and my babies weren't due until March 20 and they were born January 24 and that's like eight–ten weeks premature—and they all spent thirty-one days in intensive care and their lungs had collapsed, they had no movement and it was just terrible . . . So I stayed out of school till March and I just, I had to go back y'know, and I took just two classes an afternoon and it was alright, I didn't really miss out on any y'know—real interesting activities—I still did stuff and hung out with my friends and I did graduate—but a month later it was—now you got two babies at Mama's house and you gotta find a job and get to work.

When I was in the hospital I applied for Medicaid 'cos they [the twins] were in intensive care and I got it, so I was living with my mother, and me the oldest of six kids and it was just her taking care of the family—but then I got this job and I was working forty hours a week and they cut me off Medicaid and food stamps 'cos I was earning a few dollars over the limit, and they said—"well you live with your mother," but my mother has five other kids to take care of y'know—so I had to move out on my own, and I moved in with someone else and they walked out after two months—and like it's

you're going to bed, and you're crying and you're mad at yourself—and I
just didn't have money and no insurance so I just wouldn't take them [the
twins] to the doctor unless it's an absolute emergency. I just let my Mama
pray over them and sometimes it goes away . . . God the doctors' bills from
'89! I still owe like $549 and I think I paid $20!

Denied an abortion because of the 1988 Medicaid cutoff in Michigan,
a young mother, poor, with no child support, living on her own, working
full time, with no health insurance—Joey finds herself in an even greater
predicament by giving birth to twins and by her growing competence in the
workplace. Because she earns $38 per month over the AFDC maximum
allowance for earnings, she is cut off from benefits and rendered even more
vulnerable as the babies become sick during their first winter, running up
a pediatric bill of several hundred dollars. Because Joey has her mother
and her sister to help out with the twins, she, unlike many other single
moms, does have backup when her child care arrangements fail:

I just can't stop thanking them; if it weren't for my mama and my sister who
keep my kids—they've always been there to help me . . . it would be like
terrible if it weren't for them.

But even with their valued help, child care is an unaffordable burden;
Joey spends a minimum of $120 every two weeks out of a bimonthly pay-
check of $400 for the twins. Besides working full time, she is going to a
local college in pursuit of a social work degree and next year will have to
take more credits:

Right now I'm at the stage where everything is piling, bills and all little
things. Little things are things that do it. I can't find a baby-sitter right now
'cos I can't pay her—I try to go get help from welfare and they tell me I
make too much money. They can't go to daycare 'cos there's no space—they
can only go Monday and Friday but I need the other days too and now I
work all day Friday, Saturday, Sunday, Monday—so they went to my sister
and she keeps them and sometimes I didn't see my kids from Thursday to
Monday—but now that don't work no more and it's one thing after another
going on in my life. I gotta find a way to work, to go to school, I gotta go to
the laundromat, I try to get food—now my car broke down . . . no matter
how hard you try you're always going to be two steps behind because
whoever the force is, never wants you to succeed.

Clearly neither Joey's remarkable hard work and tenacity nor her family support have enabled her to lead a secure life with her twins. As she

sees it, "the force" is there to keep her down; a work ethic, a job, and strong motivation to succeed are insufficient to pull someone out of poverty who is young, female, and a mother. Here we see how poverty and welfare co-exist in mutually reinforcing reciprocity.

But what happens when poor families, economically stretched beyond their limits and their emotional endurance, do not, or cannot, support a young teenage mother—when affectionate support is absent, when the pregnant child is cast out as we see in Toni Crane's situation? At fourteen, pregnant and in the eighth grade, Toni becomes temporarily homeless until an aunt takes her in before the birth of her baby.

> I got pregnant when I was in the eighth grade, so I mean, already like I'm going into high school and I'm pregnant. They were shocked and they were pissed 'cos I was only fourteen and everything but they didn't give me a chance for a decision—do you want to have the baby or do you not want to have the baby or whatever. They said you are going to have the baby, you made your bed now lay in it—meanwhile all the time everyone's telling me to have the baby because they will help me—but I had to stay at my aunt— I mean I wasn't even staying at my parents, then once I had the baby she [the aunt] kicked me out because her boyfriend didn't want me and my daughter there. Already I'm in ninth grade and I missed the whole semester and I mean I'm not going back and then I come home from the hospital with my baby and they say, "Get out."

Toni's story only worsens when she becomes a victim of the Medicaid bureaucracy. Several months after her hospitalization for premature delivery, she receives a letter from the collection agency for $17,000:

> So all this time I ain't heard nothing about the bill, my mother and them were supposed to take this Medicaid card and give it to them so they could bill Medicaid. So I go—what the fuck do I do—and I'm calling these people at the hospital and they're telling me, "Well you were a minor and we don't need to speak to you, we need to speak to your parents," and I'm like, well my parents don't have nothing to do with me . . . Finally I had to go to the hospital and they had to go through my records and they say I still owe $500. Well, I didn't know I could go to DSS [Department of Social Services] and tell them I was on Medicaid and they have to pay it, so I ended up starting to pay that bill every month 'cos they said, "Well if your parents don't pay us somebody's got to pay it" . . . and there's something else— y'know when I was on social service for that time I had to sign my name on the dotted line but I never knew what I was signing—I mean after they told

me I owed them money back, I didn't even know why or what for—nobody ever talked with me and then they showed me—"If you read this right here—even if it's your fault or even if it's our fault you have to make up that difference"—and they said I was signed up wrong. I was signed up as an independent person and I should have been signed up under my aunt, because that was who I been staying with until she threw me out and she was my guardian.

Toni, a frightened child, confused and intimidated by the power and threat of the welfare bureaucracy, is left to fend for herself—alternately moving in with and out from her aunt, then her mother, then her sister, then friends, all the time holding on to her baby during the following two years. She has not been assisted by social workers or helped to negotiate her way through the maze of public assistance. For a brief period she is finally assigned a helpful caseworker, but this respite ends abruptly and Toni encounters more welfare threats:

So next thing, finally I had this caseworker and it was like working fine— she talked to me real nice—but then they fired her, they didn't tell me why— and then I got this man and I never seen him and he never called me or anything and he was sending me all those things telling me I had to go through this and through that. I thought what is going on now—then all of a sudden, like a month later, he sends me this thing when they take me and my baby off welfare—and they say I owed them like $600 or $700, because I wasn't meant to be getting that much money or whatever. I thought, oh my God you mean I owe you money! Then I had to go get one of those legal aid persons—I never seen her either—just talked to her on the phone—all I could think was oh no! Then he [the caseworker] sent me another letter telling me I didn't have to pay them, but that I was cut off. He said if I wanted I would have to come back and sign up all over next month for Medicaid and all that. But then I decided I won't go through all that, because then I'd probably owe them for all that next time.

Toni's terror of further threats from public assistance leave her and her baby with no health care, no food stamps, no shelter, and a family who are abusive and mired in their own misfortunes. Her mother, according to Toni, is "crazy," "never was a mother to us." Toni describes how her older sister, unable to have children of her own, tried to "steal" Toni's baby from her by calling in protective services and reporting Toni for neglect (after physically abusing her) and then offering to be guardian of the child,

*Because I wouldn't give my baby to my sister she reported me and she told
them I don't feed her properly, I don't bathe her right and dress her right
and then they came on me in the middle of the night—the police but they
didn't do nothing—I mean they saw my baby was okay—but you know I
been meaning to call and see if I still have a record y'know—of being a bad
mother or whatever.*

After enduring the impersonal terror of the state bureaucracy and the
personal terror of an abusive and dysfunctional family, Toni and her baby
are caught on the edges of life. Where to turn and how to find help? Because Toni is spunky and resourceful, and determined to keep her baby,
she finally locates a teen-parent center in another area. Her life and that of
her young daughter begin to change, as she returns to school (ninth grade)
and her daughter stays at the child care center. She is helped to obtain her
AFDC payments.

*I mean it wasn't just a daycare, I mean they really helped me—all of them
there is practically my mothers—I still used to cry and I used to go there
and say I'm not going back to school y'know—but they helped me do it.*

The center that was such a source of strength for Toni in 1990 has in
1991 been targeted for severe budget cuts as part of both school district
and state cuts for "nonessential" nonacademic programs. Slashing budgets
can also mean slashing young lives. In Toni's case, the program has been a
lifeline. Without it, she could not complete high school. It is not clear what
she will do if the center is forced to close.

Anna Adams was older (eighteen) and had recently graduated from
high school when she had her daughter. When asked to tell her story, she
says, "I don't really have a horror story," but instead she describes her growing disillusionment when her boyfriend deserts her and the baby, days of
work at low pay that exhaust her and that fail to make her economically
self-sufficient as she tries desperately to meet her growing baby's needs.
She is dependent on her family for help with child care, yet her relationship
with her mother is fraught with conflict. Above all, she leads a grim and
harsh life, one that she wishes fervently to escape from.

*I hate being a single mom, but there's nothing I can do about it. I hate this
life! I hate it! I hate it from day to day—I can't stand it and everyday
I'm thinking what can I do to get away from this—how can I better myself to get away from this.*

But each effort that Anna makes—and she has attempted many—meets with obstacles from a welfare bureaucracy that punishes single mothers for initiative and partial economic self-sufficiency.

see — mother who tried to save benefits for daughters college educ.

> All the time I don't think this system's here to help me, it's just to keep you right where you're at—to be poor—to make you psychologically dependent. I know a lot of people who've been on ADC for ten or twenty years . . . First, I'm like—how can you do that with your life—it's not good to sit on ADC and have baby after baby, and people like me we try and want something better but they don't help—it just doesn't work for you at all. It's like you're working—well, they want you to work—but then they take away what you make and they cut you off just as you get going—so it's like you're never on top. But I gotta find a way out of this—it's just too crazy.

Anna has experienced enormous frustration in trying to move ahead. After the baby was born, she found a job working forty hours a week at a department store and earned just over five dollars an hour. While she was eligible for health insurance, her baby was not, since there is a two-year wait period for the child's eligibility. And because her earnings exceeded the DSS cut-off, she lost food stamps and Medicaid and is now several months behind in her rent payment:

> I don't want to be on ADC but I had to get back so I could get caught up on my rent and get Medicaid for my baby . . . so I was working 40 hours and since I got back on ADC I had to cut back to 15–20 hours a week—I hate being on ADC, they make you feel so belittled I hate that! I hate going to the office and I hate dealing with the social worker and dealing with every worker that has something to say about my life . . . Sometimes they make you think that they're the one giving you this money and they're not—it's the government and they make me pay taxes so I'm the one giving the money back to myself . . .
>
> And then I was asking what if I wanted to go back to school and the worker said, "You didn't graduate," and I said I graduated! And I want to go to college—I don't want to be on ADC the rest of my life and if I keep doing what I'm doing now I'm never going to get off. I got my high hopes for me and I don't want her [my daughter] to go through the same things I have—it's terrible.

Anna's anger at the welfare system illustrates the double bind that so many single mothers are caught in. Her pink-collar job keeps her at just above minimum wage but still in poverty; there are few opportunities for advancement, particularly as she has to reduce her hours in order to protect her child's health coverage through Medicaid. She is thus all but condemned to being a permanent part-time, low-wage worker. Even if she were able to obtain private health insurance for her child in a couple of years, it is doubtful that she could carry the rental on her two-bedroom apartment, which currently runs between $500 and $600 per month. Her transportation costs are high, and while she can rely on her family for some child care, that will become increasingly difficult if she goes to college part-time as well. She worries constantly about losing her self-esteem, of succumbing to "the statistics" that make her "a nothing."

> *I feel so much better about myself when I'm working 'cos I'm also doing something for myself, and all the time I'm trying to better myself. I'm not just one of those statistics that they say just gets on ADC and sits there—especially about your being black—that's how they think you are anyway, having baby after baby as if you want to just sit all your life on ADC . . . and when you go to the supermarket I get that different treatment when I pull out the food stamps and people look at you and say you're on ADC and you're not trying to better yourself—and then I feel bad, I want to cry I want to tell them don't look like that—you don't know what's going on in our life! Those people who look at you in the line and say, "She's one of them," and I want to tell them—you just don't know—if you have a kid like this and you got no way out—see what you'd go through.*

Anna's sense of being constantly stretched to the limit, of physical and emotional exhaustion, of daily stress, creates situations in which she fears her own anger toward her daughter, particularly when she hits her and feels she can't stand her own situation any longer:

> *I just sit in the bathroom with the door shut and locked so she can't open it . . . She can beat on the door but I don't care—I have to deal with her and then she screams and howls when I run up and grab her and I start crying—and she'll sit there like she doesn't know what's going on and then I think, thank God I made it through the day—'cos I get scared I'm going to do something terrible—or I'll just call my sister and see if she can take her . . .*
>
> *You see my problem at first was that I couldn't accept being a single mother. It's just took me like until this year to realize you're a single mom and it's not going to get any better . . . It just goes by what you do and sometimes you get upset when you have friends who don't have kids, and you can't do anything . . . like I can't go out to parties and stuff or to a concert or to Cedar Point [an amusement park] . . . and now it's sunk in real hard . . . I didn't know what you had to do to be a mother when you're poor.*

Anna's insights about her own situation and her attempts to deal with her own anger toward her child have emerged as she has confronted her own personal history. Sexually molested as a child, she now fears becoming involved in a relationship with someone for fear he would molest her daughter. She feels trapped in multiple webs; daily life is a constant battle through a mine field of obstacles. She would like to go back to school while working part time, but the college child care center is unaffordable, so she plans to use a morning Head Start program, which runs only four mornings a week. Her daughter, now three, is verbal and very bright, and Anna is anxious for her to "get her education real early": "Y'know I've got a real smart kid—she's been doing everything in advance." Anna plans to take classes while her daughter is in the public preschool, but is faced with child care problems as she goes to work; for her sister will not be readily available and her mother does not support her going to school. Although Anna wants to break away from her dependence on her mother,

> If you're on ADC you can't put your kid in a good all-day preschool 'cos of your low income and it just costs too much and ADC only pays for the real cheap places.

Sara Thomas has also suffered enormously from the chronic scarcity of available and subsidized quality child care in the United States. Sara had Des when she was seventeen.

> I had graduated from high school and I finished a semester and a half of college; then I had to drop because of my pregnancy . . . When I found out I was like three or four months—the baby's father didn't care, my family didn't care—I never had a real family I was raised by my grandmother and my aunt and I ran into a lot of problems with that . . . and my aunt passed away when I was sixteen and I was on my own—that's when I had started on my own working at sixteen. So when I had my baby I had to have a C-section and one of my friends was there with me but my family never came to see me in the hospital. I stayed there five days and after that I came home to my grandmother's house, and I was like sleeping on the floor with my baby—nobody helped me—and then my uncle told me there was no room for us in the house and I had to go—so he gave me $1000 which is not a lot to live off of, so when he said that—it was like I'm grown, I don't care, I'm going to make it okay, I'll leave. I got an apartment and I left and I been out on my own ever since and six weeks later I went back to work.

Sara's boyfriend, the father of Des, temporarily moves back with her when she returns to work, but during the following months she faces the

nightmare of so many single mothers—inadequate, unsafe child care and
very few options for choice:

safe environment?

?

> *At that time my baby's father was home, who was on drugs. So it was like he
> would watch my baby, our baby, some of the time, but then the baby went to
> his great-aunt's house—it was not a safe environment, I mean it was like in
> poverty on that side. The self-esteem, the motivation was not there. Things
> that may have kept Des from being at the point he's at now maybe could
> have been prevented if I could afford proper child care . . . I mean it's a drug
> area, where dope is sold. His great-aunt drinks beer, she smokes weed.
> There's people running in and out all the time. I mean the area is just a
> criminal area—it's poverty and that's where Des had to go because I could
> not afford the child care I would want him in. I could not afford it, no, there
> was no way. I was paying her about $35 a week, but she just couldn't keep
> him rotating shifts. And I'm talking about this great-aunt is like about thirty
> or forty years old so that was like $35 a week that I had to give her—and
> say I wanted to work overtime—just to make a little more money, I would
> give her at least $45 for him staying that time and that's somebody feeding
> him, changing his diapers, spending time with him. And I worked anywhere
> from nine to ten hours a day . . . but it wasn't a good environment for him,
> but it was the safest environment I could get him in. I know that he wouldn't
> have been hurt, but I know at the same time it was not a positive role model
> in his life—but that's the best I could have him in.*
>
> *Then I had like a friend that I thought would be a really good baby-
> sitter for my son, but I come to find they were neglecting my son. They
> would like put him in a crib and just leave him in there—they never held
> him, they never cuddled him. And you know he's very affectionate, he loves
> you, but I felt that he felt like he was in jail you know and this is a $35 a
> week baby-sitter and I'm not making that much money at this time. So she
> would watch him, plus I began to float shift—I would work days, I would
> work afternoons, midnights, so it was really hard . . . and a lot of stuff later
> could have been avoided if I could have put him in proper child care but I
> couldn't afford it. And the place where I worked, they had a child care pro-
> gram, but that's designed for professionals—not entry level employees. And
> I'm talking entry level as being at the institution for like five years. I could
> not afford to send my child there. And DSS the way their program was, it
> doesn't give you any money because they go by your gross income and I
> couldn't get any help—Des didn't even qualify for WIC [Women, Infants
> and Children—a supplemental food program] and with his clothes and milk
> and Pampers and everything—the only good thing I had really going for me*

was I was blessed with a good insurance from my job that covered all his doctor visits.

Sara's life is becoming more and more complicated. Des's father has been incarcerated. At two, Des begins to exhibit severe behavioral problems, and he is switched through three different daycare settings as caregivers claim he is "uncontrollable." At this time Sara is advised to see a child psychiatrist, who diagnoses her son as suffering from attention deficit disorder (ADD) and tells Sara that she has never learned how to love and needs to stay home with her child. Put on probation at work due to her many absences, she takes a medical stress leave for a month, but once again becomes desperate when she is denied AFDC benefits because her gross income over the previous six months exceeded the cut-off by a few dollars.

So I went down to DSS and I said I'm employed but I just need a little assistance because I need to come home for a while to be a mother. So they were like, well we'll take the info but by the guidelines there's no way—so I just turned around and left . . . Well, with the stress leave from work and no help from DSS there was no way we could live—I was getting like $100 maybe a week to live off of, with a rent of $400—so nothing to eat, no pleasure, no nothing, just rent and that's not even enough to pay for electric and lights . . . so I stayed home in October and I went back end of November.

As Des has been diagnosed with a disability, he is eligible for public early childhood intervention services as a special needs child. Sara finds out that special services are far more readily available and of better quality in a neighboring school district. They move, and she enrolls Des in a part-day program with a caring and supportive early childhood special education teacher, who takes a personal interest in Sara's situation. The teacher begins to assist Sara in negotiating the maze of services and eligibility requirements with which she must become conversant in order to derive maximum benefits for herself and her child. Since the public schools offer only a half-day program, Sara must find another program for Des to attend during the rest of the day while she is at work. She experiences insensitivity to her "situation" and discriminatory attitudes toward Des at the centers:

They haven't been taught to deal with poverty—they don't say I need to learn—they didn't seek to deal with Des. Certain people did, but in order for it to work, everybody had to work with him—they wouldn't deal with him . . . They see this is a black kid in our classroom, first of all they don't

want him there, and second of all he's coming from a single-parent home—
they think his parent probably doesn't even know what's going on.

With the help of a referral from Des's special education teacher, Sara locates a trained caregiver who takes care of Des when he is not in the public preschool program; the school bus transports him to and from the caregiver. While the lives of Sara and Des begin to change dramatically in terms of their emotional well-being and short-term stability, Sara's ongoing struggles to juggle her full-time work with quality child care constitute a daily endurance test. She describes a typical day:

Well, he goes to the sitter from 7.45 in the morning and then he goes to
school at 12.30 and then he gets out of school at 3.30 and then back to the
sitter at 4 and then I get off work at 4.30 and catch the bus and get to him
about 5 and then we catch the bus again and then we get home about 6, I see
Des for bed time . . . and then we start another day.

If any part of the carefully orchestrated schedule misses a beat, everything falls apart. If Sara's job hours are switched, if the bus is late, if Des or, worse still, the caregiver or Sara becomes ill, or if the public schools go on break, enormous and unmanageable burdens descend on Sara, who navigates the precarious edges as she constantly defies the odds against her:

I got my vision, I got my dreams, and there days when I feel down like I
really can't make it, I can't go no further, I'm nothing—you know, I'm tired,
I'm tired and it's too hard. But it's like I have goals—I want to be something
different from what I have right now . . . I guess to be somebody in poverty,
to see that generation that's coming behind us—it's sad, it's real sad, what do
they have to strive for? I sacrifice now because when Des looks out the win-
dow he sees a family man taking care of his family, where if we lived in the
ghetto, if we live where my income allows me to live, Des wouldn't have
nothing to strive for—but I just got to believe I only can make the difference
. . . even though obviously the system doesn't really want you to succeed . . .
I can become what statistics has designed me to be, a nothing, or I can make
statistics a lie . . . Today, I am making statistics a lie!

Sara sees her life as having changed dramatically because she received "good help." She often speaks with appreciation of the people who intervened at critical points in her life—the public health nurse during her pregnancy, the sitter Des has now, the preschool teacher, even the psychiatrist—all of whom she used with determination and resourcefulness to help better her situation. Through all this, however, she has received minimal support from DSS for child care. She pays $280 per month (almost one-third of her monthly income) for *part-time* specialized care for Des, of which DSS contributes only $80. Had she lost her job while on probation, or been laid off, she would never have been able to sustain these costs or her eligibility for intervention services; nor could she have moved into another school district to obtain preschool services for Des. Hence we see contingency that works for some, for a while.

For seventeen-year-old Tara Mays, contingency led to desertion and a series of crises stretching from Mississippi to Michigan. She had her baby while a junior in high school in Mississippi. With neither family support nor adequate welfare to sustain her and the baby, she moved with her newborn child to relatives in Michigan.

> *At first everybody was all supportive. You know—okay—you made a mistake, we're gonna help you, we're gonna do this, we're gonna do that and this and this and this—But it's like the calls got shorter and letters less and less. I couldn't find a shoulder to cry on. At first I kind of resented it and then I kind of felt like well, you put yourself in this situation and I'm also thinking, well they got their lives. But I felt like they set me up—they told me they'd help me and then when it came time it's like—where are you guys? So I moved up here, I had to drop out of school and one of the reasons is because of the welfare system—this is paradise here in Michigan compared to Mississippi! So I came up here and I moved in with my cousin and her husband. And I was seventeen and I still had another year of high school to go after I had my baby and they had legal guardianship of me to go back to public school 'cos I'm still a minor. At first it was, they was like—you can go back to school and we'll take you this place to get this done and this done and okay, we'll help you—and it's like as a senior you have all these expectations—like prom and a ring and graduation—but on welfare you can forget it—and they said we gonna have an open house and then the plans got fewer and fewer and they lied to me. They got evicted so they decide they'll move to another city—but I just got started back in school and I didn't want to move there. So I ended up moving—me and the baby—into this apartment—and I have a baby bed, a bed, a cooler and that's it. I didn't have a stove or a refrigerator. And they left me and I'm here alone—no family, no car, no job, no nothing—me and the baby.*

Tara, alone at seventeen with her new baby, is desperate. Fortunately, through her new public school she is referred to a teen-parent center and is assisted in finding child care for her baby so that she can continue to attend school and graduate. The center has since been slated to close as part of a cost-cutting budget move, which means both the babies in care and the teen mothers risk further desertion by the education system as well as the state. For young mothers such as Toni and Tara, these centers become lifelines and temporarily sustain both mothers and their babies. The future of many other Tonis and Taras and their babies is severely threatened as closings force these teenagers to slide further over the edges. Tara's experience of abandonment and relocation in search of a better support system does not appear unusual,—it was a story repeated by several other young teenagers. Seventeen-year-old Mary Belt's is a particularly poignant one.

> I knew pretty much right away. As soon as I missed my period I knew. I didn't think anything of it because I was in love with the baby's father. I was happy. I'm gonna have this guy's baby and we're gonna be together and all that, but it didn't work out. But yeah I was happy about it for a while, I was fine, I was very content . . . My mother, I wasn't living at home at the time, and I went home when she let me come home—see, she had put me out, and I was out for like six months and when I found out I was pregnant, I thought maybe I should go back and stay with her for a while but when she found out I was pregnant she wanted to try and put me out again . . . My mother put me out just before finals, I didn't get to take my finals, I didn't get to graduate. She could at least have waited until I was eighteen and I graduated—she didn't have to take that away from me.

At seventeen, five and a half months pregnant, Mary is rejected by her mother, and is unable to graduate. The baby's father is now in prison, accusing Mary of abandoning him, although he in the interim has fathered another baby with another girlfriend. Mary, at the urging of her cousin—a single mother living alone in Michigan—decides to leave Florida and go live with her. The cousin has graduated from high school and is in her first year at a local college, struggling to work, attend school, and take care of her two-year-old daughter. The money for an air ticket is scraped together and Mary arrives in Michigan to have her baby. The two young women, longtime childhood friends, plan to pool their meager welfare resources and, when Mary's baby is born, share child care responsibilities as a family unit. Soon after Mary's arrival, however, they are given notice to leave the small apartment, as the lease does not permit such a living arrangement. They begin to search for a three-bedroom subsidized apartment but are told the waiting list is so long that they may have to wait up to four years. Mary, now in her eighth month of pregnancy remains optimistic and feels strengthened by the support and tenacity of her twenty-year-old cousin.

She's done more for me than anybody else ever done—Jan has always been there for me and she had a kid of her own when she was seventeen. I don't know what I would have done without Jan. I can identify with not knowing what a family is because when I was growing up my mother was always gone. I remember when I was four years old my mother was getting up with her boyfriends and going off to Miami for weeks on end. It was just me and maybe my aunt and she had her own kids to take care of too . . . There isn't too much that I haven't experienced so I can take one day at a time now. I've lived on the street, I've been out there, I know what it's like to sleep on a bench because you don't have anywhere to go. I can appreciate life pretty much.

Both Mary and Jan (who is currently supporting Mary since Mary receives only $92 per month from AFDC) remain hopeful that they will find an apartment before Mary gives birth and that they and their babies will pull through. Their youthful optimism and spunkiness fly in the face of the almost insurmountable odds they confront as they struggle to stretch dollars, resources, and motivation to pull themselves out of their shared fate.

The Fate of Poor Teenagers and Their Babies

According to the Children's Defense Fund, one in four adolescents today is growing up in a one-parent family. For black adolescents the number is far higher; black adolescents are twice as likely as white adolescents to live with one parent and four times as likely to live not with a parent at all but with some other relative. Among teenagers living in female-headed families, more than 25 percent have mothers younger than 35 years old. The median family income of single-mother families with adolescent children was less than $14,000 in 1988, compared to $42,000 for two-parent families with adolescent children.[1]

Today a teenage mother is typically profiled as unmarried, and current statistics predict that she and her child will live in poverty in the coming decade. While 20 percent of all children live in poor families, *almost 66 percent of children living with a parent younger than twenty-five are poor.* Almost two-thirds of all teenagers who gave birth in 1988 were unmarried. The birthrate for unmarried black teenagers is almost four times higher than it is for white teenagers (see table 1). In 1988, the proportion of babies

Table 1

Births to Women Younger than 20, 1988

	NUMBER OF BIRTHS TO WOMEN				% OF TEEN BIRTHS TO WOMEN YOUNGER THAN 18	% OF BIRTHS TO ALL WOMEN THAT WERE TO WOMEN YOUNGER THAN 20	TOTAL BIRTHS TO WOMEN OF ALL AGES
	YOUNGER THAN 20	YOUNGER THAN 15	15–17	18–19			
All							
Total births	488,941	10,588	176,624	301,729	38.3%	12.5%	3,909,510
% Unmarried	65.9%	93.6%	77.1%	58.5%			25.7%
White							
Total births	319,544	4,073	106,907	208,564	34.7%	10.5%	3,046,162
% Unmarried	53.9%	86.5%	65.9%	47.1%			17.7%
Black							
Total Births	152,508	6,182	63,833	82,493	45.9%	22.7%	671.976
% Unmarried	91.5%	98.9%	96.0%	87.4%			63.5%
Latino[a]							
Total Births	73,858	1,621	28,257	43,980	40.5%	16.4%	449,604
% Unmarried	59.2%	84.9%	68.0%	52.7%			34.0%

Note: Almost two-thirds of births to teens in 1988 were to unmarried women. The proportion for all Latino teen births hides substantial differences between various Latino subgroups. Half of Mexican-American teen births, compared with three-quarters of Puerto Ricans and two-fifths of Cubans, were to unmarried women.

[a]Only thirty states report births to Latino parents. Latinos are an ethnic group, not a race, and therefore the white, black, and Latino percentages and numbers do not equal the total for all races.

Source: National Center for Health Statistics, calculations by Children's Defense Fund. (Reprinted in CDF, *The State of America's Children, 1991*, p. 94).

born to teenagers stood at 33.8 per 1,000 births—the rate increasing particularly for fifteen-to-seventeen-year-olds.

Lisebeth Schorr has warned of the "rotten outcomes" produced by a public policy that condemns teenage mothers and their children to a lost future.[3] As Schorr argues, the risk factors that lead to later damage in children are demonstrably greater among stressed and poor families. Teenage pregnancy, premature birth, poor health, inadequate nutrition, lack of housing, instability in family relationships, and later school failure—all these factors are exacerbated by persistent poverty, for there are no buffer zones to cushion an unexpected obstacle. Stretched lives are precarious lives, and to be born to a teenage mother is to be born to a contingent life. But as both Schorr and Edelman of the Children's Defense Fund point out, the knowledge to help is available; comprehensive interventions do assist severely stressed destitute teenagers; accessible health care does reduce infant mortality, and effective contraception programs do prevent unwanted pregnancies. Teen-parent centers with child care services and programs with parent-education components are often lifelines for teenagers. It is neither the knowledge of the experts nor the desire for a different life on the part of young teenage mothers that is lacking.

How then do the stories of Joey, Toni, Anna, Sara, Tara, and Mary fit these poverty profiles? How do their lives intersect with the images of welfare queens, of unmotivated dropouts who do not value education, of the AFDC mothers, who need to develop a work ethic? The six teenagers we have listened to are scarred but fighting young women who actively have sought help, who have struggled to work, to go back to school, to provide their babies with something better. Sara says, "I got my dreams," and Anna has her "high hopes."

We see how the small interventions that these teenagers did receive— a sensitive preschool teacher, a teen-parent center, a public health nurse, a brief encounter with a caring social worker—were critical events in their lives. But the language of public assistance views such interventions only from a cost-benefit instrumental perspective, and evaluates them in terms of later economic payoffs. Perhaps it is not only a redistribution of resources that is necessary but a redistribution of sensibilities, a different way of seeing. We need to see that poor teenage mothers' lives and those of their young children *matter.* Poverty discourse has failed to give equal meaning to their dailiness, to *their* experiences on *our* horizons.

A striking theme of the six stories chronicled here is the persistently high level of educational aspirations that these teenagers hold. Two are attending college, all have gone back to high school and graduated or are

currently attempting to, and all clearly want a different future. A job at
minimum-wage level with no benefits keeps them on AFDC; but when
they take work or study initiatives to better sustain themselves and their
babies, they are punished by "being cut." The terror of the welfare bureaucracy is actual; "being cut" can virtually mean being destroyed, losing
one's future.

The widespread negative encounters of these young women with the
welfare system constantly assault their self esteem and effectively reduce
them to the status of paupers. As Kelly Sill, another teenage mom, angrily
stated:

> They want to know about your relationships about the nature of your rela-
> tionships, about boyfriends, about whether you have sex or not—they treat
> you like dirt—like you shouldn't exist—like me and my baby could just lay
> down and die and it would be like one less welfare check . . . They never gave
> me nothing when I really needed help. The system told me my gross income
> was too high where I worked so they couldn't help me, so it was either work
> or sell dope and dump your baby in some cheap low-grade child care where
> they treat your child like he's cheap, because that's all the system will pay for
> . . . It's like if you want to work and you need them they're never there for
> you. It's set up to help you fail and if you fail it's not there to help you—so
> what is the purpose in it? I don't understand it.

These young women have endured and coped with enormous stresses
in their young lives. Toni, Tara, and Mary were cast out; they suffered emotional and physical abuse, chaotic family systems, lives stretched to taut
extremes. Even when families were supportive and where mothers and
sisters assisted with child care as in the cases of Joey and Anna, daily life
was precarious. The urgent need for full-time, high-quality, subsidized
child care was an unmet priority in their lives. When child care was dependable, even if always unaffordable, their lives began to stabilize. In a
given month between one-quarter and one-half of their poverty-level earnings went toward child care costs. The fathers of the babies gave no child
support and deserted their girlfriends before or soon after the birth of their
babies. These teenage mothers appeared not to expect child support. Most
had not established paternity for the baby, and most of the fathers were, in
any case, unemployed. There was little discussion about contraception or
abortion. Joey, mother of the twins, had sought an abortion but was denied
because of Medicaid ineligibility. Awareness and use of birth control methods were absent prior to their first pregnancy, which seemed to "just happen" to them. Access to counseling services and parent education for preg-

nant teens were offered through a few innovative school-age parent programs. But both the programs which were so instrumental in helping Toni and Tara were slated to close in 1991—another successful model cut in the interests of balancing state budgets, and severely unbalancing the worlds of those it had formerly served.

When health care was available at a workplace, it was utilized and provided a vital support for a single mother. We see in Sara's situation, how she had access to high quality pediatric and psychiatric care because of her particularly good health care package at her workplace; and Sara used the opportunity to aggressively seek help for her child, to the extent of moving to a neighboring city to obtain improved early education intervention services. The need for health care for one's child is a pervasive anxiety, and Medicaid eligibility an ongoing concern.

Housing was another chronic anxiety. These young mothers were plagued by the threat of being evicted, of being unable to pay rent, of failing to balance housing and food costs, both of which were minimally and inadequately subsidized by AFDC payments. Public assistance to teenage mothers in the two-channel welfare state has failed abysmally: poor young mothers have no entitlements to health care, to housing, to child care, or to a high school education unless they meet strict eligibility criteria. Full assistance literally requires destitution, and the minimal assistance more commonly granted maintains both mothers and children in poverty. One week of the flu, chicken pox at the daycare, a snowstorm that grounds public transportation all threaten the precarious worlds of these young families.

To be poor, black, and female is to live at the intersecting points of a gendered and racist welfare system. Yet the young women whose voices we have heard in the chapter refuse to accept their placelessness in such a system. Instead, they fight desperately against succumbing to the statistics, against "being a nothing." Their resilience stands in dramatic juxtaposition to the negative images that dominate public sensibilities.

Mothers' Stories:
Contingency Continued

White and Single in the Pink-Collar Ghetto

L ORI PATTERSON GREW UP in an affluent suburban neighborhood, in a traditional two-parent family from which she feels alienated. She describes her mother as "nuts" and her sister as "weird." She did not complete her college degree and works as a full-time secretary at a university earning roughly $800 per month after taxes. She and Jim lived together comfortably since Kim's birth four years ago, but several months ago the relationship ended. Through her job, Lori has access to health care and a high-quality but now unaffordable child care center, which her son Kim attends. For the first time in her life she feels seriously threatened by her inability to pay her bills, which include, every month, almost $500 for child care and $545 for her rental apartment. Lori tells of her growing inability to manage from month to month:

> As far as ADC, I wasn't interested in that because I was just too proud. I didn't want to say that I was on ADC. I grew up as a snob you know—standing in line with food stamps—you just don't do where I grew up. And I guess one of the other reasons is that I expected to get family support. Do you know what I mean? ADC was like for people with no family to help out, or family that doesn't have the means to help out—that's what they do. When I called my parents and told them I was going to need help, I expected them—y'know after hemming and hawing—to say all right, we'll help you—but they didn't and they wouldn't. So I went to the social services department and applied and they gave me food stamps for that month—they gave me $95 and they called it emergency food stamps or whatever and they said on my income—I like make $100 over the limit—which killed me because I thought all right, I'll tell my boss to cut my wages and I'll get like $300 more or something like that. At first I contemplated it y'know—but it would also mean cutting back on my hours that I was working, which would mean los-

*ing some of my health benefits, my vacation stuff, sick pay—'cos when you
go under forty hours they change things. You're either part-time or full-time
and your benefits go according to that.*

Lori, in her mid-twenties, holds a steady job which puts her at just
above the poverty line according to the U.S.-defined poverty standard. She
receives only sporadic child support from Jim. She describes her return to
the Department of Social Services in an attempt to receive aid:

*Oh God it was hell sitting down there and filling out the forms y'know—it
was pretty humiliating. I'm a snob and I'm sitting among the homeless filling
out these forms. All these people are driving up in their rusted Chevvies and
I'm in my '87 Honda. I mean I felt really out of place—it was really horrible
. . . You have to fill out forms and they call your name and there's this security guard and she's real harsh looking. She's maybe thirty and she snaps her
gum when she talks to you and it's like—"heh, lowlifes"—y'know what I
mean. You talk through windows with holes in them, I don't know, I think it's
very demeaning. They tell you to fill out your forms and it's like you should
know to stand in this line, or that line, or what forms you should be filling
out . . . I mean I don't know how all these people do it—I really don't—I
think it takes a high IQ just to figure out all the forms. And then to get denied—my God!—after dealing with all of that and then they say you make
too much money . . . The caseworker, he filled out my worksheet and he went
to work it out on the calculator, so he left the room and I could hear him
adding stuff, and he came back and he said, "You make too much money"
and I went, "You're serious?" and he said "Well at least you have your food
stamps for this month."*

Suddenly life changes for Lori as she falls from stability into the daily
uncertainties of life on the edge, and she begins to live from paycheck to
paycheck, falling deeper and deeper in debt as the bills begin to pile up
behind the microwave. Because she began with advantages—health care,
a good child care center, a safe apartment complex, and the buffer of
middle-class respectability—her contingency is temporarily muted. Her
father helped pay her rent last month, as eviction became a serious threat.
But despite this help and sporadic child support checks from Jim, Lori
barely survives with her young son.

*I don't know what I'm going to do. My dad helped last month, but rent's due
next Wednesday and I don't have any money. I mean I don't. I just paid all
my bills. It's the end of the month now and I don't get paid for two more*

weeks. I have $2.50 in my account: two dollars and fifty cents! Rent's $545—
I get paid in two weeks again, but that will only be $400 . . . I need help—I
feel like I'm sinking.

With no college degree, Lori feels stuck in a dead-end pink-collar job
with low pay. In search of self-sufficiency, she begins to go back to school
evenings and weekends to try and complete her bachelor's degree. One of
the directors at her son's child care center, tuition for which she can no
longer afford, assists her in applying for a child care subsidy; for she now
needs child care not only while at work but also while taking classes.

I had to call this woman at social services who decides whether or not I'm
eligible for child care, and every three months I have to give them a total
lowdown on my income—where my money's at and whether Jim gives me
anything in child support—so I lied—and she said she needs a letter from
him stating what money he's given to me, and I said I won't get the letter
from him and I said what then—am I denied child care? So she said—tech-
nically the letter had to come from him but she'd take it from me—and I
only think she did that, and this is probably prejudice—because I was a
well-dressed white woman that didn't talk slang and wasn't missing my teeth
and I looked like I was serious—and I said I really need help y'know . . . so
now I get $77 every two weeks, but even that's not 100 percent of what they
can give me, that's 90 percent—according to your income or something like
that there's very very low and very low and I'm in the very very.

see Foucault

category

Lori benefits from her former white privilege and at the same time
distances herself from "the others"—those single women in poverty whom
Lori perceives as the "welfare mothers." Lori's situation worsens as she returns to school and chronic child care problems arise:

I scramble for baby-sitters—I never get baby-sitters unless I'm in school—I
can't afford it. Mindy [the neighbor] takes care of Kim whenever I'm in
school, and if she can't she'll just say, "Lori, I can't baby-sit Tuesday"; then
there's this girl Lee that the woman who cuts my hair recommended, and she
just lives down near Krogers' and she's a doll and Kim adores her. She
charges only $2 an hour, so I use her quite often. Even to go to school Friday
and Saturday nights that's $24 . . . but if I didn't have Mindy I seriously
wouldn't be able to make it . . . She's like my savior!

Despite Lori's support system, which includes her father, who has
helped out with rent, Kim's father, who sporadically pays child support and

occasionally cares for the child, and a caring neighbor, Lori faces, as do most single mothers, the major financial and child care responsibilities for her child. If Kim becomes ill, or, worse, if Mindy does, Lori's flimsy network begins to unravel. Lori also begins to perpetuate another shadow economy—low-status, low-pay jobs for women like her alternate baby-sitter Lee, who is paid $2 an hour for being "a doll" and is herself on welfare, with two young children for whom she receives inadequate public support.

Becky Jameson had her daughter Molly in her early twenties. She describes with bitterness how she lost her waitressing job when her boss found out she was pregnant:

> He kinda pushed me out the door y'know . . . So he started cutting down my hours—he wanted the Las Vegas image y'know and he couldn't have one out here y'know (gestures to her belly) walking around in a miniskirt so he just kept cutting my hours down and there was nothing I could do to fight it.

As Becky's pregnancy progressed, she found herself without health insurance. She went back to her hometown to see her family doctor and he advised her to apply for Medicaid:

> He tells me to go to social services—he goes—just downgrade your dressing, don't dress up—just wear a pair of jeans and a t-shirt and go apply for help—I said alright I'll try—I had no idea what I was getting myself into— y'know you feel like you're a piece of dirt . . . I went in there and all the kids are running around and screaming, everybody looked dirty to me—I'm sure, I guess, it's the whole image I had from the beginning . . . I'm sure these people are all in the same boat that I am, but you walk in there with a total attitude—I shouldn't be here, I don't need to be here, I can work, I'm healthy—and there's no reason why I shouldn't collect help just because I'm pregnant—so I went up and they were so snotty—they made me feel really degraded being in there—like I was asking for something I didn't deserve.

Becky has become part of the undeserving poor. Fired from her job because her body is no longer a commodity to be exploited by her boss in the bar where she works, living in a society that is one of the last holdouts among all Western democracies to fail to provide all its citizens with health insurance, Becky, carrying with her the dominant public stereotypes of poor people, suddenly finds herself one of *them* and is forced to go on welfare until after the baby is born. She and Molly's father marry after the birth, but their relationship breaks up, and her husband leaves when Molly is two. Becky finds herself once again on her own with a young daughter to support; she begins a waitressing job so she can be with her daughter during the day.

I had a lot of problems with sitters at night—I worked evenings and weekends . . . I'd waitress in the restaurant and then go work in the bar until two in the morning. So I would need somebody from four thirty in the afternoon till two in the morning and you just can't get sitters for those hours, there's no way . . . so they told me I could either start coming to work, y'know get your sitter problems taken care of or we're gonna have to let you go, so finally I just had to quit because it was getting too difficult and I had to call in too many times. You try to prearrange it y'know as early as you can in the week to get a sitter—the weekends were the hardest, the weekdays weren't too bad. But the majority of people I knew worked days, so they didn't want to be tied down to my kid in the evenings—so you get down to four o'clock in the afternoon and you have to be at work at four thirty and you still haven't found a sitter! So you call and you hear them on the other line go— oh boy! we need you here and you have to come in tonight. So what am I gonna do—bring my kid in with me? They offered me suggestions like— well, maybe you can have so and so watch your kid on her off days—well, I don't know so and so, and I don't feel comfortable leaving my kid with that person, and I would tell them and they'd say—well a friend of mine is a sitter—she'll do it at night, but if I don't know her I don't feel comfortable— I didn't want to leave my kid with anybody I didn't know.

After quitting her job, Becky is forced to move back with her parents temporarily, and several months later finds a full-time secretarial job at a corporation with health benefits. She moves into a small rented house with her daughter and two other women friends, hoping that by sharing the rent of $600 she will be able to pay Molly's high child care costs, which even with a Department of Social Services subsidy still cost her $200 per month, fully one-quarter of her monthly take-home pay. Becky's desire to become economically independent is threatened, however, when one of the housemates leaves, and Becky is forced to pick up the extra rent payment. She begins to work as a waitress on weekends, putting in a total of sixty-five to seventy hours a week and depending heavily on her younger sister to take care of Molly. But then Molly begins to pick up infections, and Becky has to take pay cuts due to her many absences from work.

Molly seems to get sick a lot more than last year—she was out a week for chicken pox, another week for viral meningitis, colds here and there—getting her in the car and having her throw up on the way to work y'know . . .

They really do need to have programs for when your child's sick—especially when your child's sick a lot. Especially being a single parent, I mean you don't have any choice but to take off work and soon that means you gonna lose your job.

Things get worse when Becky's child care subsidy is canceled because the three-monthly renewal form apparently was not received at the DSS office. In order to get reinstated, Becky must go back and reapply. So she has to make up the payments owed to the child care center on her stretched budget.

Sometimes I don't see the forms y'know—your funds can get canceled like happened to me—paperwork gets shuffled in the wrong places . . . I guess, I wonder if it don't make me feel like a loser, if I have to go back in there and be degraded and made to feel like I was the scum of the earth—y'know society sucks, it really does—when you're trying to make it and getting some help to support yourself with a child . . . I just don't think society thinks that's good enough!

Becky's life begins to close in, her job is in jeopardy, she worries about the next cold spell and Molly's susceptibility, and she is now further in debt with child care tuition payments. She receives no child support from her ex-husband and temporarily gives up plans to go to college to improve her job possibilities. While holding a full-time job within the pink ghetto— her earnings dipping and rising above the poverty line—she lives in constant anxiety of falling into the degradation of full welfare dependency.

Jenny O'Connor is in her late twenties and has lived alone with her son since he was six months old. Dan, now six, has been diagnosed as hyperactive with ADD (attention deficit disorder). He also suffers from severe asthma. Jenny's life has been a series of traumas, from childhood in an abusive alcoholic family to marriage with an abusive husband. She describes her choice to leave the marriage and become a single parent:

When Danny was six months old we left, it was very secretive. I left because I needed to avoid being pursued and followed. It was an awful wife-beating kind of relationship. When I realized that was what it was, I knew I had to leave and when I figured how to do it secretly I did. It was very difficult and depressing. Danny had never been abused and I had to get out before he got hurt. I never thought this would happen to me, but now I see there were many things in my past which predisposed me to this kind of abuse. I came from a rigid Catholic background, my parents were wealthy—they threw me out when I started experimenting with drugs and sex in school—and

*other people in my family were physically abused—my brother was a
healthy, beautiful child who was battered, totally battered, and he went to
drug abuse, now he's a very dangerous man to be around . . . So when Dan
was born I never left him with his father because I was afraid that he could
not handle the pressure, and soon after, I fled. Some abusers will try and
pursue a wife who flees. I knew the only successful way was to be completely
secretive—no communication.*

After Jenny escapes her abusive husband, she moves to another city
where her sister is living. She moves in with her, fights her own drug habit,
and begins to try and forge a new life with her baby, who has begun to
develop worrying symptoms:

*Dan was like no baby I had ever seen. He was like no other. He would not
stop crying. He had rashes all over his body—he was allergic to all sorts of
things—he was hyperactive—he didn't sleep—I thought what is wrong
with this child? At seven months they prescribed phenobarbital which is a
barbiturate. I couldn't work, because I couldn't leave him with my sister
because he was so intense. Originally we thought we'd work different shifts,
but it didn't work out and all this time I'm on welfare—but staying with my
sister—she was the only person I could turn to—she was a life saver.*

Two years later, however, Jenny's sister moves to New York to take up
a better job offer, and Jenny and Dan relocate to another city in Michigan,
hoping to find an apartment, daycare, and work. But Jenny's welfare check
goes astray and things start to fall apart.

*As soon as I got my summer apartment my welfare check was lost and they
were ready to evict me. Then my health began to suffer, Dan still needed me
and wasn't ready for daycare—it was a task to keep myself and my baby
alive! I had stopped doing drugs but now I had no one to lean on and I felt
as if I was in a trap . . . Even with cheap rent you can't believe how little
money there is after expenses. There were days when I didn't have money
for sanitary napkins—there was just nothing—there was no way anymore
for me to take care of us—my summer lease was up and we had nowhere to
go—so I take all of my things and store them in someone's garage who I'd
only known for three months, and they let us sleep on their floor . . . All this
time my health is bad, I would get my period for three weeks in a row, I
would get headaches and spells of dizziness—Dan was constantly irritable,
he would only sleep when he was totally exhausted . . . I had no money saved
and I don't understand how to get ahead with the welfare system—I had
nowhere to go—my life was in crisis.*

At this point Jenny and Dan are destitute and desperate. A caring social worker at Catholic Social Services takes Jenny and her son temporarily into her home, obtains for Jenny an emergency housing grant from the city, and, with some useful connections, helps to find her an apartment in a public housing complex. She also takes Jenny to the doctor for medical treatment. Jenny moves into the apartment.

> It was a tremendous relief to have the space. It was clean. I have a clean body. I had no money, no friends, no car, no phone, but at least I have a home—I find out that 80 percent of the people there are on welfare and there are drugs—but you just do it, you do, you would do it too. You can or you let everything else crumble . . . It was a terrible neighborhood. There is no self-respect among most of the people in my community. The amount of drug abuse is terrible and I would find used condoms and needles when Dan and I walked to the bus stop . . . Men would urinate on buildings in broad daylight—I had never seen so much depression—so much violence against women—and all this time, I would think, Gee! If I didn't have this child I could be so much more together. It bothered me a great deal I wasn't working, although I had to be with my child. There was always a struggle, you have to do both and with Dan—it was just so much harder.

As with teenage Sara Thomas and her special-needs son Des, Jenny's life is made that much harder by her son's severe asthma and his hyperactivity. Jenny becomes involved with a group of women in the housing project who, like her, want a safe and clean environment; they get rid of some of the drug dealers and begin to police the outsiders, and the neighborhood improves. Over the next two years Dan goes to four different daycare centers, and at each he is asked to leave, as the staff find him "uncontrollable." He also develops severe allergies. When Jenny takes him for psychological evaluation at the hospital, a doctor prescribes ritalin, which she is reluctant to use. During this time she has been unable to work, due to the intense demands on her time that Dan's condition creates.

> At four years old I had just about lost my mind with this child. He wouldn't listen, was constantly on the move—as much as I loved him I thought I could not deal with this anymore. I was trying to ease him into daycare so I could work, but that didn't work. By the time Dan was four I had had it with him. I was still on aid, my house had been broken into twice—everything I did have was stolen, and the social services were threatening to cut me off if I didn't take a job—I told them I was having a terrible time with my child—at one point they were trying to tell me I had to be in a work pro-

*gram for about thirty hours a week. I told them my child and I were at a
tremendously difficult point, and so I went to legal aid and they came and
represented me and said I had a special-needs child who wasn't able to stay
at a daycare center and they wanted documented proof of everything . . .
They told me I had to attend some stupid job club for a bunch of uneducated
people . . . I didn't want those dead-end minimum wage jobs. I had a 4.0
GPA for my first year at college . . . I wanted to apply for a scholarship to
get back in school.*

In the fall, when Dan turns five and becomes eligible for public school
kindergarten, Jenny begins working for the management at the public
housing complex where she lives. Her flexible hours enable her to be
around Dan when he returns from the kindergarten to which he has been
referred for special education services. Since Jenny now earns, however,
DSS cuts her benefits, placing further pressures on her.

*Originally I was getting $170 twice a month, now they've cut it down to two
$50 checks. I only make $6 an hour and I'm working twenty to twenty-five
hours a week—that's $450 a month and I get $87 in food stamps—add it up
that's not much money to live on. Rent was $310 a month here but they gave
me a break—if I didn't have that I'd be going out of my mind . . . You can
never save money like this and you can't live on $600 a month—all this time
Dan and I buy clothes at resale shops—nothing new and I buy almost nothing. If I work through the summer at a temporary job to try and earn a little
more, they will cut me off and I will get nothing—then I would have to
reapply and they have forty-five days to process the application and for that
time we would have nothing. So we can't afford for me to work at a temporary job in summer because we'll get cut during the fall—so I can't work or
I have to cheat to work! And worse, if I find a job and I get cut for longer,
after six months they cut Medicaid. So if you aren't covered through your
job, which most women aren't, you just stay poor and it's very difficult—
you're in a vulnerable position. Oh my God poverty! It's something! You just
learn to get by and then they cut you—so you can never get ahead!*

Never being able to get ahead, living in constant terror of being cut,
powerless to move beyond their situation if they have a dependent child,
with earnings that keep them in the pink ghetto and welfare that regulates
their life and that of their children—all these mothers have at different
points been a step away from homelessness. But what happens when the
most dreaded cut of all occurs? In the following section two mothers tell of
their experiences of homelessness.

Being Homeless and a Mother

There is a difference between being put out and being put outdoors. If you are put out, you go somewhere else; if you are outdoors there is no place to go. The distinction was subtle but final. Outdoors was the end of something, an irrevocable, physical fact, defining and complementing our metaphysical condition.[1] Toni Morrison - The Bluest Eye

Christy Fenton is white and in her mid-thirties. She is the mother of three children; one is a teenager and the younger two are in elementary school. Christy's "nightmare," as she describes it, first began when the father of her two younger children began battering her. After Christy had left him, he sexually molested both their young children while he was receiving visitation rights and paying child support. His parental rights were terminated, and the children received extensive therapy with the help of a domestic violence center. Christy then went on welfare and lived in an apartment rented from a private landlord. The second "nightmare" began when the landlord, having decided to upgrade and renovate the property, forced his tenants to leave. Christy describes how their lives began to fall apart:

> We were only on a month-to-month lease and the judge gave us thirty days to move out—we had no place to go—it was summer, school was out and DSS gave us this voucher for a motel and you're only meant to stay there for thirty days, but there was no housing for us so they extended it—so we lived for sixty-nine days in that motel—DSS put us there—they said there was nothing else . . . There were rats and roaches; I called the health department and told them but they never came . . . Outside they were dealing drugs and there were prostitutes walking up and down . . . My children just lost their personalities—my eight-year-old stopped eating.

Christy must show proof that she is actively searching for housing.

> So all this time I tried to search for an apartment with the $310 limit from DSS. I could find a two-bedroom that fit that but not a three-bedroom, and with three kids they said I couldn't live there—they said if you can do something about one of your kids . . . well what do you want me to do—get rid of one of my kids? And the wait for public housing is three or four years in some places.

After more than two months of futile searching, while lodged in one room with no cooking facilities and no ice-box at a roach-infested motel, at a cost of over $800 to the DSS, which nonetheless declines to raise the housing allowance to comparable market rates, the family finds itself back on the streets. A friend of a friend offers his trailer; Christy and her children move in temporarily.

> We stayed in the trailer for September and October—there was no electricity and no heat but it did have running water—we got a space heater—it was okay—at least we were together and we had a place.

At this point, just as the children have started a new school year and are adjusting to their new school, Christy is told that the trailer is needed by someone else. She manages to rent another trailer in the same trailer park.

> Well we thought we had rented it from the guy who owned it, but in the middle of January a man comes knocking at my door and tells us we have to leave—that his brother had no right to rent to us—so there we were—right back where we started—eviction—another move—and no place to go.

In desperation, Christy goes to her mother for help. Her mother owns a house but is both alcoholic and physically abusive, and Christy is reluctant to take her children there. After four months they are forced to leave when her mother becomes violent:

> We tried—we really did—and she got more and more hateful . . . She's been an alcoholic all her life—she put me through this as a child. Now she would go into the kitchen and say really mean things to the kids—she would take away their possessions and lock them in her room and then tell me, "Your kids are going to grow up to be liars just like you" . . . And then all the physical stuff broke out . . . When I came home from looking for a place I knew something was wrong—my oldest daughter was waiting for me . . . While I was gone my mother had pushed my son and knocked him into a TV, and he fell to the floor which cut the back of his head open . . . After I reported my mother to DSS, my sister—she's also an alcoholic—came round and she and my mother jumped on me, they cut my ear open and I had gouges of skin out of me everywhere, and my sister was screaming, "I'm going to kill you," in front of my kids.

After the physical abuse, DSS removes the children from the grandmother's home, and Christy is once again faced with homelessness. They are returned to the same dangerous motel, and once again the children have to change schools.

> Being back in that motel was devastating for us—we'd get up in the morning and spend all day looking for housing . . . and there's so much rejection—and you know you not gonna find anything—some days the kids

couldn't get to school and here we are right back where we started, but at least we stayed together—that's what my kids keep telling me—no matter what we've been through—we stayed together.

The family plummets into the shared fate of several million Americans who are both placeless and poor. Christy is referred to a crisis center in another area. The center puts her in touch with a community, nonprofit program dealing with homeless families. This program offers a lifeline to Christy, helping her to find housing and to negotiate the DSS regulations.

They really helped us—they took real good care of everything—the kids could go out and play—it was real safe for them—my kids began to feel a little better—they could see there are good people in the world out there— and now the kids are settled in their new schools . . . and soon I hope to update my computer skills and then maybe I can find a job—I got good records from a while back.

The two-year ordeal of Christy and her children temporarily ends as they find a home in which they will be entitled to remain for two years while members of the program's transition group. After that they will be on their own again and, if not self-sufficient, risk another fall into homelessness. Their program, too, is in danger of losing its partial state funding, which will severely limit the numbers of families to be helped in the coming year.

It takes some sound and committed public investment to make a family viable rather than contingent with a safe neighborhood, neighbors who are role models, enough money for a clean and well-maintained apartment and for food, transportation, and health care, and suddenly the world changes—the mother, stretched and straining on welfare, now aspires to return to the workforce. But Christy's aspirations will be dashed if she cannot earn a living family wage. The minimum wage, as we have seen, is a set-up for destitution, a bipartisan legislative act grievously implicated in the continuing construction of poverty and, more specifically, of mothers' and children's poverty.

Justine Wilson is black, in her late thirties. Like Christy, she has experienced the horrors of homelessness with her three children. When her oldest son became chronically ill almost four years ago, his father abandoned the family. Since that time, Justine has lived on the edges. After getting on Medicaid and weathering the crisis of her son's almost dying in the hospital,

Justine depends on her faith to get her through. She begins making plans to go back to school, whereupon her child's father returns for a reconciliation.

> He came when Jesse's out the hospital and he wanted to make things okay.
> Next thing I know I come up pregnant. When I called him and tell him—he
> wanted to say it wasn't his—I was doing fine then—I was working as a
> cashier and Jess is back in school—but now I'm pregnant too.

Several months after Justine's second child is born, the father disappears again and pays no child support. Justine, living alone with two children in a public housing project becomes very concerned about the safety of her son and baby.

> It was a drug area you know—it was very bad, and my apartment—I was
> facing the dead end street so I wanted to move and they was renting a du-
> plex in another neighborhood, so we moved over there—but one night when
> me and the kids had left—I was pregnant then with Cheri—and me and the
> boys came back and they had raided the new apartment—that's when we
> moved again. I knew when I started seeing a lot of traffic, that's when I knew
> . . . and it's dangerous if you even know they doing drugs—so we just got up
> and left and went to my aunt—but living with your folks like that is not a
> good matter—your kids are there, other people's kids—it was just a terrible
> hassle. I was just falling apart . . . We left there and we had nowhere to go.
> My brother lives in the area but he's got four kids in a trailer and he couldn't
> take us in—I never been in this situation before where I don't have no place
> for me and my kids to stay—where I been living off other people and now
> we got no place to go . . . So I said Lord, you gotta find us a place to stay.

Justine and her children are given emergency shelter through a crisis center and soon after her daughter is born, she and the three children are allocated an apartment in a housing project in another area, with a seemingly better reputation; but the safety and drug problems prove to be even worse.

> Lord what a place that was—I mean you couldn't go outside—even the
> little kids was cursing you—the parents over there they didn't help or do
> nothing—it's white people and it's black people—they all mixed in, but they
> was all selling stuff right there in front of the kids—there was shooting and
> it was dealers coming in from all over—there was no respect for the
> women—I mean I've seen them beat up people, I mean men beating the

women—black and white—how they just actually beat them and always the police took their time coming—the people be halfway dead before the police come—It was sickening to live in a place like that—we were there five months and then when Jesse almost got shot that was it!

After Jesse is caught in crossfire between two dealers behind his apartment, and Justine's brother is mugged the evening he receives his pay, Justine takes her children and leaves, declaring:

I'd rather live in a shack with my kids than have this, and I prayed and prayed to God to give us a place where me and my kids can be safe.

Fortunately for Justine, she has maintained contact with a shelter that helped her out before Cheri's birth. She applies to enter their new family program, which assists a small number of homeless families in the area with shelter, child care and job and family counseling. Justine is accepted into the program—one of the few in the state that offer comprehensive services aimed at empowering their clients—and she is temporarily relocated to a three-bedroom apartment in a safe area close to an elementary school. The family's life changes dramatically as a small measure of stability begins to undergird their existence, although they barely subsist on the AFDC payments. Although Justine has filed for child support, the Friend of the Court has achieved no results. With both her toddlers in part-time child care provided through the program, Justine begins taking classes, hoping to be placed in a corporate office after training. Just as life is on course again, however, Jesse becomes very ill and is hospitalized. By the time he is released from the hospital, Justine's credits for her coursework are lost, her chances of a job internship that summer are gone, and she faces another year on welfare. Soon, welfare is cut too, as the governor's 1991 cuts for the state go into effect.

Before, we were surviving on $135 every two weeks—my rent and electricity is vendored—plus food stamps, but now we been cut to $106 every two weeks plus food stamps—I just want to get off social services so bad—they supposed to help you but they don't give you no chance—if I start working they'll cut me—I want to take care of my own babies, but God I need a chance—any help I get I use, because I don't really care about me—my kids is me—as long as they're okay I'm gonna survive no matter what . . . You know—I've had to learn to be a survivor—as long as the kids got clothes and food and a place to live, we'll survive and slowly with their [the center program's] help it's falling into place—but God I just need a chance.

Justine and Christy, poor single mothers with children, have experienced the full precariousness of poverty as they fell through the fast unraveling public policy web into the void of homelessness. In April 1991, welfare benefits were cut 17 percent in Michigan,[2] resulting in an average overall cut of $75 to $100 per month in public assistance for a single mother and three children. Another homeless mother tells us:

The governor is cutting our benefits and his people's property taxes—so more people will be homeless and then they'll blame us after they make us homeless.

The world of homeless families becomes a world of life on the run. It is about moving about "on the hem of life" and trying to creep "up into the major folds of the garment."[3] Ironically, Christy and Justine constitute the most privileged among the homeless. Why? Because they became homeless in small cities and sought and received help from unusual, family-centered agencies, few in number and dwindling as state cuts take their toll. Were Christy and Justine to live in New York, they might find themselves in the notorious Martinique, described by Jonathon Kozol.

A woman with three children, living on the twelfth floor of the Martinique hotel, is told that she must demonstrate her self reliance by doing all she can to find a permanent apartment. If she fails to make sufficient effort, she may discover that her case is closed—her room given to someone else, her children cut off from sustenance or taken from her custody. She must therefore clip advertisements from the newspapers, use one of the telephones twelve floors below in the lobby, travel to a real estate office, fill out forms, look at apartments, and return to the hotel with evidence that she has carried out what is, in effect, "the job" of homeless people. The social worker who assigns this task also tells her that her monthly rent allowance is two hundred and seventy dollars. Realtors tell her that apartments at that rent do not exist. Her welfare worker tells her that this is probably correct, and also tells her to get enrolled for public housing. Her neighbor across the hall tells her about the waiting list for public housing. There are two hundred thousand names on the list, and the wait is eighteen years.[4]

By comparison, Christy and Justine have it good, as good as the undeserving poor should expect, if we go by the influential conservative arguments spearheaded by Charles Murray in the Reagan era. In 1985, Murray suggested that society might reduce the number of illegitimate births by beginning "to stop subsidizing the behaviors it wants to prevent" and by

[handwritten annotations in top margin: "1985~" "Helping the poor:" "A few" "modest" "proposal" "satiric" "title?"]

intensifying the unpleasantness of the pregnant mother's condition, making unwed motherhood "contemptible."[5] "Some people are better than others," writes Murray in *Losing Ground*, ". . . and deserve more of society's re-wards."[6] *[handwritten: "1984"]*

Today's poor, single-mother families are likely to be tomorrow's home-less, for the supply of housing for low-income families continues to shrink. The 1980s produced a rate of homelessness among families larger than at any time since the Great Depression. By the end of the Reagan Adminis-tration, funds for low-income housing programs had been cut by almost 80 percent.[7] The combination of decreasing income and falling AFDC grants have priced poor families completely out of the rental market. In 1988, in thirty-six states, the entire AFDC grant for a family of three was less than the amount the Department of Housing and Urban Development esti-mated for a low-cost two-bedroom apartment. People of color have suf-fered a particularly high toll in urban areas. In Pennsylvania, for example, a state with a 9 percent black population, the Coalition on Homelessness found that 64 percent of the homeless were black.[8] If current trends con-tinue, the Children's Defense Fund estimates millions of American chil-dren will spend part of their childhoods homeless. Indeed, nationwide, families with children constitute one-third of the nation's homeless, and the fastest-growing segment is one-parent, female-headed families. William Apgar has estimated that single parents between the ages of twenty-five and thirty-four pay an average of 58 percent of their incomes on rent, but for single parents younger than twenty-five, the average is a staggering 81 percent![9] Add to this the extremely high costs of full-time child care, and we see that poor single mothers are trapped in a maze: any temporary clearing is but a breathing space until the next obstacle.

The chance that Justine asks for is a chance carved out of unlikely wood. She is poor, black, female, and a mother; worst of all, she is living in the United States, one of the most dangerous democracies for a poor woman to live in as she and her children approach the twenty-first century.

The Making of a Destitute Motherhood

Justine, Christy, Lori, Becky, and Jenny share their gendered misfortunes. While Lori and Becky began their descent from the steps of white middle-class privilege, the buffer of origins was not a significant antidote to poverty. Lifeworlds a breath away from "nowhere to go" almost merge into destitu-tion. The lighting shades the actresses a little differently, the nuances of suffering are perhaps more muted here, a little brighter there; one mother stands in the foreground, another backstage, waiting; but when the winds of crisis blow, the bruising fall is not very different.

Echoed in the stories of five women portrayed in this chapter and the six teenagers in chapter 4 is a loathing of the degradation of welfare. Contrary to public images of welfare mothers, these women are workers, part of the temporary workforce. Their dependence on the welfare system comes about when men and the labor market fail them, and they are forced to become both providers and nurturers. In a society that continues to extol the ideology of motherhood and to legitimize the irresponsibility of fatherhood, public policy simultaneously promotes an economy that relegates many women to the status of second-class, secondary-sector workers—a boon for the service industry but devastating for female-headed families. Family support systems such as exist in every other major industrialized democracy—guaranteed maternity leave, universal health care, affordable, safe, subsidized housing, a universal child allowance, and fully subsidized, high-quality child care—are largely unavailable. Thus women are disempowered as both mothers and wage earners.

In the stories we have heard, critical interventions that did provide child care, safe housing, and family support enabled these mothers temporarily to get back on their feet and take care of their children. The key individuals that helped, such as a Catholic social service worker and social workers from crisis centers, were part of private, nonprofit, underfunded programs; none of these programs was part of a public-sector entitlement. Availability, access, and continued support are all contingent on *place,* on where one becomes poor and where one falls into homelessness. The lack of entitlement to such services constitutes a continuing deprivation of rights for poor women and their children.

All these public policy holes—and public policy is as much about the unmaking of people's lives as it is about the making—coalesce to form the peculiar set of circumstances that worsen the feminization of poverty.

Part
Three

In the home into which a child is born, all objects change their significance; they begin to await some as yet undeterminate treatment at his hands; another and different person is there, a new personal history, short or long, has just been initiated, another account has been opened.

Maurice Merleau-Ponty
Phenomenology of Perception

IN PART THREE OF THIS BOOK, the contingent landscape of single mothers widens as the lives of their young children become visible. How do young children experience their personal history in a world of otherness? What indeterminate possibilities lie before them as a new account is opened? How do they encounter the dailiness of poverty within their own small worlds in school? For a young child, a classroom is a lifeworld in which autonomy and powerlessness, hope and despair, all coexist as possibility. But what is life in school really like for young children of poverty? How do the youngest of these children in public child care actually fare in their classrooms? Are they too part of the undeserving poor? And how do poor children entering kindergarten and the early elementary years experience their school culture? What is their daily landscape like? How are they perceived by their teachers? Are they viewed as children at risk or as children of promise?

In the following two chapters, life in classrooms for "at-risk" poor children is presented "in vivo." The children and the classrooms profiled were observed between 1988 and 1991 in Michigan (see Appendix). In some of the compensatory education programs observed, the children of the single mothers portrayed in part 2 were enrolled, but these children have not been identified in order to protect their confidentiality. All identifying characteristics of individual children and schools have been changed, and in certain cases composite portraits have been drawn to protect individual **99** identity. It is ironic that the youngest children described here are part of the *privileged* poor—the small percentage of the poverty population who actually have gained access to public early childhood programs. These children attend Head Start and other state-funded public preschool programs. For the older elementary children, as with the preschoolers, the early years of school are an enduring and significant experience. Life in school matters.

The classrooms described in part 3 exemplify neither the best nor the worst of worlds for the children; rather they offer a window into the dailiness of *some* poor children's school lives. A searching look into the actual classrooms serving poor children may illuminate other lives lived out in other classrooms and may reveal a pervasive set of sensibilities that shape the way we look at poor children, regulate their entitlement, and consign them to the other childhood.

6

Inside Public Preschools:
A View from Below

An extraordinary economic buy.

> 1985 Report of Committee for Economic Development on
> Preschool Education for At-Risk children.[1]

Early childhood programs cost money—sometimes a lot of it. But crime
costs more.

> Governor Collins of Kentucky, National Governors'
> Association Conference on Early Intervention, 1986.[2]

Poor Children and Public Child Care

POOR CHILDREN, IT SEEMS, are deserving of public money only if
investment in their early lives has demonstrable economic payoffs.
They matter instrumentally, not existentially. Born as they are to the
undeserving poor, and many to single mothers, they, like young Oliver
Twist, are badged and ticketed. This time they are not sent to the orphan-
age or poorhouse but rather consigned to a tenuous childhood. A fortunate
few of the unfortunate many will be eligible for an "at-risk" designation,
which tickets them for access to a compensatory or pre-primary special
education program. But such an instrumental view, as Grubb and Lazerson
point out, promotes the perspective that any public expenditure which contributes to a child's development without demonstrable payoffs, or any expenditure which merely contributes to the well-being or enjoyment of children as children, cannot be justified. Hence innovative, or sometimes
merely pleasant and well-run, subsidized programs that make the world a
little better for poor families on the edge, that ease the stresses in poor
mothers' lives, have always had to fight for their continued existence. Similarly, health and nutritional programs for pregnant or nursing mothers and
their babies have been justified in terms of the avoidance of future economic costs, rather than on positive humanitarian grounds. "Malnourished

children are unacceptable because they may suffer brain damage and then become future dependents of the state, not because of the immorality of malnutrition in a land of plenty."[3] Besides, as Governor Collins and others have pointed out, crime costs more than intervention. Must we then assume every poor young child is a potential criminal in order to justify early intervention? We are reminded of Charles Brace who, in 1872, in his book *The Dangerous Classes of New York*, warned:

> Thousands are the children of poor foreigners, who have permitted them to grow up without school, education or religion. All the neglect and bad education and evil example of a poor class tend to form others, who as they mature swell the ranks of ruffians and criminals.[4]

Still, in the late twentieth century, it is the poor who are considered to have only themselves to blame. The Pygmalion[5] predictions persist, implicating poor young children as the "dangerous classes." Early education becomes another form of cost-effective crime prevention. Indeed, part of the much-hailed success of the Perry Preschool Intervention Program is the claim that the arrest rate of participants was 40 percent lower than control-group children. But a different question hovers above this instrumental discourse—Do poor children's lives matter? How do we reconcile our "progressive" democratic language about educational equality, equity, access, and opportunity with cost-benefit analyses of intervention efforts on behalf of poor babies and young children? Do we retain our democratic sensibilities when we confront the poor and their children? Or, put another way, are poor children cheap?

The history of child care and early education in the United States reveals that a two-tier system has always existed. Public custodial care in the form of day nurseries was available for poor children from the late nineteenth century, while the nursery movement of the early twentieth century offered part-day developmental enrichment to middle-class children. The day nursery, an integral development of the Child-Saving era, emerged from the cult of motherhood and domestic feminism, a period in which upper-class women and philanthropists efficiently organized day care for the children of poor mothers in several large urban slums. While reaching only a fraction of needy children, these programs nevertheless provided not only hygienic and custodial care, but often employment and domestic training as well. The Leila Day Nursery in New Haven, for example, ran an "intelligence department" for widows and the abandoned wives of drunkards, and provided a work referral service. Habits of obedience and cleanliness were fostered, and many nurseries provided after-school care. The sentiments expressed by the Armitage Day Nursery in New York City capture the prevailing attitudes toward the mothers of the children in care: "Who has not felt disheartened when visiting among the poor, at the incapability of the mothers to make and keep a home in the truest sense?" Or as a caregiver in another nursery stated, "slum babies would all be better off in nurseries."[7] Both the day nurseries and the charity kindergartens were directed at poor children whose mothers were forced to work; yet the nurseries came under strong criticism. Opponents argued that they loosened family ties, that they encouraged laziness and irresponsibility by mothers who should be caring for their own children; that female work depressed male wages and, furthermore, loosened the father's tie as sole breadwinner, even though he was already absent!

After World War I, a clinical perspective prevailed in social work. In caring for poor children, "problem families" became the focus. Grace Caldwell, addressing the National Conference of Social Work in 1919 on the admission standards to day nurseries, cautioned her audience to see the poor children of working mothers as members of disturbed families:

> That we spend the greater part of our funds for the care of children does not alter the fact that the reason we do so is because of some maladjustment in the families of which they are members, and it is to get at the cause of this maladjustment and to build up normal family conditions that our nursery care works towards.[8]

From maladjusted to culturally deprived; from the family as a tangle of pathology to broken, non-intact, and dysfunctional; from the pauper child as potential criminal to the at-risk student delinquent—this is a discourse embedded in time and in the American ethos. The "poverty problem" is framed as individual and private, grounded in intrapsychic or intrafamily deficits but not in the politics of distribution, not in state-constructed poverty, not in a conception of positive state entitlements withheld from certain of its citizenry. When a War on Poverty was finally declared in the 1960s as part of Johnson's Great Society vision, one of the most far-reaching and ambitious efforts undertaken to address the issue of child and family poverty in this country, how then did public child care fare?

In 1965, funded by the Economic Opportunity Act, Head Start was launched as a massive early intervention program in the lives of poor children to inoculate them against the ill effects of poverty. During an era in which the elasticity of the child's developing intelligence was touted by educational psychologists, the view was widely promulgated that heavy doses of cognitive enrichment would boost poor children's IQs. Although, as Edward Zigler points out, Head Start was a comprehensive program which focused on social competence as well as cognitive outcomes and broadened its mandate to develop an ecological perspective on the child,[9] the measurement of cognitive gains has continued to dominate the assessment of the program. Head Start differed too from other compensatory, deficit-oriented enrichment programs of the time because of its holistic perspective. The development of the child was emphasized through four major components: education, health, nutrition, and social services. An integral facet of the successful educational intervention was parent education and involvement. Polly Greenberg, one of the founding team members of Head Start, tells how in 1964 Sargent Shriver, who launched Head Start, argued that it was more important to provide large numbers of children with nutritious food, health care, social services, early education, and opportunities for parent education than to serve fewer children with model cognitive development programs, which previously had been promoted as part of the compensatory education movement.[10]

As in many other progressive educational mandates, the distance between theory and the reality of children's lives in classrooms was vast. Under intense scrutiny to prove that it is worth investing in young children's lives, Head Start has employed conventional quantitative measures to assess essentially qualitative changes in children's and families' lives. IQ testing and batteries of other standardized tests have assaulted Head Start children despite growing evidence of racial and cultural bias and the dubious validity of test scores when applied to the developing range of young children's social and cognitive competence. In 1988, the National Association for the Education of Young Children took a strong stand against the institutionalization of standardized testing.[11] Yet testing continues to afflict early childhood classrooms, particularly those serving at-risk children. Herbert Ginsburg, in a clear critique of compensatory education and the myths it engenders of cognitively deprived, linguistically deficient poor children, describes his experiences as a psychologist testing Head Start children in the late 1960s, as part of a federal evaluation of Head Start programs across the country:

> Young children, in nursery school or kindergarten, often appear quite apprehensive when a strange adult—who is sometimes called "doctor"—puts the question to them. It is, after all, an absurd situation: strange adults do not often seek the company of children for games or anything else; the request must be threatening or at least unsettling . . . I began with 4-year-old test items. The first item at this age level is "picture vocabulary." The child is

shown a series of pictures on 2 by 4 inch cards—e.g., cup, book, jacket, etc.—and he is asked, "What's this? What do you call it?" In the examiner's manual, some examples of correct and incorrect responses are given. For example, when shown a picture of a coat, the child may answer "coat" or "jacket," but he is wrong if he says "suit or shirt" or "overcoat" . . .

Then I placed three of the objects—for example, lion, ball, block—in a row and said, "Now shut your eyes tight so that you can't see them." I placed a screen, also part of the standard test equipment, in front of the objects just in case the child did not close his eyes. Then I covered one of the three toys with a small box. "Open your eyes. Look! Which one did I hide?" The child must say the name of the hidden object and not just point to it. I repeated the procedure twice, each time of course with different objects. The child must succeed on at least two of the three problems to pass the hidden-object test.[12]

And thus a four-year-old's cognitive abilities are scored. If the child were to tell a story about an overcoat, she would be scored down because of failure to label correctly. If her brother calls an overcoat "a big shirt," as I once had a child tell me, she fails too! Hence the rich linguistic context and the imaginative world of the child are denied as is her ability to extend her thinking beyond the label. If she were to point and become playful, hiding the object from the examiner—that too is an event to be negatively scored. The Stanford-Binet is still a widely used test, despite its linguistic and cultural biases. What Ginsburg portrays in the late 1960s has not changed much in the late '80s and early '90s as Head Start evaluations have relied on psychometrically limiting constructs for interpreting children's intellectual and social competence.[13] The results of such quantitative evaluations often drive classroom practice; activities and routines for young children begin to mirror the antidevelopmental perspective displayed in psychometric testing. Exclusive emphasis is placed on labeling and sequence drills and little time is devoted to children's self-initiated talk, so that what Piaget terms figurative knowledge is promoted rather than the operative/transformative knowledge that is constructed by the children themselves as part of their inventive mastery of the classroom world.[14]

While the original Head Start objectives stressed a comprehensive and ecological view of the child in his or her family and poverty milieu, the deficit assumptions of the compensatory education movement were still present in objectives and practice. Cognitive and social deficiencies were assumed to be present, as we read in the 1965 National Head Start Recommendations. Objective 1 stresses the critical importance of the early years of the poverty cycle as a period in which "the creation of learning patterns, emotional development and the formation of individual expectations and aspirations take place at a very rapid pace. *For the child of poverty there are clearly observable deficiencies in the processes which lay the foundation for a pattern of failure* [my emphasis]—and thus a pattern of poverty—throughout the child's entire life." Objective 5B refers to the need for "helping the emotional and social development of the child by encouraging self-confidence, spontaneity, curiosity, and self-discipline," and 5C targets *"improving the child's mental processes and skills with particular attention to conceptual and verbal skills"* (my emphasis).[15] In many ways these early recommendations lay the ground for the proliferation of programs aimed not only at intervening in the child's intellectual developmental cycle, which is seen as deficient in comparison to that of the middle-class child, but also at regulating and ordering the child's milieu. What kind of spontaneity and curiosity is permitted—that which conforms to the classroom routines or that which initiates a novel activity that goes beyond the daily lesson plan?

This regulation extends to the child's family. When does parent education become invasion of another cultural milieu and set of interaction patterns? Consider the different forms of talk and "ways with words" in terms of how mothers speak to their toddlers that Shirley Brice Heath has documented in the Piedmont Carolinas,[16] or the research on cultural and linguistic diversity in the analogical or referential styles adopted by white and black children as they communicate in classrooms.[17]

The deficit assumptions, criticized by Ginsburg, that educators and psychologists make about poor children are manifest in the class and ethnic arrogance of the remedial education projects such as the Klaus and Gray Programs. These are still lauded as a successful early-training project of Head Start, designed to alleviate the "progressive retardation" of the black children who lived in "spatially and temporally disorganized homes,"[18] where young children were seen as "noticeably deficient in perception, concept formation and language" (presumably this deficiency is inferred from the children's not succeeding on test items requiring standard English and correct labeling responses). In these early intervention programs there was a heavy emphasis on reinforcement theory. Children were required to speak "correctly" so that a request for milk, for example, would be rewarded only when the child spoke in a complete sentence. Mothers were to be trained to respond to their children in "correct" and appropriate educational ways, leading Ginsburg to conclude that such programs were aimed at modifying "the very foundations of family life among the poor." The drafters of the program, argued Ginsburg, "believe that lower class mothers are so incompetent at childrearing as to damage their children's intellect and destroy their chances of academic success."[19]

While Head Start programs have not all embodied the deficit assumptions of the early-training projects, and while there is a growing consciousness among early childhood educators about developmentally and culturally appropriate practice, which is now recommended in current Head Start guidelines, the pervasive deficit view about poor children—a mirror reflection of public perceptions of the poor—remains as an invidious frame into which much of early intervention falls. Teachers themselves are not necessarily free of class and race prejudice. Teacher training institutions offer very little in the way of antibias education, and Head Start teachers are not noticeably different in their orientations, being graduates of the same institutions or recipients of the Child Development Associate (CDA) credential approved by Head Start. Although Head Start clearly has helped children in significant ways in term of health, nutrition, social services, and parent education, it too has been a participant in the construction of at-risk, deficit perceptions of poor children.

Deficit perceptions lead many educators to propound a highly structured and rigid environment for poor children, with respect not only to cognitive and verbal abilities but to socialization skills as well. Teaching the children of poverty confronts many teachers with a world they would rather not confront, for such children reveal the inequities and injustice that shape their young lives in the other America. Their poverty is frequently condemned as the fault of their parents' immorality, irresponsibility, drug habits, or dependence on social services. When children are poor and of color, they are doubly disadvantaged. Blaming the victim has not disappeared; the discourse has changed, and the labels have turned, but at-risk children are still seldom seen as children of promise.[20] In order to see such children differently, we need to examine the possible pathology of the classroom rather than the assumed pathology of the child or family. Another question needs to surface from a complicit educational discourse— are poor children experiencing classrooms which place them at risk for *later* promise? In the classroom observations that follow, the diverse worlds of poor children in public child care are portrayed.[21]

Inside Head Start Classrooms

Red Oaks

The Head Start program in Red Oaks public school district is part of an
early childhood education center that houses several kindergarten rooms,
a developmental kindergarten, and two Head Start classrooms; the latter
are staffed by two experienced teachers certified to teach at the early childhood level, who have been teaching at-risk children for over twelve years.
Both teachers are white and both classroom assistants are black; each
morning a parent volunteer is present to assist the staff. There are eighteen
four-year-olds in each classroom with an even mix of white and black children; no other ethnic minorities are present. Thirty of the thirty-six enrolled children are from single-mother households.

> *In Mrs. Roby's room the brightly colored art adorning the walls, painted
> shapes, train frames, alphabet pictures, number people, is striking. It is all
> adult-made. The children's art is confined to one corner of the side wall with
> written descriptions by the teachers labeling what the children have drawn
> or painted. Mrs. Roby sits at a table in the center of the room with a basket
> filled with clothespins, hangers, and number cards. Individually the children
> are called over to hang the correct number of clothespins on the hanger that
> corresponds to the number she selects for them from the basket. "It's your
> turn, Kashara." Kashara willingly comes over to the table, and Mrs. Roby
> selects number four. Kashara seems uncertain and begins to play with the
> clothespins. Mrs. Roby removes the clothespins from Kashara's hand and
> counts each clothespin very distinctly, "one, two, three, four," which Kashara
> repeats obediently. Mrs. Roby guides her hand and places four clothespins
> on the hanger, "how many clothespins do we have," she asks Kashara, mov-
> ing her face right up to Kashara and mouthing the number four. "Four,"
> mumbles Kashara, squirming in her seat. "Rrright," responds Mrs. Roby,
> "now you may go over to Mrs. Crane's table." Kashara sits down at Mrs.
> Crane's table and is handed a precut, heart-shaped Valentine card. The
> words "I love you" are on a connect-the-dots paper for Kashara to trace.
> Mrs. Crane then guides Kashara's hand to cut along the lines by placing her
> pencil beside the scissors while Kashara is told to "cut it right." The cut-out
> heart is then glued on to the precut card. Kashara is then directed to dictate
> her message, which Mrs. Crane will write on the card before it is sent home
> in Kashara's backpack.*
>
> *After these two activities take place, during "free choice" time Byron,
> who has been reprimanded by both teachers for running in the room and*

using his "too loud outside voice," pulls me by the hand and asks me to play with him at another table. He selects a bin with differently shaped and sized colored blocks. I begin to build a tower, which he watches silently. "Don't you want to make something too?" He shakes his head and continues to watch Mrs. Roby, shifting uneasily from foot to foot as if in anticipation of being stopped. He is right, as two minutes later Mrs. Roby rings a bell and announces "We're going to clean up in five minutes." With the exception of a number of soft blocks on the floor, the clean-up for "free choice" time is contained on three tables. Five minutes later the lights go off, and Mrs. Roby says, "If you're in your seats I'll know you're ready to go to the bathroom." Chris comes running over to Mrs. Roby, and she bends down and places her hands over his legs, asking sternly and quietly, "Where do you run?" "Outside." "Right." As the children line up in silence, they are told, "Okay, tell your feet to walk." In unison, the children reply, "Walk feet," and they march through the door to the bathroom.

At this point, halfway through the morning program on a typical day, the children have spent more time being prepared for various teacher-planned activities and being drilled in the correct clean-up and line-up procedures than actually engaging in these activities. As long as the children obey the temporal and spatial norms—no running or loud voices inside, no mixing of activities from one space to another, no interrupting the teacher, no playing with friends inside, no self-initiated activities—they are pleasantly treated. However, any child who transgresses such classroom norms quickly becomes a problem and threatens the well-regulated world of the teacher's classroom. There was little time or space for a child's initiative. Valentines had to be made the right way, numbers were a counting drill, allowing the children very little opportunity for hands-on learning. Byron's sense of unease about building in the allotted time frame was disturbing, he seemed not to want to try, because whatever he began had to be undone in clean-up time, which followed rapidly with clockwork efficiency. This same problem reemerged on subsequent visits:

Sarah was asked by Mrs. Roby during circle time, "What choice are you going to make today?" On a flannel board in front of the teachers were three picture cutouts of three choices—housekeeping, blocks, and the arts and crafts table. "I want to go to housekeeping then painting," said Sarah. "Well you need to choose one—make one choice," said Mrs. Roby, her tone becoming a little impatient as the remaining eight children in the circle became restless, awaiting their turns. "Umm-ummm I don't know," said Sarah, putting her finger in her mouth. "Well, why don't you choose the art table to-

day," said Mrs. Roby, glancing at her chart of the week and noting Sarah's
previous choices. "Okay," said Sarah, "I think I'll paint"; but when she went
to the art table, a leaf-pasting collage activity was already in place, and
Sarah was handed her leaves, paste, and paper by a parent volunteer, who
said, "Hurry up! We only have a little while longer to make this project."

Choice time ran for approximately forty minutes in a three-hour morning program. The objective for choice time was to help the child make
independent choices, and one of the desired outcomes was active,
discovery-oriented play, "the building blocks of later thinking skills," according to the stated curriculum guidelines. Yet there was neither space
nor time for little Sarah to discover or invent her own world that morning.
Play was reduced to three choices, all teacher-defined and teacher-
planned. Even as Sarah accepted her teacher's choice for her, art was
changed into a preplanned art project, and an expressive activity was denied in favor of a more ordered, less messy project. As long as Sarah and
her classmates acquiesced with docility, their daily experience appeared to
be repetitious, dull, ordered, but pleasant. As poor children, they were
being trained in the routines of regulation and compliance, which the
teachers believed they needed for later school success. As another kindergarten teacher in the building told me, "When they come out of preschool,
they should known how to behave and follow directions because those type
of kids don't learn it at home!" Accordingly, training in disciplined routines
occupies a central aspect of the entry and exit rituals of the classroom.

The lights go off, and the children are asked to line up in silence in one
straight line behind Mrs. Crane to go home. "Push your chairs under the
table and make one straight line . . . Okay, what did we do with Mrs. Crane
today?" Some of the children answer that they made Valentines. "What did
we do with Mrs. Arne today?" "We ate snack," answers Amanda. "Say good-
bye," says Mrs. Roby nodding, and the children chorus, "Goodbye
Mrs.Roby, Goodbye Mrs. Crane, Goodbye Mrs. Arne," and Mrs. Crane
leads them down the hall in line to the bus. Byron is out of line talking to
himself and dawdling, so Mrs. Roby forcefully pulls him aside and sends him
to the back of the line.

Mrs. Roby, who controls the carefully sequenced day with efficiency,
punishes the children who dawdle or move "off-task." She creates a regulated world for the children and describes the classroom as "a balance between carefully structured play and teacher-directed activities." She con-
ducts all teacher planning, and she instructs her assistant, Mrs. Crane,

and the parent volunteers accordingly. She has a reputation throughout several districts as one who runs one of the best classrooms for at-risk preschoolers.

During storytime about Sylvester, a donkey who discovers the powers of a magic pebble, Duke feels in his pocket and excitedly exclaims, "See, I have one too—maybe it can make magic like Sylvester," and he begins to rub the pebble and say, "biggledy boo." "Sit down and hush," says Mrs. Roby sternly, and a new student teacher is instructed to hold Duke on her lap as he is now jumping up and down, saying, "See, see, it's magic," to the other children who have moved out of the circle and are trying to touch the pebble. As Duke continues to disrupt story time, he is given another warning and then sent to the time-out chair at the far end of the room. He is now defiant and begins to shout "Nooo, leave me alone, you fucker" as he kicks the student teacher, screaming "Gimme, gimme" and trying to snatch his magic pebble back, which has been taken away from him. Duke is removed, screaming, from the classroom. Mrs. Roby later tells me, "I've had it up to here with him. He comes from one of the housing projects, his mother's on welfare, and he'll end up in prison or on drugs like his older brother. I don't know what kindergarten teacher here is going to take him—we'll have to get him referred to developmental and special ed."

Duke indeed was a deviant black child within that classroom. He constantly sought recognition but rarely received positive acknowledgment. His excitement about his pebble could have been incorporated into the storytime in a more flexible classroom, but a rigid teacher agenda did not allow for that. When I later inquired about the possibility of recognizing Duke's contributions, even if they were out of order, both teachers told me, "These kids have to learn to follow classroom rules—Duke's one of the really disruptive ones." This negative and punitive attitude toward Duke and the other "out of order" children created a daily experience of harassment for the "troublemakers." They were constantly under surveillance.

Today Tommy and Byron are in the block area during playtime, and they began to "vroom-vrrooom" around the block area with their wooden trucks. Tommy drives his truck noisily to the housekeeping area and begins to stack plates and cups from housekeeping into the back of the truck. "Oh yeah! We can drive the stuff," said Byron and rummages in the dress-up box for two hats, which he places on his and Tommy's heads. As the two "deliverymen" begin to drive their trucks in the direction of the block area, Mrs. Roby rushes over, saying, "We don't move stuff from housekeeping into the block

area; if you want to play in housekeeping, leave the wooden trucks," as she
begins to dismantle the boy's careful "deliveries." Byron lies on the floor and
begins to cry and kick the truck. He throws the blocks over the floor, shout-
ing, "Don't—no—gimmee" as Mrs. Roby separates and reorders the two
areas. Byron, as a "last warning," is told to "settle down" or "you'll have to
go to time-out until you can behave."

Not only did Mrs. Roby violate the children's cooperative and imaginative play, but she also failed to recognize the cognitive value of such inventive play. Byron and Tommy were engaged in complex representational,
multidimensional play—they created a situation, found props, elaborated
their play as they put together functions and objects, and created a plausible make-believe world. Not so for their teacher, who saw transgression
of the separate-spaces rule and in fact promoted unidimensional play,
thereby denying the inherently constructivist nature of their child-initiated
activity, which Piaget argues is central to the development of later intellectual operations. In such a classroom, specific activities are permitted only
within strictly defined temporal and spatial frames. Violation of the spatial
and temporal frames *is considered* creates non-normative or deviant behavior. Boundaries between activity areas are strictly maintained, so playing in two spaces
violates the strict demarcation of objects-in-their-place rule, which is an
implicit norm of the classroom.

Stated adherence to developmentally appropriate practice in such
early intervention programs is reduced to a set of regulatory practices that
control initiative, imaginative symbolic play, and active engagement in stories. The practice of drilling students in labeling and counting objects promotes static and figurative knowledge rather than inventive exploratory
learning, and trains the children to produce unidimensional correct responses rather than encouraging flexible and transformative thinking.
"Studying the ways young children think is a matter of listening to what
children say and paying attention to what they do," Millie Almy and Celia
Genishi remind us. "It is also a matter of respecting their thinking while
providing them with activity and experiences to nurture and challenge it."[22]
How Duke's magic pebble might have woven a magic tapestry of dramatic
play around Sylvester's story remains a mystery—to be discovered unfor-
tunately in too few early childhood centers, which across all socioeconomic
lines, for children of the privileged and the poor, suffer from a pervasive
erosion of play under the compliance agendas of teachers.[23] Despite the
discourse of developmentally appropriate practice, child and classroom
management is still a dominant preoccupation of the American educational

landscape. When this imperative is applied to poor children, some of the most disturbing aspects of early intervention become apparent.

Shady Trails

The Shady Trails Head Start Program is housed in a pleasant, well-equipped, one-story building in the center of an urban metropolitan area. The program offers part-day classes for four-year-olds Monday through Thursday, and parent education and Home Start visits on Fridays. The children served in the three classrooms are predominantly black (of the fifty-six children, four are white, and ten are Hispanic), and all the teachers are black. There is a high degree of parent involvement in the program, although not many volunteer as aides in the classroom. Because the Head Start program is not part of the public school district, teacher salaries are accordingly much lower. The Head Start teachers, who have CDA credentials, earn an average salary of approximately $13,000.

In one of several visits to Teacher Lisa and Teacher Mara's classroom, I observe the group time. From 2.45 to 3.30 the children are expected to sit in a chair and do work. Today the planned activity involves the children's tracing the first letter of their names with glue and then sticking marshmallows on it. Before they are permitted to begin, Teacher Lisa gives each child a name card and asks them to look at the first letter of their name. Holding up an alphabet letter she announces, "If this is the first letter of your name, come on up here." As each child comes up, Teacher Lisa individually writes out their first name on a colored piece of paper. Meanwhile the children fidget in their seats, throwing their name cards around, poking their neighbors, kicking their feet up and down, and sliding off their chairs. Without looking up, Teacher Lisa says, "People are not paying attention . . . I'm gonna have to move you . . . I'm gonna have to move you." After about fifteen minutes, every child has a piece of paper with his or her name on it, and the children are instructed to take their chairs back to the lunch/snack tables and sit down. The two teachers circulate, pouring glue over the first letter of the children's names. Teacher Mara lets some of the children trace their own first letter with glue since she has a glue bottle with a spout, but Teacher Lisa does it for the children. Both teachers give each child a handful of marshmallows. Several minutes later the children are done with their "project," and several begin sliding under the table and giggling. Teacher Mara: "Let's get back in our seats please. I want you back in your seats." As the children continue to fidget and play under the table and the noise level increases,

Teacher Mara moves to the front of the class and loudly says, "Keep it up, keep it up and we'll see if we'll have snack." The children quiet down. "I hear talking, I don't know who it is but it's gonna get you in trouble." The room becomes silent. One by one she sends the children to the housekeeping area with their hands in their lap. "I said sit down and put your hands in your lap." André giggles and is called back to sit in the snack area. A few minutes later, Teacher Mara says, "André, do you think you can go over and act like you should?" André nods and is sent over to the other children, who are now doing finger plays with Teacher Lisa.

Most of group time was spent ordering and organizing the children, policing their behavior and ensuring their compliance. The children actually spent only ten minutes of the forty-minute group time involved in their project. Although both teachers were constantly directing and ordering the children, when compliance was achieved and the room was quiet and ordered they warmly complimented the children, saying, "You kids have been real good today," or "This is my best class of kids," and they frequently hugged and cuddled the children. But the overriding focus was on teacher-planned activities with a constant emphasis on labeling and "doing it right." The marshmallow project was fun for the kids because it was gooey and sticky and they could sneak some marshmallows when the teachers' eyes were diverted; but this was short-lived. The constant stress on drilling the children in letter and name recognition extended into other parts of the day as well. There was little room for inventive, child-initiated activities, and silence was constantly required for classroom activities. A "school-like" atmosphere prevailed for these four-year-olds, who were subjected to the early intervention rigors in a developmentally inappropriate classroom structure to prepare them for school. Teacher Mara had attended a High/Scope training workshop and claimed to base her classroom practice on the plan-do-review model, designed to involve children in the planning of their day, the making of choices, the doing, and the later telling.

Today I was present for the full plan-do-review as Teacher Mara presented the day's project. She sat in a chair with the children facing her and demonstrated how to drop different colors of paint on a piece of paper and fold it in half, making what she called an "African abstract." The children were instructed to carry their chairs back to the snack tables, each of which was supplied with forks and three colors of paint. Stacey drops blots of paint from a fork onto her paper. She trades colors and forks with Jimiel and begins to pour red and black paint onto her paper, giggling. Teacher Lisa notices the large blots of paint on Stacey's paper and scoops it up, saying

"That's too much in one spot—here's another." In spite of Stacey's protests, she throws away Stacey's paper and tells her to "do it over." Stacey does, and is then told to fold her paper in half and smooth it over with her hand. She opens the paper, and Teacher Mara applauds while Stacey stares blankly at the result. As Teacher Mara turns away, Stacey folds it twice over and notices the new smudges with interest. Teacher Mara turns around, "Stacey, leave your picture alone [as she tries to add more paint]; don't touch it; leave it there and get up . . . Stacey, you'll ruin it," as Stacey continues to fold it. The picture is removed and pegged on the line. Meanwhile, Teacher Lisa walks over to Jimiel, who is carefully dropping green paint only on the top righthand corner of his paper. "Here Jimiel, spread the paint all over the picture. Fill it up with paint." She takes the cup of paint and puts several blots of paint in the empty spaces as Jimiel begins to squirm in his seat. When she leaves, he throws his fork under the table and climbs underneath to retrieve it. He does not return to his spoiled painting, which is folded by Teacher Lisa the "right way" and pegged on the line to dry.

Following a ten-minuted cleanup the children are gathered in a circle. Teacher Mara says, "What did we do today?" "Painting with forks," replies one of the children. "We made African abstracts and how did we do that?" The children are fidgeting, and Teacher Mara recaps the project saying, "That's what we did and now we're going to learn an African song in Swahili . . . say S-w-a-h-i-l-i," and she proceeds to point out the letters of the alphabet, which they repeat after her.

The original High/Scope curriculum is organized on the premise that children are active learners who construct their own knowledge from activities they plan and carry out themselves in a plan-do-review session.[24] In this classroom, the teachers both planned and carried out the activities and then drilled the children in the correct review response. Noticeably absent was any space for a child to actively pursue a thought, such as Stacey's experimentation with how increasing folds made more smudges, or Jimiel's aesthetic experimentation with his own green drop design. The rigidly planned activity and directed teaching precluded child discovery. Although the children sometimes persisted with their ideas, they eventually yielded and became compliant as the teachers managed their world of learning. Even the attempt to introduce the Afrocentric curriculum was adult-directed and rigidly managed, with little attempt to contextualize the meaning of the activities for the children. Even during choice and free time, the dominant emphasis was on order and cleaning up, not on doing and making and experimenting.

Several children are playing with clay at the table, talking and commenting,
"Let's see," "Lookit," "See what I made." Ryan rolls out a long snake and gets
up to show his snake to Teacher Mara. "That's nice Ryan, now take it back
and put it on the table." Chris gets up too to show his truck of clay. "I said
keep it on the table—keep all the play dough on the table." Ben is sitting on
the floor of the housekeeping area with all the pots, plates, cups, and other
sundry objects spread around him. In an annoyed tone Teacher Mara says,
"Ben, what are you doing?" "I'm making something for myself." "Well be
sure to put all those things away when you're done." Teacher Mara tells me,
"He always does this, he takes them out and never wants to put them away."
She then announces, "We'll start clean-up in ten minutes," but goes back to
housekeeping and tells Ben to start cleaning up. "But I'm not done," he pro-
tests, guarding his little circle of household wares, which he has now orga-
nized in piles of plates, cups, pots in ascending order of sizes. "You heard
me," says Teacher Mara, and she dismantles his carefully organized struc-
ture. Ben throws a pot across the floor and begins to cry, and he is sent to sit
by himself at the back of the room.

Containment, order, and control are the key experiences of these
young children. When they comply, they are treated affectionately, but a
child's action that deviates from the classroom norms reaps punishment.
Because the order orientation is so dominant, the teachers often cannot see
what the children *do* to demonstrate their own learning and interest. Ben's
ordering of kitchen objects was a clear example of a preoperational child's
growing mastery of classification. The violation of Ben's organizational
structure, which he himself had initiated with kitchen objects, led to his
resistance; yet his protest was seen only as a resistance to clean-up, which
in fact was given far more importance than play. Ironically, when Ben was
verbally tested on his labeling and sorting skills, he performed poorly; yet
it was clear his competence and motivation were present if only he were
allowed to experiment *his* way. But both teachers believed it was their responsibility "to train these kids so they can make it in school." Directed
instruction and lessons in compliance constituted the major part of their
educational landscape.

Birch Glen

The Head Start programs in Birch Glen, a small city, are part of the public
school district which enrolls approximately one hundred four-year-olds in
three sites housed in the public schools, and a home-based program for

three-year-olds. Teacher Jackie, who is white, is a certified early childhood teacher, and her black assistant, Teacher Mae, is enrolled in the Head Start CDA Program. Teacher Jackie's classroom, in an elementary school, also has the services of the school's teacher consultant, who works with "special needs" children as well as parent volunteers who regularly help with classroom activities. The children are ethnically diverse; of the eighteen enrolled, three are non-native English speakers, eight are black, three are Hispanic and four are white; eleven are from single-parent families.

During my first visit I am struck by the small size of the classroom, buzzing with diverse activities, and the spread of four-year-olds in every nook and cranny of the classroom: two little girls drawing on paper under tables, several children sprawled in the reading corner, two hiding in a fort, three clustered in the block corner, arguing about whether the road is "curvey enough," and four, silent and with captivated faces, watching their growing tadpoles almost leaping out of their "pond." The walls and blackboard are covered with children's art, several "invented spelling" stories, and pictures of each child's "family and people who we care about." The room hums with the "busyness" of children's play; a multitude of activities appear to coexist simultaneously in the room. It takes a little while to find Teacher Jackie, who is hiding in the fort with two children to test whether it's "real dark and scary inside." Teacher Mae is in the adjoining bathroom, helping several children clean paint from their hair after a particularly boisterous fingerpainting activity, which Teacher Mae tells me "turned into hair and face painting too." The morning is loosely structured around free play, circle/storytime, snack, choice activity time, and outside time. There is only one official clean-up time at the end of the morning, but I notice most children need little reminding to clean up their individual activities as they move from area to area. Derek and James are building a fort; and after they are done, they make a picture, which they tape onto the fort with a red stop sign after laboriously copying the letters from a poster on the far end of the blackboard. After the sign is taped onto the fort, the fort is allowed to remain standing for the rest of the day.

The fort, built by Derek and James, began during free play and becomes more and more elaborate as materials from both the housekeeping and the block areas are imaginatively utilized. As Teacher Jackie calls the children to the rug for storytime, they initiate the stop sign and continue to work on it while the rest of the children are already in the circle. After they have taped up the sign, they join the circle independently without reprimands. After the story they return to the fort—at this point it has become a social matrix for

the room—and the boys have initiated turn-taking rules: "Only two kids at
a time and no jumping 'cos it will break down." Their classmates appear to
follow the rules, and the teachers look on without intervening.   *Cf. mexican*
teachers

The flexible structure of this classroom fostered creative and elaborated play that embodied social cooperation, decision making, creative
child initiatives, and a built-in cognitive component, spelling STOP in order to protect their creation! I observed a number of other child-initiated
extended play activities in which children made choices and built imaginative worlds. While many of these young children were stressed by their
poverty and fragile early lives, in this classroom they became children of
promise. Children who might have been labeled troublemakers in other
Head Start classrooms found a place here. Daren was one such child.

Daren is a startling presence in the room, wild-eyed with an intense look,
almost like a grimace over his face, constantly darting about, tenaciously
gripping the tractor and riding it through the room. During circle time he
sits either on one of the teachers' laps or on the little rocking chair next to
them, rocking himself back and forth in a rhythmic motion. He often points
at objects and stumbles as he tries to reach them, bursting into tears and
collapsing in Teacher Jackie's arms, who holds him until he is comforted. To-
day Annie and Sandy and Ron are playing in housekeeping. Ron "eats" from
a pot in which the children have cooked "stone soup"—they giggle and dress
themselves in wigs. Daren darts by, stops, smiles, and slowly takes a wig and
puts it on his head, and the four continue to eat the soup. They take plastic
cutlery and pretend to cut the vegetables with the knife. Daren takes the
knife and runs it across his throat several times, as if to slit it, staring with a
strange look into the distance. He then chases one of the children with the
plastic knife, repeating the slitting action across the child's throat. Teacher
Mae comes over and calmly removes the knife from Daren, and he cries. She
picks him up and takes him to the book corner and settles him down with
one of the fifth-grade helpers, who reads him a story. After the story he finds
the tractor and sits back on it, silently watching the other children, who are
busily involved. As he begins to ride the tractor, he suddenly needs to go to
the bathroom and starts pulling his pants down and dragging the tractor
with him to the toilet as if afraid another child will take the tractor. Teacher
Jackie notices and tells him, "It's okay, you can go to the bathroom, I'll save
the tractor for you until you're done."

Both teachers treat Daren with gentleness and care and are acutely
tuned to his every movement. Teacher Jackie describes him as a sweet,

traumatized child, who "until the age of three and a half basically raised himself." Upon entry into the classroom eight months ago, he apparently didn't speak. He "growled," cried, bit the teachers and other children and frequently messed in his pants. Reports indicate his mother was destitute and drug-addicted when she was pregnant with him; when a toddler he was found by police wandering the streets shoeless in the snow. His grand-mother took over guardianship when Daren was three and a half, and soon after he became eligible for Head Start. But since the program runs only four half-days and the grandmother works full-time at minimum wage, she suffers from a critical child care problem in the afternoons. Both teachers appear to have a very positive relationship with the grandmother and feel that they have all worked collaboratively to help Daren, who receives pe-diatric follow-ups, speech therapy several times a week, is now toilet trained, and is starting to communicate verbally and participate in the classroom activities, although from the fringes of the room. Because the classroom is relaxed and flexible, a demanding and disturbed child can be accommodated. Teacher Jackie has resisted having him transferred to a special-education preschool classroom in another building, for she believes he has made remarkable progress. With the grandmother's approval, she will keep him another year in her classroom.

> During choice time the speech teacher comes into the classroom and plays a lotto game on the rug with Maria, Farhad, Ishmael, and Hy-Jung. When it is Maria's turn, she stares intently at the cards but doesn't answer. Farhad an-swers for her and the game continues in this fashion. Maria sits involved but doesn't talk in the group. Later, when the children shift activities, she goes to the lotto box and takes out the cards and begins to talk to herself, naming the different cards and objects. Teacher Jackie tells me that they have noticed that Maria wants to participate but talks only after the children have gone. Teacher Mae corroborates Maria's progress, saying "When I made a home visit she did everything—she counted and drew and sorted blocks and re-cited a 'Curious George' story from memory." Maria also uses the toy tele-phone in the room in novel ways. She holds long conversations in Spanish and English on the telephone, gesturing fearfully and shouting, "No, no" and "Leave me alone." The teachers both remark that she seems to be talking far less on the telephone and participating far more in classroom activities than she did in previous months.

Maria too has a troubled history, as revealed in her telephone talk. Her mother was physically abused by her father and escaped with her three children to a safe house in Michigan. The family is on welfare and has moved three times in the past year, trying to find an affordable apartment. Their telephone has been cut off, and they are unable to pay their rent. The social services coordinator is trying to assist the family, now on the brink of homelessness. Maria, however, has blossomed this year in her pre-school. She is an active little girl who is constantly busy in the room and is given both time and space by the staff to become involved at her own pace. Apparently their patience has borne fruit, for Maria has slowly changed from a passive, withdrawn, and fearful child to one who is developing confidence and tentative participation in her classroom world. In short, this program represents Head Start at its best, where early health screening, speech therapy interventions, and parent education all *work* in collaboration with sensitive teachers.

These diverse Head Start classrooms in Michigan illustrate, with one notable exception, the difficulties that beset a much-needed early intervention program. Head Start, consistently underfunded, has been plagued by high rates of staff turnover and uneven staff quality. Nationally, 47 percent of Head Start teachers earn less than $10,000 per year, and the national average for all Head Start teachers was $12,074 in 1989. Salaries for support staff, including parents working as aides, are minimal, and Head Start training funds have not matched overall expansion.[25] The Silver Ribbon Panel report released by the National Head Start Association in May 1990 recommended that by 1994 all eligible three- to five-year-olds be served, and that, by the year 2000, children under age three be served and full-day programs be developed.[26] Yet in 1990, Head Start served only 27 percent of income-eligible children, with four-year-olds constituting the major constituency.[27] The reauthorization of funds for Head Start by the 1990 Congress called for more than seven million dollars by 1994 to serve all eligible three- and four-year-olds and up to 30 percent of eligible five-year-olds.[28] But it should be noted that most Head Start Programs for four-year-olds are part-day, running only four mornings or four afternoons a week, and that programs for three-year-olds are usually "home based," which means the child and mother (who is required to be at home) receive one weekly visit from a teacher and one classroom session per week. How mothers on AFDC are expected to find work during Head Start hours remains a mystery, as does the care of their young children under three until the year 2000. But even if this goal is achieved, improvements of part-day child care services will actually be minimal for young children; for expansion of high-quality programs requires commensurate training as well as radical shifts in teacher salaries, both of which are totally inadequate at present.

Furthermore, we must continue to question the grounds on which Head Start was founded, despite its well-intentioned holistic perspective. Deficit assumptions about the "culture of poverty" and poor children's intellect still predominate, and instrumentality rather than entitlement has prevailed in terms of how poor children's experiences in public care are mediated. The component that most needs to be addressed is also the most invisible: the persistent sensibilities, even at their most charitable, that make poor children *other* and justify an educational perspective of remediation. Neither Head Start nor other compensatory programs for at-risk children escape this contamination. In the following section, two non–Head Start preschool programs are profiled. These programs are funded by federal Chapter I funds and other state monies for Compensatory Education.[29]

Inside Public Preschool Programs for At-Risk Children

Bennington

The public preschool program in Bennington public school district is designed for low-income children diagnosed as at risk. Eligibility is dependent on a risk index screening as well as on a family interview, and there is a waiting list of children in the district. Classes are offered four mornings or four afternoons a week; each of the six classrooms serves fifteen to twenty children and is staffed by a state-certified teacher and an assistant with early childhood experience. Five of the six head teachers are white, and one is black. There are four black assistants and two white. The racially mixed classrooms include about 60 percent black children, 25 percent white children and 15 percent other ethnic minority children. I observed two of the six preschool classrooms—those of Mrs. Naly, a white teacher, and of Mrs. Berry, a black teacher.

Mrs. Naly's room is divided into several carefully made play areas—there is a beauty shop, a fire station, blockbuilding, a quiet corner, an arts and crafts center, and a popular loftspace. The walls are brightly decorated with signs, alphabet pictures, book company commercials to promote reading, and teacher-made charts of the weather, of the days of the week, and other announcements. No child-made art is immediately visible; it is confined to a small pin-up board on the side of the classroom, under a sign, "Look what we made today." Each day certain children's work is selected by the teachers for show. Necklaces hang above each area, and children are required to wear one round their neck when entering each carefully picture-labeled area. When all the necklaces are taken, no more children may visit the area at that time. During my visit I notice that many children play in the house area without necklaces and that several leave the area forgetting to place the house corner necklaces on the hook. But the loft is a different story. There are two necklaces, and the teachers constantly check to see that these are returned or passed on before a child leaves.

Jen and Danny are playing in the loft. Danny leans over and waves to John, who is looking up and waiting for a necklace to be returned. Mrs. Naly calls out, "On your knees Danny, otherwise you'll be down here." Dan sinks to his knees, but minutes later Jen stands up to choose some red shapes for her design. "Down on your knees—you know the rule," calls Mrs. Naly. Over the next few minutes I count ten more "on your knees" reprimands directed at the two children, whose heads constantly pop up above the railing in what appears to be a perfectly safe high place for the children to stand. After the children have been there for ten minutes, Mrs. Naly's timer rings. She directs the two children to come down and return their necklaces to the hooks, and directs John to go up. Danny doesn't come down when told to. Mrs. Naly speaks sternly: "Danny, you heard me; come down right now or you'll have no more free play time this week!" Meanwhile John, who is now kneeling alone, looking rather forlorn up by himself in the loft, climbs down again, replaces his necklace, and joins Danny in the blockbuilding area. The loft stands empty, and I hear Mrs. Naly telling Molly and Marissa, who have made a colorful design of tiles and are now hopping over them, "You may not jump in this area, jumping is for outside or on the mats . . . Molly and Marissa, come over here, can you match this for me?" She removes part of their design and places three red tiles in a row. "What color is this—can you match this?"

It appears that free play is neither free nor playful for the children. The list of rules that extend to every space and activity in the classroom was difficult for even an adult visitor to memorize, and some, such as kneeling in the loft, appeared patently silly, given its sturdy construction, the ample guard rail, and the foam mats below. For the children there would have been an excitement in being high and looking down on the world; instead, they were forced to crawl and hobble over the large surface on their knees. Their play was timed by a timer and abruptly terminated at ten-minute intervals, and for John, who wanted company, it was no fun to be there alone without his buddy, Danny. The opportunity for the children to engage in some decision making about sharing turns in the loft space was effectively removed by Mrs. Naly's timer, which made no allowances for individual children's needs or for the context of their play. When I asked whether the timer had been instituted because of earlier problems, Mrs. Naly responded, "No—but these type of kids need a lot of structure. They're all at risk, you know, and they just aren't very polite; we need to teach them basic social skills." This perception of the need for "structure" frequently converts classroom activities to a constant policing and surveillance of what some others might consider "normal" behavior of four-year-olds.

> The lights go off and the room becomes silent as activity stops. "It's time to line up to go to storytime." The children line up as Mrs. Naly orders, "Put your hands in some place where they don't touch your neighbor." A few children are still talking. "I can tell we are not ready to go." Danny is shoving two boys who are whispering; all three are pulled out of line (all three are black) and sent back to the classroom to sit silently. "Now what are the rules to remember? No talking, don't touch the walls, don't touch your friend, sit quietly for the story." The children silently file into Mrs. Berry's classroom and sit crosslegged on the floor. Jesse says, "Hi Chris," to a friend, and Mrs. Berry sternly calls out, "No talking." Story time lasts twenty minutes. Mrs. Naly walks around the room making sure there is no fidgeting while Mrs. Berry reads several stories. The stories are dramatic and engaging, and most of the children appear interested but are constantly reprimanded for lying down, fiddling with velcro shoe snaps, sucking thumbs, and touching neighbors. Twice Mrs. Berry stops and stares silently, this time at Debbie, who is softly saying the name "Abiyoyo" to herself and playing with her hair. Debbie is listening intently, and at the end of the story about the giant Abiyoyo, who is made to disappear, the children have a bevy of questions. Debbie has her hand up and stands up to be noticed. "Mrs. Berry, Mrs. Berry," she waves excitedly, "I want to ask something." She is told to sit down and wait. "But how come—how do you disappear—was it magic?" she says to Annie next to her. "Debbie!" reprimands Mrs. Berry and hushes the other children who are also animatedly asking about the giant, but none are to be answered. Instead, the children are silenced and are questioned by Mrs. Berry on a chronology-and-sequence review of the stories. Mrs. Naly constantly shakes her head as other children raise their hands out of turn; and in a few minutes they are told to walk in silence back to their rooms.

When children's experiences of stories are vitiated and de-storied, when their encounters with books are reduced to a boot camp, their early literacy experiences become an unpleasant drill, their bodies constantly under surveillance and their imaginative engagement eroded in the interests of regulation and control. Why, we might ask? Is a training in compliance and docility a developmentally appropriate experience for any four-year-olds, and when at-risk four-year-olds are targeted for assistance and intervention, does remediation become an early erosion of curiosity, of liveliness, of imaginative play?

fruitage of compensatory remedial framework, assumptions

In Mrs. Berry's class, the same highly structured and rigid program is continued.

> During circle time Mrs. Berry reads It Looked Like Spilt Milk. *The story reflects an image of a moving cloud which changes each time you look at it. When Mrs. Berry reaches the picture of a pig, Jeremiah (who is black) starts snorting. Very slowly Mrs. Berry lowers the book and says, "Jeremiah, just listen." When the picture of an owl is shown, Mrs. Berry stops the story and sternly says, "Jeremiah, we're listening only."*
>
> Three boys are at the painting easels during choice time, Chris, Jeremiah, and Yasser. Yasser and Chris have pocketed small wooden cars from the block area and secretly sneak them over to the easel area. Jeremiah has painted "a curvey road" with a series of arrows pointing in one direction and a stop sign in red. Chris and Yasser are trying to drive their cars on the road made by Jeremiah without touching the wet paint, saying, "we going to Chicago—vroom." Mrs. Berry strides over and snatches the cars from the boys, saying, "We do not drive cars over the easel, this is for painting only—you boys never pay attention; go over to the table and sit with your arms folded." Chris and Yasser run away and collide with each other, and Chris shouts "You dummy, you asshole" at Yasser as Mrs. Berry physically separates them and places them at opposite sides of the table, telling them they will miss outside time today. She tells me, "These two boys are real problems. Chris has no father and his mother is always running around, and Yasser doesn't understand anything you tell him."

Jeremiah, Chris, and Yasser are Mrs. Berry's "problem" children; she pointed them out to me the first day I visited the class. Jeremiah's curiosity seems constantly to irritate her and she keeps reprimanding him for his disruptions. Chris, who is the white child of a single teenage mother, is seen as the repository of his mother's "immoral" ways, and Yasser, an Arab child, is assumed to be cognitively deficient because of his language differences. The inventive play of the children that preceded the incident was not even seen; all that was focused on was the boundary violation and the breaking of a rule. The fact that the three boys had cooperatively played together, integrating their play and using Jeremiah's road representation (which, interestingly, resembled a primitive map) as a route to Chicago for their cars, was ignored. While Mrs. Berry seems equally irritated by these three ethnically different boys, and reprimands them consistently, Mrs. Naly seems to target three black boys exclusively in her classroom. In both classrooms the children who are targeted are little boys, who in some way fail to comply with the management agendas of the teachers. Whether by their liveliness, their playfulness, or their curiosity, these boys are at risk for scapegoating and labeling, and little positive attribution comes their way. The following incident with Dan, Ryan, and Jomo, who are Mrs. Naly's black "troublemakers," illustrates how playfulness is recast as deviance:

> Jomo goes over to the piano and sounds a note. Mrs. Naly rushes over. "Can you tell me what that says?" she says, roughly pulling Jomo so that he turns and faces a hand-lettered sign which has a frowning face. "No playing," he says, squirming under her grasp. "Right," she responds, and walks back to the art table. Danny and Ryan, who are playing on the floor, tickle Jomo, and he falls on top of them laughing. The three boys roll on the floor giggling and tickling each other, and Ryan's foot catches a shelf with stacking blocks. The blocks fall on top of the boys, and more giggling ensues as Ryan says, "Quit it man—I'm building," and starts to build a structure on the floor. As the other two follow, Mrs. Naly approaches from the other side of the room. "You three are misbehaving again—you're just going to have to learn to settle down, and until you do you'll be in trouble from me—no outside time today!" For the third day that week the three "troublemakers" are kept inside while the other children go out. Mrs. Naly tells me that none of those three is ready for kindergarten: "They're real problem kids and their families are a mess." I later find out that all three are from single-parent families and that Ryan's family spent two months homeless in the back of a truck before finding temporary shelter.

In this program the children designated as at risk were children who indeed were put at risk in a rigid and unfriendly school where the teachers were unforgiving of any childlike transgressions. The classroom was not a child-friendly landscape, nor were any comprehensive services offered as in Head Start. The parents of these children were seen as problems, and the children were perceived as the repositories and perpetrators of their family's suspect life styles. One of the other teachers in the preschool program, whose classroom I did not observe, said of the free lunch program, "Some of these mothers only send their kids here so they don't have to feed them." Such were these children's experiences—an early education without compassion, in which remediation erased the possibilities for play and provided for many of the children not enrichment but an early initiation into a rigid and discriminatory schooling experience.

Belton

In the community of Belton, the preschool at-risk program is funded by Chapter I and state education grants for low-income children. Many of the children come from destitute families who have experienced frequent episodes of homelessness. The four classrooms of eighty students, serve a mixed population of black (50 percent) and Hispanic (30 percent) four-year-old children, and a smaller number of white children (20 percent); all receive breakfast, snack, and lunch but no other comprehensive services. Many of the children in this program appear hungry and arrive at school unwashed.

> As I enter the room, Teacher Peggy (who is white) tells me, "These kids are real problems—I don't know if I can work here much longer." The children receive breakfast, snack, and lunch at the program, which runs four mornings a week. I notice that several of the children have insatiable appetites and constantly ask for seconds and thirds. Snack is served at mid-morning, and Teacher Dee (the black teacher aide), with two child helpers, prepares crackers with peanut butter. The remaining sixteen four-year-olds are required to sit in silence, with their arms folded, as snack is passed around. Teacher Peggy twice reprimands Greg for comments that the snack "looks real yummy." As Greg has talked out of turn, he is passed over and has to wait for his snack until the children at the table behind him receive theirs. Greg begins to protest, "Gimme mine—no fair—gimme," and he grabs at the tray. Teacher Peggy grabs Greg and wipes his runny nose with a look of distaste and takes him to the time-out chair. At this point Greg is sobbing and yelling "no fair" and is forced to sit on the chair for fifteen minutes as he hungrily looks at the others eating. Teacher Peggy comes over to tell me this is part of her classroom management plan with Greg, as "food is what he really cares about."

In this incident Greg is stripped of his child dignity and reduced to the mechanistic behavior modification schedules reminiscent of Watson's notorious experiments with Albert and the white rat. This becomes even more problematic when we realize that Greg has very little choice; he either complies or goes hungry. This becomes a particularly disturbing in-

cident when we realize its impact in the life of a hungry child. Meted out
to any child, such practice is clearly unethical. But snack is of major importance when you have no food at home, as in Greg's case; he is living in a
welfare motel with his mother and two sisters since the family has been
homeless for over a month.

Although disciplining by means of food deprivation is unethical, and in
violation of early education guidelines, it happens. It happens because children like Greg are condemned before they enter their classrooms. Teachers like Peggy and many others in the educational profession share the
general public's social perceptions of the poor. The fact that one teaches in
a preschool program for poor children is no guarantee that one is free of
prejudice toward the poor or, for that matter, free of racism. Later that day,
Teacher Peggy tells Greg's mother, who is black, "You people better do
something about your kids." She also tells me that her aide Teacher Dee,
whom I have observed hugging the children frequently, "is too soft on these
kids."

> *Casey came in crying today, and the bus driver told Teacher Dee as she met
> the bus that Casey's father literally threw him screaming onto the bus this
> morning and that a neighbor had told her his mother had been beaten last
> night by Casey's father. Casey has bruises over his back, which Teacher Dee
> shows to Teacher Peggy, while holding Casey. Teacher Peggy sighs and says,
> "These migrant workers really shouldn't have children," and tells Teacher
> Dee to go to the office and have the director call protective services. She
> directs the children into a circle and begins with a song and finger-play.
> Kelly lies down on the floor and sucks her thumb. "Kelly, sit on your bot-
> tom," says Teacher Peggy sternly, and Kelly obediently sits up. A few minutes
> later as the choices for the day are being reviewed: "blocks, housekeeping or
> pasting at the art table." Kelly goes to the library corner and quietly lies
> down with a book in her hands. "Kelly, get over here right now," shouts
> Teacher Peggy; "the book corner is closed today and circle time is not over."
> Kelly walks back sucking her thumb and sits in the circle, playing with her
> velcro sneaker. The velcro tie comes off in her hand and she begins to cry.
> "Kelly, you'll have to go and sit outside the door until you can quiet down,"
> orders Teacher Peggy. Kelly sits crying outside the door, still holding the bro-
> ken velcro snapper in her hand.

The visits made to this public preschool classroom revealed a continuing pattern of harsh and punitive practice by the head teacher, Peggy,
whose contempt for the children and their families was evident on every

disturbing occasion. The abused child Casey, was not treated with any compassion or concern but rather confirmed Teacher Peggy's stereotypes of poor Latino children, some of whom were from migrant families in the area. Teacher Dee somewhat ameliorated the harsh classroom world by treating the children with gentleness, but she too was intimidated by her supervisor. Kelly, a recently homeless child, was often dirty and smelly when she came to class and increasingly became the target of Teacher Peggy's wrath. There was little that Kelly could do right in the classroom; appearing constantly sleepy and near to tears, she found it difficult to respond to the rigid classroom routines, particularly the large group circle time, when she was frequently reprimanded for lying down, not participating, or playing with objects in the wrong space at the wrong time. She kept gravitating toward the quiet reading corner, probably for a cozy cushion to sleep on. She was living in a crowded shelter with her mother and two younger brothers, the family having been evicted from their apartment because of unpaid rent. Even more troubling was the educational experience she was subjected to; it was another obstacle in her young life, which further stigmatized her as a child with nowhere to turn. Like her classmate Greg, who had been punished for his enthusiasm over food, Kelly was classified as an at-risk child and trapped in a harsh landscape of failure.

Poor Children's Pedagogy

In the Head Start and public preschool programs just discussed, we have seen that for many children their early education becomes another stressful experience in a severely stressed young life. Yet it need not be so. We saw how one program, sensitive and nurturant, promoted rather than impeded young children's development.

In our historical two-tiered system of child care, the children of the poor were destined to custodial care, and those of the privileged to educational enrichment. In contemporary practice a two-tiered system means that poor children go to Head Start and other at-risk public preschools (if they gain access), and middle- and upper-income children attend fee-based child care centers where parents choose the kind and quality of program they wish their children to enroll in. Not only does this two-tiered system create economic and racial segregation, but it also ensures that children, in their earliest developing years, are placed in stratified educational landscapes. Cost-benefit accountability for poor children's early education is demanded, whereas fee-based centers do not have to prove their right to provide a place for children to play and to learn. In the absence of a national child care system, public early education becomes a gift bestowed by the haves upon the have-nots. It is not surprising that the two-tiered system is fostering a separate and unequal education—a pedagogy for the poor.

The fact that a program may be harsh and discriminatory does not necessarily prevent a child from showing cognitive gains as measured by standardized, norm-referenced tests. A rigid classroom structure can train children in naming and classifying and matching tasks, which standardized tests will measure. Whether those tests should be seen as a pedagogically sensible and accurate indicator of children's competence is another question. Even more fundamental is the question whether a classroom that demonstrates a gain in IQ points is a successful classroom. Might it not be a damaging child landscape in which the child feels scapegoated rather than nurtured and encouraged?

When the experts and the policy makers cite the results of the Perry High Scope Project, the Cornell Consortium data, and the Head Start evaluations, early intervention is described as a cost-effective method for combating the effects of early poverty.[30] But what have not been confronted are the effects of a far-reaching set of negative sensibilities that contaminate the way children in poverty are seen and that shape their classroom experiences in multiple ways. The concealed, unspoken narrative of classroom worlds also must be addressed as part of the necessary advocacy for early intervention.

While the Developmentally Appropriate Practice Guidelines of The National Association for the Education of Young Children and the Anti-Bias Curriculum are important and progressive steps forward,[31] it is only by looking at the actual lifeworlds of poor children in classrooms, that the current distance between a democratic discourse and pervasive practice is seen. When we consider the critical lack of early educational services for children, we see a minimal alleviation of the present crisis, despite the fanfare of reform in the 1990 child care legislation. The Child Care and Development Block grant[32] and the amendments to Title IV-A of the Social Security Act ("At-Risk" Child Care), authorizing new federal funds to assist families with child care costs and channeling funds to the states to improve the quality and supply of child care services, represented a severely diluted version of the original ABC Child Care Bill. As already discussed, Head Start served only 27 percent of income-eligible children in 1990; despite the much-needed reauthorization of funds by Congress, vast numbers of children will continue to be denied access because they are too young or need full-day care. Of the thirty-five states that now fund diverse preschool programs for children, few offer Head Start's comprehensive approach. A stated educational commitment to early intervention combining minimal services with minimal resources is destined to provide minimal quality. The highly regarded Perry Preschool Program was estimated to cost $5,000 per child per year in 1981 and, given inflation, $9,600 in 1990—a far cry from the $3,640 per-child program cost that Congress estimated for 1991. Sharon Kagan rightly complains "America *over*expects robust results from programs it consistently *under*funds."[33]

My critique of some of the assumptions and practices of Head Start should *not* be misconstrued as an argument against providing early education and intervention services for poor children. I support the comprehensive ecological perspective of Head Start; but at the same time, an early childhood advocacy that promotes equity must involve access for all young children to a non-segregated, high-quality, generously subsidized national child care system which is in the best interests of all children.

A pedagogy of the poor ensures that poor children have no entitlement to early education; rather, they must be classified for eligibility. They experience their *other* status in the kind of programs they have access to, and their lives become commodities to be priced in terms of worthwhile investments. For, after all, we are serving these children at taxpayer expense. We educate them to contain them so they do not endanger our privileges. We compensate them for what their families have failed to give them, not for what we have taken away from them. We remediate their behavior because, when we create poverty, it becomes necessary to manage it, and in cost-effective ways. Hence young lives are contingent lives, contingent on our munificence—or our meanness. And snotty noses and dirty faces and hungry eyes continue to represent their problem, not ours.

The Classroom Worlds of At-Risk
Children: Five Portraits

Tyrone

TYRONE IS A FIVE-YEAR-OLD BLACK CHILD [1] who attends a developmental kindergarten. For the previous year he attended a Head Start
Preschool classroom housed in the same building. Tyrone was placed
in the "Young Fives" program as a result of his performance on the Gesell
Developmental Screening Test and a language interview. Mrs. Wright, his
teacher, explains that "these children are just too youthful, they are just still
too impulsive to be in the regular kindergarten program . . . Young Fives is
designed for children who are chronologically 4.9 to 5.9 years by September but who are functioning developmentally on the 4.0 to 4.9 range . . .
The Gesell measures the developmental age of a child. It allowed us to
determine Tyrone's readiness and make decisions about his placement."

Tyrone lives in a housing project in a school district of ethnic and socioeconomic diversity. I notice that the developmental kindergarten draws
two-thirds of its eighteen students from low-income families. With one exception, all the Head Start children appeared to graduate into the "Young
Fives" developmental kindergarten. Mrs. Wright tells me, "We find that
kids like Tyrone do better with the extra year; they're just not ready for the
regular classroom." In the regular kindergarten across the hall I glimpsed
the children seated two to a table, in rows one behind the other. The
teacher was standing in front of the room, saying, "Turn your workbooks to
page 6." Mrs. Wright's classroom, by contrast, was divided into activity
areas—book corner, arts and crafts, housekeeping, blocks, nature corner—
and a daily schedule which included both small group and large group activities.

Tyrone was identified by Mrs. Wright as "a problem child—I think
we'll probably find that he's ADD [attention deficit disorder] as he moves
into first grade." Tyrone's problem, from his teacher's perspective, was that
he came from the housing projects, where "these kids just don't live a normal family life—there's drug dealing and constant crisis and their mothers

are all on welfare." Yet she attributes to Tyrone's mother a strong interest
and concern in his school progress: "She does care—I see that she's real
concerned about him, but these people lead such chaotic lives and none of
these women are married, so the boys have no role models."

Tyrone occupies an ambiguous place in the classroom. On the one
hand, he is under constant surveillance by his teacher, who feels it necessary to socialize him effectively for entry into kindergarten. On the other
hand, Tyrone is a large, active child who constantly disturbs the order of
the room; when he tries to participate appropriately, his efforts often mis-
fire. The following series of observations give a flavor of his day:

*During the art project, the boys and girls are seated at separate tables as is
customary during Mrs. Wright's planned activities. Tyrone exclaims excitedly, "Look what I made" (referring to a trace-the-dots-to-make-a-bunny activity), "look at my vampire," and he holds it up for all to see. Mrs. Wright,
who overhears from the other side of the room, calls out, "Tyrone, I want
some nice bunnies, no vampires—Do you hear me?" After Tyrone completes
his picture, now corrected, he takes it to Mrs. Wright for approval, saying,
"See, the vampire turned back into a bunny." Mrs. Wright takes the picture,
commenting only on the fact that "You wrote your name backwards," and
she returns it to him for correction of his name.*

*Later, during snack, Tyrone keeps tipping on his chair and twice falls
over, laughing. Mrs. Wright becomes increasingly annoyed; she glares at him
and shakes her head, frowning. Tyrone turns the chair around and sits
astride, with the back of the chair facing the table. Mrs. Wright goes over,
roughly pulls him up, and turns his chair around the right way, saying,
"There, now sit!" Two minutes later, Tyrone tips his chair again and falls
over. He begins to laugh but goes silent as Mrs. Wright shouts, "Tyrone!" As
the children finish snack, they go outside for recess. Tyrone is punished by
Mrs. Wright, who takes ten minutes off his recess time.*

*Today the children have a large group activity focusing on math readi-
ness. The teacher has several frames with numbers of different-colored dots.
The children are asked to count the number of dots of the same color and
write the correct number in the frame. Several hands go up, including Tyrone's. "Me, me" he calls, standing up and waving his hand. "Sit down,
Tyrone, and wait your turn," says Mrs. Wright. She continues, "Who can tell
me how many there are here . . . very good Marcy" as Marcy correctly identifies six. Tyrone by now has moved out of the circle, and Mrs. Wright says,
"Tyrone, back in the circle." "But I want a turn." "Well, put your hand up*

*and wait your turn." Tyrone sits down and puts his hand up, but he is not
called on. Five other children are, and he is still waiting, now lying across
the rug. He notices a little girl having difficulty with number five, and he sits
bolt upright shouting, "I know, I got it, pick me." "Tyrone, be quiet or miss
your turn," says Mrs. Wright angrily. Tyrone is now pulling his sweatshirt
over his head, muttering, "No fair, no fair," as the activity is almost over. The
bell rings, and some children start moving to the edge of the circle. "That is
not what I asked you to do," says Mrs. Wright. "I am going to wait until
everybody sits down, and then you may move on." "But I didn't get no turn,"
shouts Tyrone. "All right Tyrone, you come up here with me, and the rest of
you go to your tables and get ready for gym."*

Tyrone is a <u>marginal</u> child in the classroom, and his sense of not belonging is increased by the time he spends with a special education teacher,
who pulls him out of the classroom for remedial activities each day. On
several occasions I observed Tyrone staring at the door and becoming very
fidgety as if anticipating that he would be required to leave for a period of
time. On one occasion I overheard him talking to himself saying, "That lady
is here for me." His sense of not belonging seems to be emphasized in his
experience with his classmates:

*Today the children play "duck, duck, goose" in gym. Several clamor to be the
leader of the game, including Tyrone, who is shouting, "Pick me, pick me."
He is not chosen and shouts, "I never get no chance." The child in the center
goes around and taps various children on the head, but not Tyrone. After six
rounds, Tyrone stands up and shouts, "Pick me, pick me," but the other children ignore him and choose the gym teacher. When the gym teacher goes
around the second time, he taps Tyrone, who is calling out, "Hey, you
missed me."*

*Three children are in the block area, building. Tyrone hovers at the
edge of the area, watching. "You can't play with us," says Jim. "Yeah, Tyrone,
we already made our stuff," continues Ben, and Shawn adds, "Yeah, you
can't be our friend." Mrs. Wright overhears the children. She calls Tyrone
over and redirects him to the book corner, but does not react to the children's
comments. A few minutes later Tyrone is back in the block area and kicks the
road the three boys have made. He is reprimanded by Mrs. Wright and told
to ask, "May I play too?" He runs over to housekeeping and disrupts several
dressup activities. Mrs. Wright calls out, "Tyrone, in five minutes Mrs. Green
[the special education teacher] is coming for you," rolling her eyes at the
prestudent teacher and muttering, "I've had it with him this week."*

It appears that the music teacher also views Tyrone as a problem and constantly monitors his behavior, anticipating disruption. As the children enter the music room, they are told to go sit on the floor in a circle. One of the children shoves Tyrone, saying, "You can't sit here," and covering the spot to keep a place for his friend. Tyrone shoves him back, stomps over to the desk outside of the circle, and sits down. The music teacher, Ms. Clay, tells Tyrone to sit on the floor. He sits on the edge of the circle and lies down, kicking other children with his feet. Ms. Clay walks over, roughly pulls him up, and seats him "the right way," saying, "This is your last chance, now look and follow what I say." Noticing that Tyrone has a runny nose, she says in an irritated tone,

> "Go over and get a kleenex and wipe your nose," and sighs to herself. Several other children have colds and runny noses, but she does not react to them. As the children learn "The old lady who swallowed a fly," Tyrone asks "Why don't she spit it out?" Ms. Clay reprimands him: "It's not question time now, be quiet and follow."

The classroom is a lonely place for lively little Tyrone. He is only five, and yet his childlike transgressions are treated with harshness. Viewed negatively by his teachers and his classmates, he has few friends in the classroom. Although his speech is sometimes difficult to understand, he is certainly a verbal child with no noticeable speech impairment. Yet he is receiving speech therapy, and his teacher says he has "speech problems." Frequently his questions are dismissed or he is reprimanded because of inappropriate timing on his part. He becomes aggressive when frustrated; an ongoing frustration for him appears to be his sense of exclusion, of never being chosen. To his credit, he is very persistent and complains openly about not being picked. While part of his need to be chosen may be attributed to a kindergartner's developmental egocentrism, I considered, as an adult observer, that his perception was also accurate, founded in a concrete experience of marginality in the classroom. The teacher's negative treatment appeared contagious and was passed on to the children. While exclusion behavior may be seen as a fairly typical dynamic in a classroom of five-year-olds, the teacher made little attempt to encourage inclusion and social cooperation among the other children.

If we consider Tyrone's experience of exclusion at five years, the labels already attached to him—"too youthful," "speech impaired," "ADD"—and the fact that he is both poor and black, we see that his place in the world of school is hardly promising. The use of the Gesell Screening is a highly questionable practice currently under severe criticism for its "high stakes testing." While its developers claim that it provides reliable identification for children at high risk for school failure, thereby determining school readiness, promotion, and retention, few convincing data support these conclusions.[2] Furthermore, the bias involved in the language proficiency interview which was also used to screen Tyrone and his classmates raises the specter of cultural and racial bias when children who speak nonstandard English are viewed as language-impaired. The issue of readiness, interlaced with the unquestioned assumption that the child must "fit" the classroom rather than the classroom should be made to "fit" the child, makes for a rigid, formalized curriculum and turns the developmental kindergarten into a training ground for compliance. More significantly, the developmental kindergarten seems to have become a receiving room for poor children whose economic disadvantage marks them as cognitively and socially deficient; they are being acculturated into monocultural passive learning norms in preparation for formal schooling. What will happen to Tyrone as he moves through an increasingly marginalized schooling? At five years old, on the brink of his public school career, his potential has already been thrown into question; his initiative and desire to participate have been restricted. He is scarred before he has a chance to be otherwise.

Carrie

Carrie is six, the daughter of a white mother and a black father. She, too, is a child of poverty—the oldest of three, whose mother has been hospitalized twice for a serious illness. Carrie lives with her mother and two siblings in a subsidized rental apartment. Her mother has lost her part-time clerical job at a local company due to chronic illness, and the family is struggling to survive on welfare. Carrie's kindergarten teacher, Ms. Juno, describes the family as being "in constant crisis" and expresses her concern about Carrie's two younger siblings, who are waiting to be accepted into Head Start, though all available slots are filled. Carrie, according to Ms. Juno, "has problems, but what child wouldn't after what she's gone through." Ms. Juno describes her classroom as a "play-based kindergarten," which she runs as a balance between "my planning and their playing." Carrie appears angry and hostile toward other children in the classroom and does not participate readily in large group activities.

> The children sit on the rug and listen to the story "The Very Hungry Caterpillar." All are in the circle except Carrie, who sits at the arts and crafts table cutting paper. "Ms. Juno, Carrie's not in the circle," says one little girl. "I

know," replies Ms. Juno; "she'll come when she's ready." When the story is over, Ms. Juno announces she has a surprise. She goes into the closet and emerges with a large tank filled with sand. "Guess what I have in here." "A caterpillar," says Travis. "Right," replies Ms. Juno, "all sorts of worms and caterpillars." In twos the children take turns at the tank and fish out worms and caterpillars. Carrie, after watching from her vantage point at the table, slowly edges closer until she is in the circle. Ms. Juno calls her up together with Annie, a child who sometimes plays with Carrie. After the hands-on caterpillar activity, the children are given a choice of painting, drawing, or writing a story about caterpillars. Carrie chooses painting and goes straight to the easel; with deep concentration she spends almost fifteen minutes painting a picture of a "caterpillar family" and then counting all their legs.

After a field trip to a park with a boardwalk over marshy land, the children are once again drawing and writing about what they saw. Carrie takes a black crayon and scribbles over her page while remarking to her neighbors, "I don't like yours," "That's yukky," and grabbing markers from the center. She says to Jeremy, who is drawing a rainbow, "That's not how you do it," and scribbles over his picture. He protests and tries to grab her marker, but she throws it on the floor. Ms. Juno comes over and tells Carrie, "I think you need to draw at this table for a while," taking her over to an adjacent table. As she helps Jeremy find markers and paper to draw another rainbow, she tells him, "I know you're mad at Carrie for messing your picture—it was a real nice rainbow. When she's feeling calmer, we'll all talk about it." During recess Ms. Juno asks both children to come and sit with her by the fence, and she asks each child to talk about what happened and how they feel.

During small group time, when Carrie is sitting next to Pat, she takes his colored marker and pokes him. Pat moves away, saying, "I wish I didn't have sat next to you." Carrie tries to write on his shirt with the marker. Pat shouts, "Quit it," and calls, "Ms. Juno, Ms. Juno, Carrie's writing on my shirt." Ms. Juno comes over and moves Carrie, saying, "Carrie, you cannot write on people's shirts, that really makes Pat feel bad—now come over here with me by my table." Carrie goes to Ms. Juno and pleads with her tearfully, "Don't tell my mother, she got sick again in the hospital." "Your mother will be real pleased to hear how well you've been doing, Carrie. Yesterday you were real helpful, and today's been hard for you, but we'll work on it."

When Carrie initiates a conflict with the other children, she often frowns and clenches her teeth, and her eyes fill with tears. Ms. Juno handles her aggressive behavior toward other children by removing her from the situation and giving her some time to calm down without punishment. She then uses a conflict-resolution approach with the children, helping them to recognize each other's feelings. It is difficult for the other children in the class to recognize Carrie's, for they often become the unprovoked targets of her anger. But Ms. Juno tells them, "Carrie is worried about her mommy and sometimes she feels sad or mad because she's going through a hard time, and we all need to help her." Consequently, some children are very solicitous of Carrie and take care of her in class, while others reject or avoid her. Ms. Juno worries that other children will notice her special treatment of Carrie and feel it is unfair, although she tells them, "Anyone in this class can always ask for a special time with me if they feel sad." Over a period of three months I observe noticeable changes in Carrie. She begins to participate more willingly in large group activities and becomes excited about her growing mastery of reading. She begins to spend increasing amounts of time in the book corner. Usually Ms. Juno leaves her alone if she is quietly reading and does not want to participate in a planned activity, telling her she can choose to do it later. If other children request the same option (and two that I observed did), Ms. Juno agrees, telling them they may choose to make the activity up later. And they do. The flexibility in the room allows options that work particularly well for a stressed child like Carrie. Ms. Juno's warmth toward the little girl is a critical factor in her development, and a strong emotional bond with her teacher carries her through each day.

It is clear that a child such as Carrie does not fit easily into a classroom environment, but with a sensitive teacher, accepting of her needs, Carrie gradually becomes a nontargeted participant in the classroom. In many other classrooms Carrie might already have been classified as emotionally impaired and her label would condemn her to constant surveillance. By being granted some time and space, in which she can find her place, Carrie initiates several improvements in her behavior, such as volunteering to be the clean-up helper and the office messenger, as well as a marked decrease in her aggressive interactions with other children. At recess she begins to play with two girls with whom Ms. Juno has tried to pair her. Ms. Juno continues to give her that little bit of extra attention, saying, "If I can give her an extra hug and a little special time when she comes in every morning, I notice the pattern of her day is far more positive." Ms. Juno also views Carrie as a child with much promise. "She really tries, and I've noticed she loves stories, so I try and give her as much encouragement as I can with books." While Carrie's classroom world is a caring and positive landscape, it is also a buffer against an increasingly harsh world outside as her family encounters crisis after crisis, including eviction from the apartment and a temporary cutoff of their Medicaid insurance. When Carrie comes to school, she plays out these stresses; yet she also shows signs of a growing self-esteem. She tells me enthusiastically, "I can read real books now, and Ms. Juno said I get to read my book I made to the whole class in circle time." Carrie has found a place in this classroom—her presence, while problematic, is valued and she matters. As she nears the end of her kindergarten year, there are questions, seeded with meaning, that hover above her: Whose eyes will see Carrie next year? Will she be given the space for promise? Or will she, too, become another casualty, another child at risk?

[handwritten margin note: why not remain in Ktn another year?]

Heather

Seven-year-old Heather was easy to identify as a problem second-grader as she sat at her desk pushed out into the hallway. The children passing by told me that they were not allowed to speak to her, neither was she allowed to speak to anyone. She could not go to recess or eat lunch with the others in the cafeteria anymore. What had the child done, I wondered, to receive such harsh punishment? The teacher, Mrs. Mack, claims:

> *"This child just does not know the difference between right and wrong—she absolutely does not belong in a normal classroom with normal children." I look at Heather, now being sent to the principal's office, awkwardly slipping in her flipflops three sizes too big for her, walking down the corridor—in the middle of a snowy December—dressed in a summer blouse several sizes too small and a long flimsy skirt. What had Heather done? "I've given up on this child—she's socially dysfunctional—three times now we've caught her stealing free lunch and storing it in her desk to take home!"*

Heather's crime was indeed noteworthy. The white child of a single mother, she lived with her sister and mother in a trailer park. The children appeared chronically hungry, particularly when food stamps ran out before the end of the month. Apparently Heather had been caught stealing extra free lunch on three Fridays, knowing that she and her sister would have to wait until Monday for their next free meals. Mrs. Mack has tried repeatedly to have Heather removed from her classroom, claiming "she's LD (learning disabled) and EI (emotionally impaired) and I'm tired of having these children placed in my room." Mrs. Mack is also angry with Heather's mother, who has refused to have her tested. But Heather's mother says:

"Yes, I am very upset. The teacher says she does not know her blends and she
wants to have the school psychologist test her because she does not know her
blends and because she's a problem in the classroom. Ever since I became
separated and we moved here and applied for free lunches, you know, I've
had nothing but problems with this school, and now with this teacher—she's
always thinking there is something wrong with Heather. I don't see it; I told
them I'd help Heather if they told me what to do, but they keep insisting I
sign the papers. I told them I would not sign those papers, and they said if I
don't sign the papers they would fail Heather. Now I don't know what to do."

Heather eventually is evaluated and assigned to special education,
which causes her to be pulled out of class for certain remedial activities
each day.

The children are doing math worksheets, and Heather is sitting away from
the grouped desks because "she always falls behind." About ten minutes into
the math period, a teacher walks into the room. "Heather has to go with
Mrs. King" announces Jan. "Jan, thank you, I'll tell Heather what she has to
do," responds Mrs. Mack, signaling to Heather to leave. Heather is taken out
and goes to the special education room for remedial reading. When she re-
turns, math is over, and the children begin a social studies unit about Japan.
"Sit down and pay attention so you can make up what you missed," says
Mrs. Mack. Heather stands looking lost next to her desk as the children are
busy gathering papers. She has to miss recess so as to make up her lost social
studies time, and never does get back to her math sheet that day.

Heather is permanently set up for failure in this classroom. She cannot
complete many assignments because she is pulled out of class for remedial
teaching. Although she can read, she does poorly on her phonics tests and
worksheets. She is given no reading assignments in remedial reading and is
placed in the lowest reading group in her class, a group that is given worksheet assignments rather than actual reading. When Heather lags behind
in math because she is pulled out and does not have time to finish her
assignments, her mother is told that "Heather has poor work habits." She is
also labeled by the other children, who know that she's "a special ed kid"
and shun her because "she smells and dresses weird." Mrs. Mack targets
Heather constantly, blaming her for her absence from class:

Today Heather returns from the resource room to a desk piled high with the
morning's work. Mrs. Mack tells her, "you'll have to do your work during
lunch and recess because going to the resource room isn't a special privi-

lege." I stayed in with Heather at recess and looked at her work. Three of the papers were without errors, but the teacher had only written a small "OK" at the top. By contrast, I noticed that the papers correctly completed by other children had smiley faces and "good job" written on them. Heather's other papers, which had errors, were marked with large check marks and negative comments. Mrs. Mack also sent home a note at the end of that day informing her mother that a conference should be scheduled to discuss Heather's poor work habits. Interestingly, Heather is an accurate, if slow and halting, reader with good comprehension, which she demonstrated as we read together during lunch. She feels marginalized by her teacher and her classmates and is very self-conscious about her appearance. She tells me that "Mrs. Mack always picks on me and I hate her . . . I hate this school and I don't got no friends here."

In Mrs. Mack's eyes, Heather has no positive potential. Since she is a quiet and rather obliging child, it is difficult to fathom the depth of her teacher's animosity. Heather rarely misbehaves—she moves almost furtively about the room, as if waiting to be pounced on. Her marginalization is emphasized from every angle. Not only is she a "free luncher," as Mrs. Mack once described her, but she is also denied full participation in classroom activities as well as recess and lunch in the cafeteria. In addition, she is unable to participate fully in class projects.

The children were instructed to bring four dollars for a rock and minerals project that was planned by Mrs. Mack. On the due date, Heather did not have the money, and Mrs. Mack said, "Well, I guessed you wouldn't bring in the money, so you'll have to do some other work." Heather was in tears, being the only child in the class who didn't make a rock and mineral collection; nor did she go on the field trip. On another occasion the children were instructed to buy folders for their social studies worksheets, of which there were many. Heather did not have money for a folder, so she folded her homework paper and put it in the textbook. When she handed it in, Mrs. Mack crumpled it up and threw it in the basket, saying, "I told you to place these in a folder, not to fold it up like this."

Not only does Heather receive harsh treatment and emotional abuse in this classroom, where almost 80 percent of the directed teaching focuses on drill and worksheets, but she is denied equal access to classroom activities that should be part of her public education. She is one of the poor children bussed to Blake Elementary, in a predominantly middle- and lower-middle-income school district, where several classroom teachers express negative perceptions about "those trailer park kids." One teacher who worked as a substitute in that school commented, "They really look down on the welfare kids. I saw a lot of things in that school that really bothered me; some teachers really have a hard time separating their negative perceptions of the parents from the children—they always see the children as problems."

Heather's world, circumscribed by her destitution, is increasingly narrowed in school, where she faces daily humiliation and miseducation. A pedagogy for the poor assigns her an increasingly marginalized place in the classroom. Whether sitting in the corridor, banished for stealing food, or inside the classroom, subject to constant harassment and reprimand, Heather is marked for failure. At seven years old, in second grade, this little girl is already a condemned child.

George

Why is Heather's color not mentioned?

George is a ten-year-old black child, a fifth grader, who midway through the school year is transferred from a predominantly black school district to the district of Addington, a blue-collar community with a substantial population of poor southern whites and a small number of blacks and Hispanics. George is rather small for his age, having been born prematurely to a young single mother. In the past four years, George has attended schools in five different school districts. In two of these schools he has been tested for special education but has not received services. George is placed in Ms. Donovan's classroom; she too is new to the school and the district. In the following narrative, George's school experiences are seen through the eyes of his new teacher.

> My class consisted of fifth-grade students . . . When I was told that I would be getting a new student in mid-December, the teacher's lounge reverberated with negative comments: "Now you will have a chance to compare black and white students and you'll see how terrible these black students are." "You're lucky we only have a few at this school . . . they can't read, barely even speak, you'll see . . ." All this was said to me before I even met the new student. I was appalled by my colleagues' comments. I knew racism existed in the teacher's lounge but not to this degree."

Within this racist school climate, George is assigned to Ms. Donovan's room and, after being given the standard reading equivalency test, is placed in the lowest reading group, taught by Mrs. Crim. Ms. Donovan is concerned about this placement, for Mrs. Crim has made derogatory remarks

"the reading teacher"

142

to her about students in poverty, describing them as "all the bad low-skilled kids . . . [who] come from broken homes . . . They are either hillbillies or blacks from the poor section where those run-down apartments are . . . and that means trouble." George, however, according to Ms. Donovan, is a warm and friendly child who adjusted quite easily to her classroom routines, though she notices that he lacks basic skills and struggles to keep up with some of the math assignments.

> *I discussed this with one of the teachers, who said, "It doesn't surprise me. Why not have him tested? He is probably LD [learning disabled] or Comp. Ed. [compensatory education]. Most blacks in this district fall into one of the two categories." When I asked the school secretary why the records from George's previous school were not there, as I needed them to prepare an evaluation for the compensatory education program, the secretary responded, "Karen, consider where they're coming from . . . These people don't care. We may never get them."*

" predominantly black school district " 141)

If it were not for his classroom teacher, George would be a condemned student. His dual identity as both a poor and a black child in a school structure that is openly racist and filled with prejudicial stereotypes about children in poverty puts George at the mercy of a forbidding and accusatory adult world; fortunately he has one advocate who sees him with different eyes. Ms. Donovan also notices that George, despite his low performance levels in reading, has a gift for poetry, which she encourages:

> *As a group project, the fifth graders were designing and publishing their own book. When George first joined the class he was somewhat intimidated by the group project. But, once the other students realized that he had such a creative sense of phrasing, they asked him to write for the book. And for a class assignment on personification he produced this poem, which was selected as the book's opening page:*

> > *The willow tree became a harp*
> > *in the gentle fingers of the wind.*

> *In passing I mentioned the poem to Mrs. Crim, the reading teacher, and told George to show her his work because I felt it was very good. He returned quickly and did not say a word to me about what her reaction had been. Since she never said anything to me about his visit, I finally asked her if she was not impressed with his creativity. "Oh, it was nice," she responded. Then with her usual cynicism she asked, "Do you think George really made up*

that poem or did he copy it?" When I told her that George actually dictated
the poem to the other kids in the group, word by word as he was composing
it, she said, "I doubt it. He probably heard it somewhere before."

George is not permitted to succeed in the eyes of his reading teacher. Even when he succeeds, his successes are reduced by suspicions of cheating. As the end of the year approaches, Ms. Donovan is put under increasing pressure to retain George as he has consistently failed in reading. George has also not completed his reading assignments and is now being punished by Mrs. Crim and forced to miss recess. He says he has not done his assignments because he cannot read them—an accurate complaint since the ditto sheets that he has been given are illegible. Mrs. Crim claims that George entered school too late in the year for her to request a new workbook and adds, "What difference would it make. He can't do the work and he doesn't care." At this point Ms. Donovan makes several attempts to contact George's mother, who, it has been claimed, is completely unconcerned about her son's problems, having failed to respond to notes sent home. Ms. Donovan continues:

> *I asked George if it would be possible to reach his mother by telephone, and*
> *he said, "Yes, but she sometimes works until nine at night." I began to call in*
> *the evening as late as 10 PM but I could not reach her. I asked George if he*
> *was alone at home at night, and he said, "Yes, but it's okay, I'm used to it." I*
> *was becoming increasingly concerned. When I mentioned to another teacher*
> *that George's mother was at work until late, he responded, "How do you*
> *know she's at work? She might be out on the streets. You know what these*
> *black women are like—the more kids they have, the more money they get*
> *from ADC." I tried to explain to him that George's mother worked, and from*
> *all records it appeared he was an only child. He simply smiled and said, "I*
> *can't believe you're so naive."*

Ms. Donovan then approaches the principal and requests that retention proceedings be delayed to give her more time to observe George and to explore the possibilities of additional educational help. The principal reluctantly agrees, cautioning Ms. Donovan that George might not be there much longer, "considering how many times *these* people move around."

After Ms. Donovan's limited but successful advocacy on behalf of George, which includes a plan worked out with his mother, who has managed to change her work schedule to help George with his assignments at home, George is conditionally promoted to sixth grade. But Ms. Donovan is transferred to another school district, and one year of promise in George's school life abruptly comes to a close. Where is George now? Who cares for him and the countless others who find themselves victims of a continuing educational assault on their young lives? To be black and poor in a condemned landscape—is this to be George's fate?

Tim

Tim is another child consigned to otherness in his educational landscape. His withdrawn and chronically exhausted appearance conjures up images of Hugo's little Cosette, "the poor lark [who] never sang." Tim never sings either, nor does he smile much. He is white, nine years old, and placeless. He has no home; nor has he found a place in his classroom. Living with his twenty-four-year-old mother and a younger sister, Tim has attended four different schools the past year as his homeless family moved from a truck to a shelter, from a shelter to a trailer, from a trailer to a welfare motel, and now to a transitional shelter. His fourth teacher this year describes him as "socially maladjusted with real learning problems." In the third-grade classroom Tim is also shunned by his classmates.

> During social studies, Mrs. Devon tells the children to select a partner and to begin working on their maps. There are twenty-six children in the class, but Tim is left without a partner, as a threesome forms amid whispering. I overhear one of the three saying, "Yuk, he's an asshole, can I be partners with you guys?" Mrs. Devon calls Tim over and says, "Well, I guess they want to work in a threesome, so you'll have to do it by yourself after you come back from reading." At that point a reading aide comes to call Tim out of class, and he goes to remedial reading. I follow him and find a certified remedial education teacher assisted by several aides, one of whom can barely read. That makes no difference, however, since no reading takes place. Tim is given worksheets to complete. Later, during lunch, I follow Tim to the lunch room. No child sits with him, and he goes to sit at the other end of a large table, hungrily eating his free lunch and looking at the wasted leftovers on other plates. When no one is looking during clean-up, he quickly takes an apple, from which a small bite has been taken, and slips it into his pocket, making a noticeable bulge. On the way back to afternoon class, Tim slips the apple into his locker without being caught.
>
> After school, Tim is particularly upset because two children called him

*names during gym and made fun of his socks, which are worn, with holes.
He says, "They think 'cos I haven't got no home that I haven't got nothing
inside of me—they won't play with me—they won't be a buddy when we go
on trips either and no kids will be my friends . . . Also they all think I'm so
dumb and I hate this school, and Mrs. Devon keeps saying she got no time
when I ask her things."*

*A week later, on another visit to the classroom, Tim's name is up on the
board; he is being punished and cannot go to recess because he did not complete or return his homework assignments. Mrs. Devon describes Tim as
"lacking motivation—he's always staring out the window, and he has not
completed any of his assignments this week." Tim says, "She hates everything I do—she made red checks on all my worksheets and anyhow I can't
do homework and stuff in the shelter—there's always noise and stuff going
on." I notice that Tim seems to fall asleep several times in the afternoon and
is jerked back to attention by Mrs. Devon's voice loudly calling his name.*

Tim is a nuisance in Mrs. Devon's room. He entered late in the first
semester, and she has made no effort to assist him in making yet another
transition. Although he qualifies for Chapter I funds for compensatory education, she believes he should be in special education as "he's definitely
learning disabled." Tim's basic skills are understandably lacking since he
has attended four schools in different school districts with different curricula; it is hardly surprising that he should need some extra tutoring. When
he receives a student tutor, through a local university tutoring program, he
shows marked progress. Because he is chronically tired and hungry, he is
often inattentive at school. He describes the best part of his tutoring lesson
as "snack," which his tutor, Julie, brings with her each week. Depriving Tim
of recess also takes away the few opportunities for exercise on a play-
ground. After school he is cooped up in a shelter with no safe outside space
to play.

Mrs. Devon's attitude towards Tim improves after Julie begins tutoring
him and taking an active interest in his educational progress. Mrs. Devon
tells Julie, "I'm very pleased you're working with Tim; I just don't have time
for these kids on top of my teaching—they transfer in and out and we're
meant to educate them too—it's just too much of a burden, and their mothers move them from place to place—they don't have proper records and
Tim's the third one of them I've had in the past two years."

Tim, as "one of them," has little entitlement to an education, despite
the passing of the McKinney Homelessness Act in 1987.[3] Homeless chil-

dren are lost in the educational bureaucracy. Records do not follow them, school lunches often take a week or two to activate, and their pressing needs and daily stresses of destitution are compounded by homelessness. Tim is also homeless in school. He exists on the margins of a social world in which his peers discard him and he has no place other than as a burden in his classroom. It is clear that Tim is an intelligent child. With a little extra attention on the part of a caring tutor, he was capable of making significant progress. Yet his teacher was unwilling to make any effort for Tim; she wanted him out. His selfhood was of no value to her, for a destitute child is a nuisance child, a disrupter of ordered routines. Tim's diminishing entitlement to an education brands him with the visible humiliations of his placelessness and augments the construction of his at-risk status.

Contingent Children

The stories of these five children chronicle the making as well as the unmaking of early educational failure. In their fragile lives, the world of a classroom becomes a landscape of promise or a landscape of condemnation. The well-stocked armory of at-risk labels, which serve as proliferating weapons of exclusion, are part of the language of otherness. To unpack the language of otherness is also to peel away the complicit educational layers that conceal the appalling consequences of a pedagogy for the poor. Neither the "scientific" neutrality of an educational discourse that consignes poor children to the hem of classroom life, nor the blighted gaze that keeps them clinging to the edges, is much different from the ways of seeing that have long characterized our perceptions of the undeserving poor. The children of the poor, like their parents, and specifically their mothers, are constructed and located in the poverty-as-a-private-affair myth, where public intervention is premised on deficiencies, not rights. As Grubb and Lazerson argue, "we so desperately distrust and dislike lower-class adults that we are willing to let their children suffer as well."[4]

Teachers do not live above their culture; they too are participants in the pervasive poverty discourse that conceals economic and educational inequalities, state-induced destitution. At-risk children are constructed in classrooms that place them at risk for consignment to the other America. Once consigned, they find few exits to the promised land. Having consigned them to the unnamed landscape, we find that poverty, like the plague, spreads across many landscapes, theirs and ours. As Tarrou tells us in Camus's *The Plague*, "It is in the thick of a calamity that one gets hardened to the truth—in other words, to silence."[5] Confronting the silence, naming the classroom world with different forms of talk, shifting our ways of seeing, opening up spaces for possibility can shift the tenuous ground on which young children of poverty stand. It is the question of existential value that confronts the silence.

Poor Children's Pedagogy: The Construction of At-Risk Students

This oversimplified account of educational trends over the last two decades highlights two important lapses in our thinking about equality and excellence. The first lapse is that in our search for the solution to the problems of educational inequality, our focus was almost exclusively on the characteristics of the children themselves. We looked for sources of educational failure in their homes, their neighborhoods, their language, their cultures, even in their genes. In all our searching we almost entirely overlooked the possibility that what happens *within* schools might contribute to unequal educational opportunities and outcomes . . . The second lapse is in our current view of educational excellence. In our quest for higher standards and superior academic performance we seem to have forgotten that schools cannot be excellent as long as there are groups of children who are not well served by them."

> Jeannie Oakes
> *Keeping Track*[1]

NO CHILDREN ARE WELL SERVED by a pedagogy for the poor. What happens *inside* schools matters and what happens *inside* classrooms matters—early tracking, sorting and classifying, scapegoating, marginalization are not isolated experiences particular to the classroom worlds portrayed in these chapters. And these are not the worst of worlds for young children. Neither physical nor sexual abuse is present, and the physical school environments are relatively safe. Rather, these classroom worlds are telling landscapes that reveal shared stories of exclusion, humiliation, and neglect—narratives of experience that speak to broader educational issues. National studies have chronicled the failure to educate "disadvantaged youth," who are consistently described as belonging to the socially, racially, and economically disadvantaged groups in our society. As Kenneth Clark puts it,

1988

their expendability begins in the early stages of their education where they
are subjected to inferior schools and low standards of learning. Early in their
lives they are programmed to be victims of the prophecy that they cannot
benefit from the standards and quality which are provided for children from
more privileged groups. This pattern of inferior education, of low standards
and expectations, continues through secondary schools and culminates in
failures, dropouts, and pushouts.[2]

A 1990 federal study of effective academic instruction for the children
of poverty points to poor children's schooling as an increasingly urgent concern. The authors, Michael Knapp and Brenda Turnbull, claim that despite
extra resources from the Chapter I Compensatory Program, and despite
educational reforms, "the children of poverty experience failure disproportionately in their early school years."[3] Such children, it is inferred, will
travel predictable paths to the bottom track: retention in grade, transition
room placements, and enrollment in remedial or special education programs.[4] Richard Allington argues that school failure among the poor is generally connected to literacy learning difficulties. In his extensive review of
the school experiences of poor children participating in remedial and special education, he concludes that few children who need greater amounts
of high-quality instruction actually have access to it. Most remedial interventions yield predictable outcomes; the programs organized for children
of poverty are designed to provide the minimum amount of the least expen-
sive instruction allowed under federal and state guidelines.[5]

Poor children are cheap. That is not a surprising finding. Nor is Allington's cited research that remedial and special education interventions
rarely result in improved academic achievement. Poor children are disabled by remediation that places them within a disease/pathology paradigm. The conventional educational psychology literature expounded by
well-known experts such as Jere Brophy and Thomas Good is replete with
arguments that such children require a different and more controlled instructional program, in which order and compliance are to be fostered:

> Low-SES–low-achieving students need more control and structuring from
> their teachers: more active instruction and feedback, more redundancy, and
> smaller steps with higher success rates. This will mean more review, drill, and
> practice, and thus more lower-level questions.[6]

And when these children, having used up the limited public monies spent
on their behalf, reach adolescence and still continue to fail, the pathology/

genetic argument returns to haunt them, this time in the official federal education discourse, as articulated by Assistant Secretary of Education Chester Finn in 1987:

> To the degree that dropping out is caused by factors beyond the school's control, the symptom is not likely to be eradicated by school-based remedies, insofar as it is a manifestation of linked social pathologies and inherited characteristics.[7]

Whether the causes are seen to lie in the individual deficits of the child—his race, her class, his family, her culture—one theme has been consistently articulated by mainstream educators and by policymakers: the blame lies everywhere *but* inside in the landscape of the school—and certainly *not* outside in the politics of inequity. Hence to begin to question the meaning of "at-risk" is also to question the meaning of schooling for poor children; it entails reframing the at-risk label in order to ask who is at risk—the child, the teacher, or the school? And, moving beyond the school building, it entails tracing the formation of deficit images actively perpetuated in the college classrooms of teacher training institutions and disseminated through educational institutes, research publications, and training workshops sponsored by major research associations such as the American Educational Research Association. All these institutions are implicated in the framing of poor children as *other,* and in institutionalizing the legitimacy of their *otherness* status. Once named, once funded. Once funded, remediation of at-risk children's deficits becomes a lucrative trade.

Consignment to the Edges: Classrooms at Risk

In the majority of the preschool and elementary classrooms described in this book, there was a pervasive ethos of containment and regulation—drilling children to produce the correct responses, regulating their imagination, presenting them with tasks to be completed rather than learning encounters. Teachers, with the exception of three sensitive ones, saw obedience and compliance to the routinized tasks as indicating success. The classrooms were, for the most part, rigidly segregated by gender and ability groupings, and out-of-order children, often young black boys in poverty, rapidly became classroom deviants. Even when they exhibited giftedness, as did young George with his poetry, they were not seen as gifted by those who had already condemned them as impaired. In many such classrooms, children's well-being was placed at risk. The classrooms become at-risk landscapes that impair young children's self-esteem, increase the stresses already present in their vulnerable lives, and offer remediation services that impede development. When remedial literacy in the early elementary grades results in never encountering an actual children's book, how can children develop comprehension skills, and, more important, what is there left to enjoy of reading? Apparently the whole-language approach and literature-based instruction do not form part of poor children's pedagogy; their remediation experience consists largely of phonics, decoding skills, and endless worksheets. The arbitrary nature of the referral and evaluation process by which children are designated as eligible for special education services is also deserving of scrutiny, for many of the children referred by teachers were out-of-order students in rigidly managed classrooms. One concerned Head Start teacher I interviewed told of her former experience as a second grade teacher in a low-income neighborhood.

> *After the year I taught second grade at that school the teacher in third grade referred all but four of my kids for psychological testing! I loved those kids—they were great kids—but when she got through with them they all needed help!*

Children who are different—poor, many of them bright and lively and talk-ative—are constructed as impaired when they disrupt rigid classroom routines that permit neither time nor space for imagination, for transformation of the given.

Rigid classrooms are not limited to poor children; they cut across the socioeconomic spectrum and across all age and grade levels. In a study of over one thousand classrooms across the nation, John Goodlad has pointed out that students in those classes rarely were given the opportunity to make any decisions about their learning, and that almost 100 percent of elementary classrooms were teacher-dominated with respect to seating, grouping, content, materials, use of space and time, and learning activities. These same patterns were found in 90 percent of the junior highs and 80 percent of the senior highs. Goodlad also raises concerns about the dominance of "teacher talk" in classrooms, where teachers talked for about 70 percent of the class time devoted to instruction,[8] demarcating the classroom world as a directed site for passive, noninteractive learning. When we begin to analyze the dominance of passive learning and directed teaching, which places little value on children's talk or questions, we realize how damaging this management ethos becomes when applied to the teaching of at-risk children. Such children have two strikes against them: they are poor and they do not fit. They come to school fragile and enormously stressed from coping with the daily struggles of life in poverty. Because they are not easily

balance needed between tchr- and student- centricity

incorporated into the normative patterns of traditional classrooms, their presence demands recognition and action. The remediation programs devised by the mainstream compensatory educational researchers for over three decades have relegated poor children even further to the fringes.[9] The distance between their world and the world of the classroom has widened, as their prior experiences have been devalued and targeted for reshaping.

ethnographic research   *statistical studies*

When research is done *in* classrooms rather than *on* classrooms, a qualitative perspective reveals inequity *in vivo*. Ethnographic and field-based research during the 1980s has found that poor children receive a differentiated, class-based education which focuses on drill and rote learning and emphasizes mechanical skills.[10] Jean Anyon's study of classroom instruction in elementary schools in contrasting socioeconomic communities demonstrates that distinctions of social class are evident in both differentiated curriculum and process. Activities and tests for poor children were geared to lower-level thinking skills, to retention of subject matter, while activities in the affluent schools tended to foster creativity and independent thought.[11] Disturbing differences in children's own perceptions of their school identity and future are illustrated in Oakes's *Keeping Track:*

> I want to be a lawyer and debate has taught me to dig for answers and get involved. I can express myself. (High Track English)

> To understand concepts and ideas and experiment with them. Also to work independently. (High Track Science)

> Behave in class. (Low Track English)

> To be a better listener in class. (Low Track English)

> I have learned that I should do my questions for the book when he asks me to. (Low Track Science)[12]

The differences in students' self-perceptions mirror the predictions of the educational experts who, years before these tracked students ever reached high school, consigned many of them to low-level classes with minimal expectations—a grand Pygmalion conspiracy of successive self-fulfilling prophecies which, as we have seen, begins very early in a student's schooling. At four and five and six years old the Tyrones and the Heathers, the Dukes and the Gregs, and the Kellys and countless invisible others have already been named ADD, EI, LD—sanitized, medicalized labels that conceal the power, class, and ethnic differentiation pointing "these children" to the exit. *9. Teenage Wasteland*

Decoding the At-Risk Label

Who belongs in the gray zone between normality and abnormality, between health and pathology? In a recent Phi Delta Kappa study conducted in 276 schools, the authors begin with the assumption "that children are at risk if they are likely to fail—either in school or in life."[13] Who decides what constitutes failure in life? Have poor children already failed in life because they are dispossessed, or have we failed them by consigning them? Elizabeth Swadener, examining the etiology of the at-risk construct, cites 1,047 citations in a recent bibliographic search using the descriptor "high risk." She asks who the stakeholders are in the continuing construction of at-risk groups, and whose interests are being served by the maintenance and perpetuation of the classification.[14] The descriptions of at-risk students and their families are all too familiar, grounded in a two-hundred-year history. As early as 1805, the New York City Free School Society declaimed:

> These miserable and almost friendless objects are ushered upon the stage of life, inheriting those vices which idleness and the bad example of their parents naturally produce. The consequences of this neglect of education are ignorance and vice, and all these manifold evils resulting from every species of immorality by which public hospitals and alm-houses are filled with objects of disease and poverty.[15]

While educators and public officials have continued to attribute poor academic achievement to defects in individual character or to parental dysfunction, Larry Cuban points out, few question the culture of the school, "which ignores or degrades their family and community backgrounds," singles out poor children for being different, and promotes a pedagogy that serves to "crush the self esteem of students and neglect the strengths that these students bring to school." As dropout rates approach 50 percent among the ethnic urban poor, the conventional educational discourse, which assumes there is something wrong with the poor child's intellect, language, and social interactions, must be replaced. "It is time," argues Cuban, "to consider a less popular way of framing the problem: that the inflexible structure of the school itself contributes to the conditions that breed academic failure and unsatisfactory student performance."[16]

It is essential that not only the structure of the school, but also the sets of assumptions governing the psychological structuring of poor children's learning, be critically examined. Economic deprivation and disadvantage do not *necessarily* imply cognitive deficits; this faulty cause-effect relationship must be rethought. In 1972, when Ginsburg wrote *The Myth of the*

Deprived Child, he raised this issue at the height of the compensatory education movement. Ginsburg takes a Piagetian-developmental perspective—as pertinent now as it was in the 1970s—arguing that poor children's cognition is very similar to that of middle-class children. Certain cognitive universals develop irrespective of culture and class, and the differences that reflect one's heritage and linguistic/cultural community are relatively superficial. What really matter are the forms of knowledge that are validated in school settings—forms largely monocultural and middle-class in orientation.

The assumption that the poor child's environment is deprived of intellectual stimulation undergirded the original Head Start guidelines and the compensatory education training curricula. Ginsburg argued that there was no evidence to support that assumption in 1972; neither is there evidence now. In some respects children who are poor are required very early to develop forms of practical intelligence and code switching, from Black English to Standard English for example, or from Spanish to English, which white Anglo children do not necessarily encounter. The ghetto is a stressful place for a child to endure, but that does not mean it is a sensorily or linguistically deprived environment. Both Labov's early sociolinguistic research and Ginsburg's have demonstrated the contrary.[17] What really is at issue is school-validated knowledge and constructed norms of success that favor middle-class lifestyles and communication patterns. Poor children "must solve problems that middle-class children cannot even imagine; they suffer special kinds of oppression; they often live in despair. These are all distinctive conditions with which the poor, but not some others, must cope and for which they develop special accommodations, unique ways of behaving and thinking."[18]

In monocultural classrooms such differences are made pathological; exclusion patterns are entrenched in order to manage difference. When poor children are tested and classified in "soft" categories such as EMI (educable mentally impaired), vastly disproportionate numbers of poor minority children are placed there. As the Black Child Development Institute points out, "There is something wrong when Black children make up approximately 40% of the educable mentally retarded (EMR) population in schools when they are slightly more than 10% of the population at large."[19] If we examine the working definitions in use, we find the narrow evaluations are based almost exclusively on psychometric testing with all its attendant bias. The revised Michigan Administrative Rules for Special Education,[20] which apply to the children portrayed in this book, document the following behavioral characteristics as a basis for the determination of EMI (educable mentally impaired):

a) Development at a rate approximately 2 to 3 standard deviations below the mean as determined through intellectual assessment
b) Scores approximately within the lowest 6 percentiles on a standardized test in reading and arithmetic
c) Lack of development primarily in the cognitive domain
d) Impairment of adaptive behavior

Although the guidelines state that "a determination of impairment shall not be based solely on behaviors relating to environmental, cultural, or economic differences," the caveat clearly leaves open the possibility that such factors can and do play a role. What is an adaptive impairment? Not adapting to a passive, inflexible learning environment? Why are these psychometric tests being used when so much evidence, accumulated over three decades, testifies to their dubious accuracy and, further, to the active harm they cause to poor and minority children? In the even murkier category of EI (emotional impairment), only one or more of the following behavioral characteristics need be manifested over an extended period of time:

a) Inability to build or maintain satisfactory interpersonal relationships within the school environment
b) Inappropriate types of behavior or feelings under normal circumstances
c) General pervasive mood of unhappiness or depression
d) Tendency to develop physical symptoms or fears associated with personal or school problems

Consider the situation of little Heather, who was persistently scapegoated by her second grade teacher, Mrs. Mack; she eventually developed tummy aches (symptom *d*) before going to school and felt friendless (symptom *a*) and appeared sad (symptom *c*). Is she emotionally impaired or is her teacher? How often does the child become the victim of disabling and impaired classrooms? If "these kids" are already perceived as problems before they even enter school, the damaging effects of their labels track them for continuing impairment in a school setting. Just as the "at-risk" label has drawn from the public health model,[21] so the immunization metaphor has found a ready home in both compensatory and special education, with early diagnosis and intervention seen as instruments of inoculation against maladaptive behaviors of poor and minority children. The metaphor breaks down, however, when we realize that, unlike polio vaccines which actually inoculate against polio, intervention programs merely segregate and confine the "contaminated." Poverty is not eradicated, nor are its consequences—hunger, homelessness, unprotected illness, and the badge of humiliation that ticketed children wear to school every day.

Because our youngest children are being screened for "at-risk to fail" characteristics before they even enter public school programs, and because deferred diagnoses for at-risk developmental delays are permitted under Public Law 99-457, more sifting and sorting are likely to further segregate young children. The two-tiered system begins when early screening for public child care takes place. Susan Bailey, of the Educational Equity resource center, warns that "every equity problem we've seen in elementary and secondary schools is being repeated in the early childhood programs. But the equity problems seem to be less recognized in early childhood programs than in other areas of education."[22] Equity, it appears, has a great deal to do with fit; who fits and who doesn't, whose actions are disruptive and whose are inventive. The same set of behaviors exhibited by a lively poor child, such as Duke, who became entranced by the story of Sylvester and who imaginatively reconstructed and transferred the magic powers of the pebble to a stone in his pocket, is "impaired behavior"—possibly early signs of EI behavior! Yet I have seen similar imaginative behavior validated in classrooms where children have been identified as gifted. Simple nuances of seeing and framing and naming permit or constrain the possibilities of young children. As Humpty Dumpty tells Alice,

> "When *I* use a word . . . it means just what I choose it to mean—neither more nor less."
>
> "The question is," said Alice, "whether you *can* make words mean so many different things."
>
> "The question is," said Humpty Dumpty, "which is to be master—that's all."[23]

Education for Compliance

The capability of banking education to minimize or annul the students' creative power and to stimulate their credulity serves the interest of the oppressors, who care neither to have the world revealed nor to see it transformed . . . It follows logically from the banking notion of consciousness that the educator's role is to regulate the way the world "enters into" the students . . . And since men [and women] "receive" the world as passive entities, education should make them more passive still, and adapt them to the world. The edu-cated man [woman] is the adapted man [woman], because he [she] is better "fit" for the world

> Paulo Freire
> *Pedagogy of the Oppressed*

[margin handwritten note: see mama's remarks on "well-adjusted" mentality]

Banking education, argues Paulo Freire, creates a culture of silence, de-signed to perpetuate domination and compliance. A pedagogy for poor children does likewise. Poor children are required to fit the world created for them by school structures that violate their promise and devalue their resilience. They become impaired when they fail to fit the regulated world to which they are consigned. The worst result of their miseducation is the diminishing of selfhood. Compliance imperatives that construct deviance from children who do not fit promotes in classrooms what Roland Barth has termed "a field of well-trained sheep."[24] An educational landscape is created that reminds us of Camus's fictional town of Oran, "a town without pigeons, without any trees or gardens, where you never hear the beat of wings or the rustle of leaves." In this stripped and barren landscape, "how the people in it work, how they love, and how they die . . . are done on much the same lines," cultivating habits not of the heart but of an empti-ness.[25] In such a leveled American educational landscape, poor children are at risk of being beaten down by every institutional encounter, of receiving the empty shell of an education from which the fruit of meaningful learning has been stripped. If we are to promote developmentally appropriate prac-tices, we also need to think with Piaget about how to "create the possibili-ties for a child to invent and discover"; for "learning that is not the result of the child's own activity will be deformed."[26] Rarely are at-risk children given extra doses of talk-time, of expressive activities, of discovery-oriented projects that they themselves control. Lacking autonomy in almost every other part of their world, they are further denied it in school.

[margin handwritten note: see Foucault]

Thinking, imagining, inventing, hands-on learning threaten to subvert the order of what Foucault has termed the discipline of docile bodies,[27] the structuring of a child's consciousness and the vitiation of expressive possi-bilities. "To accomplish his object," the narrator tells us in Moby Dick, "Ahab must use tools; and of all tools used in the shadow of the moon, men are most apt to get out of order."[28] Children too are apt to get out of order when they think and talk and question and invent their world. Ideas are unruly, they often create disorder. Enthusiasm may be contagious. Yet it is an order paradigm of compliance that circumscribes the educational experiences of poor children.

The microcosmic classroom practices of regulation and containment portrayed in this book embody macrocosmic traces; they implicate the structure and training practices of teacher-certification institutions. As long as educators continue to make the burden of adaptation fall solely on the child, it is unlikely that classroom practice will meet the diverse developmental and social needs of students, and at-risk children will continue to be harmed in schools at alarming rates.

Perhaps we should listen more closely to the words of Ivan, in *The Brothers Karamazov*, as he tells his brother Alyosha, "Though I may not believe in the order of the universe, yet I love the sticky little leaves as they open in spring."[29] These sticky leaves can help to free us from the burdens of order, for a little stickiness, a little messiness make possible a going beyond—a beginning of autonomy. This is the developing autonomy that Anna, a second grade at-risk child, expressed after she wrote and acted out a story with her classmates in a flexible child-centered classroom: "It made me feel all warm in my tummy—kinda powerful and like I want to make another one tomorrow."

For Anna to become a meaningmaker in her classroom, an author of her own developing world, what Maxine Greene terms "wide—awakeness" must be present in the landscape of the classroom.[30] A dialogue of existential encounters must take place between teachers and their students, between students and their texts of action. Children must find a place in their classroom so that the ground upon which they stand *matters.* Poor children deserve a pedagogy of compassion and challenge that nurtures, not impairs, their development. Another language is necessary, a counterlanguage, in order to create educational landscapes that offer "the capacity to surpass the given—to look at things as if they could be otherwise."[31]

Finding a Place That Matters in School

In his *Philosophical Investigations,* Ludwig Wittgenstein poses an intriguing question—when does a town actually become a town? How many houses or streets does it take before a town feels like a town? When does the collection of houses create a composite image so that we begin to see a town, and sense the atmosphere of a town? At what point do we no longer look at a motley collection of houses and winding streets but rather begin to breathe the air of a town? And when does it become *our town?*[32] As educators we might well ask, When does a school become a *place*—a place that is more than the sum of its routines, its rules, its schedules, its scores? When does it become a place where children feel they matter, not instrumentally in terms of attendance and head counts, but existentially, because it is a landscape in which they have meaning and a sense of belonging? And, most significantly for poor children, when does a school become *their* place, where they find acceptance and possibility?

If we are to adopt an ecological perspective on development as Bronfenbrenner first urged,[33] the child's entire lifeworld must be taken into account. As John Dewey pointed out in 1897 in *My Pedagogic Creed,*

> Much of present education fails because it neglects this fundamental principle of the school as a form of community life. It conceives the school as a place where certain information is to be given, where certain lessons are to be learned, or where certain habits are to be formed. The value of these is conceived as lying largely in the remote future; the child must do these things for the sake of something else he is to do; they are mere preparations.[34]

For children designated as at risk, the school cannot abrogate its role as a form of community life. Educators must become informed about the context and meaning of the lives of children in poverty, destitution, and homelessness. They must recognize that the lack of entitlement to healthcare, housing, nutrition, and child care create stressed and powerless lives; that problems often diagnosed as emotional impairments or learning disabilities may be reactions to conditions of stress and want. In Abraham Maslow's hierarchy of needs, physiological and safety needs lie at the base of the developmental pyramid; belonging, self-esteem, and self-actualization emerge when these basic needs are met.[35] At the present time fully 25 percent of our youngest children and 20 percent of school-age children have not experienced either of those basic levels. We need to look at what the child can do and likes to do, rather than emphasizing what the child cannot or should not do. Standardized assessment instruments currently in use create deficiency constructs because the child's prior knowledge is valued not for what it is but for what it should be.

In order to build a pedagogy of equity for poor children, we need an "opening of spaces as well as perspectives," a different way of seeing and being with poor children. We need to promote their autonomy and dignity, "with everything depending on the actions we take in the course of our quest, the praxis we learn to devise."[36] The most telling stories of at-risk children's success over the past three decades have been narratives of teachers as child watchers, sensitively tuning the classroom to the developing child's questions—an existential pedagogy in which the child is encouraged to become a meaningmaker, a builder of thoughts, an expressive and curious actor experimenting with the avant-garde of knowledge.

Sylvia Ashton-Warner's remarkable work with Maori children, the discarded ones of New Zealand's educational system, shows how a generative literacy attaches profound meaning to the child's engagement with words and experiences drawn from "the dynamic life itself," from the personal/familial culture in which the child resides. Long before "whole language" became an educational buzzword of the eighties, Ashton-Warner was saying, "First words must mean something to a child. First words must have intense meaning for a child. They must be part of his being."[37]

We see the same incorporation of students' existential lifeworlds as part of classroom life and text in Herbert Kohl's *Thirty-six Children*, portraying the language and literacy development of sixth-grade poor black children in Harlem.[38] Kohl watched and listened to what the children could do and liked to do, and wove classical mythology, journalism, chess, and novels into the open spaces created by a pedagogy that permitted children's strengths and self-esteem to flourish. Yet these children had previously been judged at risk for academic failure by conventional compensatory approaches.

The child observation studies conducted by Patricia Carini and her colleagues at the Prospect Center in Vermont have constructed qualitative portraits of children as part of "the art of seeing and the visibility of the person."[39] Carini's *School Lives of Seven Children,* a five-year study tracing the school lives of children in the New York experimental PreKindergarten Program, presents children of promise whose competencies are highlighted as clues to understanding how to help those same students master areas of struggle.[40] The early identification of strengths through careful sustained observations by a collaborative team of teachers and consultants, allows the children to be seen as rich in promise, as artists and storytellers, as writers and problem solvers, as lively communicators. To begin to teach from the assumption of competence rather than of deficiency, Carini reminds us, is to teach from the child's strengths, with attention to what is of value and what matters to the child; for "a child has a right to come to school," and to other child care settings, not as a 'case' but as a person."[41] When at-risk children are seen in this light, they become capable of shedding their sheath of condemnation. This does not mean that their lives inside or outside school lose their vulnerability. Neither the teacher nor the school can cure the ravages of poverty; but a classroom can become a buf-

fer world, firm ground on which to stand, a place to belong, to feel empow-
ered to question, to experiment with entitlement. *?*

The work of Shirley Brice Heath, conducted in the Piedmont Carolinas with black and white children in two communities, demonstrates once
again how diverse linguistic and cultural traditions can be celebrated and
incorporated into elementary classrooms, so that the children's diversity is
viewed as a source of strength rather than deficiency.[42] Brice Heath, who
worked in intensive collaboration with the teachers, chronicles the changing frames of the teachers as they become ethnographers of their own
classrooms. Their increasing knowledge of the children's "ways with words"
sensitizes them to the children's communicative competence.

see earlier reference to this study

These four educators, whose ideas and practice span several decades,
provide instructive examples of another way of seeing. They share a competence view rather than a deficit view of children; they honor the children's cultural and class and ethnic differences as styles, perspectives, ways
of being that represent lifeworlds in the classroom. They recognize that
external realities become internal classroom realities, that "sociopolitical
and ideological visions are brought to the classrooms through the values,
attitudes, and behaviors of teachers," as Sarah Lawrence Lightfoot demonstrated dramatically in her *Worlds Apart*.[43] These educators also exemplify
the sensibilities outlined in the development of an anti-bias curriculum,[44]
which calls for children to learn the beliefs, values, rules, and language of
their own culture as well as those of the dominant culture in which they
live, and in a learning style that fits their personal/cultural landscape. In an
anti-bias, flexible classroom, multiculturalism is integrated into the educational landscape. As James Banks has shown, multiculturalism actually demands reforming the schools so that meaningful learning for all children is
made possible, and that reforming the curriculum means that *all* children
develop multicultural perspectives.[45]

Yet the issues embedded in the development of an anti-bias curriculum, the debates over an Afrocentric versus a Eurocentric curriculum, and
the researched differences in cognitive styles between culturally different
students should not obscure what Asa Hilliard describes as the systematic
inequities of low-expectation teaching, meted out to certain groups of children:

> In short, I believe that the children, no matter what their style, are failing
> primarily because of systematic inequities in the delivery of whatever peda-
> gogical approach the teachers claim to master—not because students cannot
> learn from teachers whose styles do not match their own.[46]

Hilliard denounces "the failure of researchers to document the differential pedagogical treatment that children receive based upon income and race."[47] Part of the differential pedagogical treatment consists of disciplinary practices disproportionately meted out to black students, which lead to exclusion from classes, alienation and rejection, and, ultimately, dropping out. Black students nationally are two to five times more likely than whites to be suspended.[48] In Michigan for example, minority students as a group are suspended at far higher rates than whites: the suspension rate of minority students is 141 per 1,000; for non-minority students, only 56 per 1,000. The highest rates recorded are for black students at 167 per 1,000 students.[49]

Schools have traditionally favored and legitimated Eurocentric learning styles and landscapes.[50] It is critical, however, to recognize and support diversity in order to restructure an education inimical to students from different cultural groups who experience "self-alienation."[51] We need to recreate the spaces for diversity in field-sensitive classrooms. The child's lifeworld must be opened and incorporated; a personal/cultural/familial ground structure must be validated and used as an invitation for self-development and expressive activity, for a dialogue in diversity that enriches both child and community. The traditional schooling model—white, middle-class, male-biased, and exclusionary of low-power groups—historically has mirrored the pervasive class, racial, and gender inequities of the society. Such schooling produces well-managed, docile bodies to be "subjected, used, transformed, and improved" as part of its disciplinary technology,[52] but breeds concentric spirals of inequity. What is called for is "a pushing back of the horizons of silence . . . , the opening of new frequencies for ears willing to risk new sounds,"[53] if poor children are to gain access to a pedagogy committed to their development as children of promise.

A classroom for a young child is a lifeworld; each year brings new forms of power, of possibility, of despair. As educators we are responsible for making school a place in which a child matters—a place away from the edges.

9

Lives on the Edge

I even think now that the land of the entire country was hostile to marigolds that year. The soil is bad for certain kinds of flowers. Certain seeds it will not nurture, certain fruit it will not bear, and when the land kills of its own volition, we acquiesce and say the victim had no right to live. We are wrong, of course, but it doesn't matter. It's too late. At least on the edge of my town, among the garbage and the sunflowers of my town, it's much, much, much too late.

Toni Morrison
The Bluest Eye

IT IS TOO LATE TO AVERT the 40,000 infant deaths of 1988, of which approximately 23,000 are estimated to be the result of low birthweight, largely preventable by adequate prenatal care. It is too late to change the infant mortality rate of 1989, in which 10 babies died for every 1,000 live births. Black babies died at the rate of 18 per 1,000 live births. While the United States ranks second in the world in per capita gross national product, it has a higher infant mortality rate than twenty-one other nations. It is too late to prevent the measles epidemic that the National Vaccine Advisory Committee reports was due to the failure to immunize vulnerable preschool children on time—a failure caused by an undersupply of vaccine, overcrowded and understaffed clinics flooded with sick and uninsured children. Among the poorest sections of the population, specifically among black and Hispanic urban children, the immunization rate is estimated to be lower than 50 percent. It is too late to prevent the number of babies already born to teenage mothers, or the rate increase for fifteen- to seventeen-year-olds, for whom the rate rose from 31.8 births per 1,000 to 33.8 per 1,000 in 1988.[1] It is too late to repair the damage caused by the slashed budget for low-income housing, cut by almost 80 percent during the Reagan years, which, together with sweeping cuts in federal assistance and soaring housing costs, had by 1987 created a situation where one-half

163

of all renter households in poverty were spending more than 70 percent of their income on housing.[2] That situation has contributed in large measure to the swelling number of homeless families. The National Coalition for the Homeless estimates that on any given night there are one-half million homeless children,[3] and that families with children make up one-third of the nation's homeless population.

It *is* too late to prevent the ravages of poverty that have blighted lives already here. It is not too late to prevent further ravages, to begin to understand the full impact of living on the edges, and to devise, in Paulo Freire's words, a new praxis.[4] This praxis must involve a refusal to acquiesce in the continuing construction of private greed and public squalor. It must involve changing the discourse, reframing the "problem" of poverty in a way that does not vitiate the existential character of destitution and that places responsibility for destitution on an impaired society in which its most vulnerable citizens, poor single mothers and their children, are at risk every day of their lives. Only when we can confront the meaning of constructed inequity as something that has been made by public policy and can be *unmade* by public policy can we begin to address the question of civic entitlement in the other America. Once again we need to question why? Why is there a failure to act with purpose almost thirty years after Michael Harrington wrote:

> Yet those who could make the difference too often refuse to act because of their ignorant, smug moralisms. They view the effects of poverty—above all, the warping of the will and spirit that is a consequence of being poor—as choices. Understanding the vicious circle is an important step in breaking down this prejudice.[5]

Is poverty necessary in one of the wealthiest and most advanced industrial nations? Why do we accept its inevitability? As these questions are raised, old attitudes harden. An article in the *New York Times* of September 2, 1991, "Shift in Feelings on the Homeless: Empathy Turns Into Frustration," describes the increasingly intolerant public and civic attitudes in several major cities—Atlanta, New York, Santa Barbara, Miami—with resulting punitive measures. In Miami, panhandlers who approach motorists to wash windows, for example, face fines of up to $500 and sixty-day jail sentences. In The District of Columbia, voters repealed a 1984 law requiring the city to shelter all those in need, closed two emergency shelters, and restricted the number of nights for shelter availability in remaining shelters. As more and more homeless adults and children fill the cities, one

New York advocacy worker is quoted as saying, "The problem is just enveloping us . . . How big a rug are you going to need to sweep them under?"

Once more it is *they* who infest our cities, *them* we must get rid of rather than the dehumanizing policies and sensibilities that make other people *other.* Only when we analyze the multiple ways in which poverty results from the politics of distribution—and not from natural law, or mere fate, or vice, or an inherited condition—can we confront the social and economic and political bureaucracies, which require both new visions and new organizational structures. Above all, we need the courage to confront private greed and the ideology of consumerism, the "rugged individualist" ethos that fails to see success as tied to the privileged histories of class and gender and color.

As we begin to think through the critical obstacles facing poor women and their children, the disabling events that cause fragile systems to crack, the daily unmet needs, the shocks of life on the edges, a clear set of issues emerge that point the way either to *inside* or to *outside,* either to entitlement or disenfranchisement. Concerning the issues that are uniquely female in their interrelated combinations, it is instructive to look at our neighbors across our northern borders and across the Atlantic, as alternative paths are mapped.

Entitlements or Benefits   *168*   ?

As Diana Pearce has pointed out, *single, maternal* female poverty is unique because mothers bear the burden of economic responsibility for their children;[6] when mothers are poor, their children are poor too. Since women also bear the burden of economic discrimination in the workplace, low-paying jobs in the secondary sector create pink-collar contingency, without benefits or health insurance. Women still only earn 68 cents to the male dollar, a figure that has changed very little in the past decades. William Julius Wilson has argued that solving the problem of male joblessness is the key to urban policy reform affecting poor black families,[7] but that solution does not take account of the special contingency of women in relation to male control and male power. Viable employment as a means of establishing economic autonomy for single mothers is vital. Yet an ongoing child care crisis is created when woman-as-worker is not also recognized as woman-as-mother. The care of her young children creates enormous stresses for a mother when workplace demands and child care needs conflict, where child care is viewed as a private affair rather than a publicly supported entitlement. A teenage, single mother such as Anna, forced to cut back her forty-hour-a-week job in a department store and anxious to obtain a college degree, cannot get ahead unless she is provided with high-quality child care. As Anna told us earlier, "You can't put your kid in a good all-day preschool 'cos of your low income and ADC only pays for the real cheap places." Her child, although eligible for Head Start, is still in need of supplementary child care, for Head Start only runs part-day four mornings a week. For Jenny and her son Dan, child care was an even greater problem because of his health and behavioral problems; in turn, she was almost cut from public assistance because, due to her son's special needs, she failed to participate in the mandatory state job-training program.

Thus, in the absence of publicly subsidized, full-time child care and a universal child allowance, a single woman's ability to take care of her children is severely undermined by the inequities she faces in the labor market, as well as by the gendered inequities of the welfare system.[8]

The United States holds a unique position regarding its dearth of social insurance policies for working mothers. It stands alone among more than one hundred other countries (including all the industrialized Western democracies) in having no national legislation that grants specific pregnancy-related rights to its female labor force.[9] Maternity leave, job protection while on leave, cash benefits that equal (or amount to a significant portion of) one's wages, health insurance—none of these are entitlements in this country. All western European countries provide a minimum of three months paid maternity leave; West Germany provides six and Sweden fifteen months (to be used by one or both parents). In addition, several of these countries have legislated paid sick care leaves for parents to stay home and take care of sick children. In Sweden, for example, a working parent can take up to sixty days a year to care for an ill child if medically necessary.[10] A far cry from the primitive efforts that exist in the United States, where in 1990 President Bush vetoed and the business community opposed an *unpaid* parental leave bill that would have permitted mothers (or fathers) to stay home after the birth of their child, after adoption, or when a child becomes sick.[11]

In 1988 there were 10.2 million children (51 percent) with mothers in the labor force, and by 1995 that number is projected to rise to 14.6 million. Yet in 1987, for employed mothers, only 25 percent of children under five were served by child care/preschool centers and 22 percent by family daycare homes.[12] Furthermore, despite voluminous research studies documenting the components of good quality care for young children[13]—a consistent and nurturant staff trained in early childhood development with whom the children develop secure attachments, low employee turnover, low child-staff ratios, play-based developmentally appropriate programs, cultural sensitivity, parent access and education, a safe, healthy physical environment and adequate staff salaries—approximately 43 percent of all children in centers are unprotected by even minimal state legislation. While places that receive public funds are generally regulated, licensing requirements vary enormously from state to state. According to a recent Health and Human Services Study, caseloads for state licensing inspectors exceed almost twice the recommended levels.[14]

Child care costs are prohibitive not only for poor single mothers but for many middle-income women as well. The average child care costs in selected cities around the country vary from $3,900 a year for full-time infant care in Dallas (Texas) to $6,604 in Boulder (Colorado). For a single mother working full time at minimum wage, this would constitute between 45.9 percent of her income in Texas to 77.7 percent of her income in Colorado. In Boulder, the average annual cost for a four-year-old is $4,472, or 52.6 percent of a single mother's minimum wage income (see table 2).[15] The Michigan mothers portrayed in this book spent one-quarter to more than one-half of their income on child care. Lori, for example, paid almost $500 a month out of an $800-a-month net salary for four-year-old Kim to attend a high-quality preschool. She received only a partial DSS child care subsidy of $144 a month. Like the other single mothers portrayed here, Lori is overwhelmed by her financial morass: "I don't know what I'm going to do . . . I need help . . . I feel like I'm sinking." In Michigan, the average monthly cost for full-time child care for preschoolers is $308, and that figure almost doubles in some areas of the state. Although the Family Support Act of 1988 has set monthly minimum rates for federal reimbursement, for children older than two (like Kim) the rate is only $175 per month in Michigan, and this subsidy is far below the cost of actual care.[16] $\rangle$ –

Our western European neighbors have invested a great deal of state planning to serve young children of working mothers. Sweden, Denmark, and France offer instructive examples.[17] Sweden has one of the best-developed and most progressive child care systems; subsidized care is offered in the form of public child care centers at or close to the parents' workplace, as well as small, neighborhood family daycare homes which are municipally licensed. Denmark's system is run on similar lines to that of Sweden. In France, the *écoles maternelles*, since the 1950s, have enrolled almost all the nation's three- to six-year-olds; in addition, for babies from six months to three years of age, crèches are available, which are partially or fully subsidized with parents paying on a sliding-fee basis. Since all the

Table 2

Average Fees Charged in Licensed Child Care Centers, by Age Group, in Selected Cities, 1990

	OAKLAND CA	BOULDER CO	DALLAS TX	ORLANDO FL
Average annual cost of child care for a one-year-old child	$5,773	$6,604	$3,900	$4,212
Percent of income low-income parents would have to pay for average child care for their one-year-old child if they were:				
single parent working full time at the minimum wage	67.9%	77.7%	45.9%	49.6%
two parents working full time at the minimum wage	34.0%	38.8%	22.9%	24.8%
Average annual cost of child care for a four-year-old child	$4,836	$4,472	$3,380	$3,120
Percent of income low-income parents would have to pay for average child care for their four-year-old child if they were:				
single parent working full time at the minimum wage	56.9%	52.6%	39.8%	36.7%
two parents working full time at the minimum wage	28.4%	26.3%	19.9%	18.4%

Source: Data analyzed by the Children's Defense Fund. Average cost data collected from various Resource and Referral agencies, and reported in the April 1990 edition of *Child Care Information Exchange* (Reprinted in CDF, *The State of America's Children, 1991,* p. 43).

western European countries provide paid maternity leave with child allowances, the crisis in early infant care is averted.

A study by Sheila Kamerman of eight industrialized countries—Sweden, the Federal Republic of Germany, France, Canada, Australia, Israel, and the United Kingdom—showed that the United States stood alone in providing no universal child allowances.[18] Child allowances in these other countries involve payments to all families irrespective of income and employment. The payments cover infants through late adolescence or, in some cases if students are in postsecondary schools, until age twenty-five. The amount of the payments vary from country to country, and because they are not income-tested, they are not stigmatized. Existing as a statutory benefit, the allowances usually constitute between 13 and 27 percent of the family income if the mother does not work, and between 10 and 24 percent if the mother earns a modest salary. France, in addition to its child allowance, adds an income-tested supplementary allowance with a ceiling sufficiently high that over 75 percent of families with three or more children, or with a child under three years old, qualify. The child allowance is particularly significant for single parents, because it exists as a statutory government benefit. It is both dependable and continuing. Sweden, the most progressive in its family policy, also has a program of advance maintenance support for single parents and offers tax-free, non-income-tested cash benefits equal to 40 percent of the Swedish reference wage, which is an indexed amount. These support payments are extended to single mothers for each child under eighteen. Approximately 27 percent of Swedish families are single-parent households, and these advance maintenance support payments are designed to ensure that the child is not penalized by the absent parent's lack of support. It is estimated that roughly 50 percent of the costs will be offset by the absent parent responsible for the child support. This benefit is viewed as equivalent to, or higher than, the amount one parent would pay to support a child. Swedish family policy assumes but does not require labor force participation by mothers, yet makes it possible for single parents to live comfortably, work, and receive support for their children. Despite the substantial increase in single parent families in Sweden, Swedish single mothers, like most Swedish women, work either full time or part time.

Kamerman also points out that the universal child allowance is part of a general package of housing allowances and health care benefits that are statutory, benefiting both low- and middle-income citizens in these societies.[19] The Swedish housing allowance, primarily directed to families with children, makes up between 20 and 30 percent of family income for single mothers. In France the benefits make up 15 percent of single-mother families' income, and about one-quarter of families with children receive the benefits. Because the income ceiling is high, the stigma of welfare does not exist, and most single-mother families of middle-income status qualify as well.

Kamerman's findings indicate that in countries with strong family policies—and all countries in western Europe have such policies in place—citizens make less use of "welfare"; for several of their benefits are seen as universal entitlements, as rights rather than stigmatized public assistance. The combination of a universal child allowance, national health care, housing allowances plus maternity benefits, and subsidized child care is effective in reducing family destitution and child poverty. These entitlements provide single mothers and their children with a tolerable standard of living, so that the links between poverty and single parenthood seen in the United States lose their persistence.

The 1991 recommendations from the National Commission on Children,[20] cognizant of the United States' pariah status among Western industrialized nations, which all have active family support policies in place, has proposed some far-reaching changes to attack childhood poverty. Many of the proposals are influenced by the successful programs already in place in western Europe. At the beginning of the 1990s, 35.7 million Americans lack health insurance, including 9.8 million children,[21] or 15.3 percent of all American children. Typically the uninsured are disproportionately poor, despite ties to the labor force. The commission, chaired by Democratic senator John D. Rockefeller IV, recommends a universal system of health coverage for pregnant women and children to be financed by both government and employers. The commission also recommends the creation of a $1,000 refundable child tax credit for all children through age eighteen, and the elimination of the personal exemption that currently exists for dependent children. This change is designed to benefit all families regardless of income or tax liability. For low-income families who earn too little to pay federal income tax, it would result in a cash payment from the Internal Revenue Service. The commission's recommendations form part of a comprehensive package, which includes a cash allowance in place of the current restrictive food stamp program; the establishment of uniform eligibility criteria for AFDC, Medicaid, and other federal public assistance programs; as well as the streamlining of programs and providers in order to simplify the current maze of different bureaucracies. Also proposed is a demonstration project to evaluate the feasibility of an insured child-support benefit plan, already widely in use in Europe. The Family Support Act of 1988 has already mandated collection of child support through automatic withholding of wages when absent fathers fail to pay, and has determined child support payments based on uniform state guidelines. The proposed plan would guarantee minimum support for a child irrespective of the delinquency of the father.

While the commission's proposals point in a more progressive direction, the long overdue reforms are, in actuality, minimal. The financial benefit levels are low by comparison to those in western Europe, which lacks the widespread and persistent childhood poverty that exists in the United States and whose calculated poverty standard far exceeds our own. Yet despite the modesty of the reforms called for, nine of the thirty-four commissioners wrote a dissenting chapter in the report opposing the health care recommendations. Official response from the White House was described as "tepid" by the *New York Times,* which quoted press secretary Marlin Fitzwater as saying, "Big ticket items for any purpose are going to have a very tough time being enacted. The fact is the money's not there." The same article quoted one of the Republican commissioners as criticizing the lack of fiscal restraints in the wide-ranging recommendations: "There was no reality check, no sense of what can be done realistically for children." The Heritage Foundation's response from Washington expressed concerns that some of the proposals would serve as "a big new subsidy for single mothers."[22] Thus, after the fanfare celebrating what America is doing for its poor children dies down, *Beyond Rhetoric: A New American Agenda for Children and Families* returns to its rightful place on the shelves of public policy proposals gone astray with idealism—to be debated, diluted, downsized, and dissolved in doses of fiscal realism that render visible only certain realities, and mask the textured horror of daily destitution.

And worse is to come if we look at policies currently being proposed in the states. In Michigan, where childhood poverty rates are 22.7 percent, with high concentrations in the cities—in 1989, the child poverty rate in Detroit was 46.6 percent. AFDC benefits were cut by 17 percent effective May 1991 and later partially restored, wreaking months of havoc in many families' lives. The 1991–92 Executive Budget proposed a federal waiver to establish Learnfare in Michigan, which would reduce AFDC levels further by withholding portions of the benefit payment if the child should fail to attend school. A further devastating proposal in the Executive Budget would be the elimination of child care payments for parents in education or job training programs.[23] Proposals in New Jersey and Wisconsin recommend cutting federal and state aid to single mothers who have subsequent pregnancies by denying them the minimum increase for an additional child (an extra $64 per month). These proposals are apparently designed to discourage poor mothers from living off the "fruits" of AFDC "as if the thought of life on $520 a month for a family of three in Wisconsin, and $424 a month in New Jersey, was not discouragement enough,"[24] writes Martha Davis of the NOW Legal Defense and Education Fund. Not only do such proposals punish single women for their "other motherhood" status, attempt to control their sexual behavior, and reinforce traditional gender stereotypes by rewarding them with benefits if they marry, but they fail to address the critical issues that mire single mothers in poverty, reducing them to modern-day paupers, undeserving wards of the state. Hence, in the last decade of the twentieth century, the entitlements guaranteed to single mothers and their children as civil rights in all other Western democracies are not present in the United States—not yet; wealthy, powerful, technologically advanced, but dismally failing to adequately protect its most vulnerable citizens. They are reduced to grubbing for worms in the shadows of the private garden.

The Old Story Revisited

Oliver's mother dying in the streets of nineteenth-century London; Fantine abandoning her little "lark," Cosette; Hester Prynne emblazoned with her scarlet letter and clinging desperately to her "witch child" Pearl; the earth refusing to bear marigolds this year; the pain of Anna, Toni, or Sara, of Justine, Christy or Jenny—the stories fade, but new voices echo in the caverns of invisibility, locked in the language of concealment, which becomes more strident as the meaning of entitlement shrinks. And what of their children, of Tyrone, Heather, and Tim, placed at risk in classrooms, impaired by a pedagogy of the poor?

Statistics do lose their power after repeated onslaughts on conscience and consciousness; we become inured to figures that prefigure lives outside and childhoods in shadow. Yet to act and see differently means to develop an understanding that enables us, in Sartre's words, "to change, to go beyond oneself."[25] And to go beyond oneself is to build another way of seeing, beyond the deficit pathology frames that have made poverty an individual problem and a private affair—not a public responsibility, not a consequence of the political economy of distribution, of public policies that have constructed the poor. Reconstruction of the state, of employment policies, of supply-side economics; elimination of sex-gender-racial inequalities, of workplace inequities, of unfair housing policies; availability of health care and child care and early intervention; restructuring of the public schools— all these changes and reforms have been proposed by leading critics and social and public policy analysts, many of them discussed in this book. But until private interests give way to public responsibility and to a notion of civic entitlements rather than undeserving poor benefits, poor people will remain poor in a land of affluence. Those who live in the other America live in another country—disenfranchised, disempowered, and with no civic voice.

Single mothers and their children are a growing constituency in the other America, and it is their lives that I have attempted to illuminate in this book. Countless others live on the outside edges of America—young black men, Hispanic and Native American youth, single adults, mentally ill people, old people, poor two-parent families—whose stories too need to be told. My choice, however, has been to trace the lives of some women and some children, to show the face of poverty among its resilient survivors, to link their stories with the larger story, to create the experiential encounters that reduce the distance between them and us. When we cancel interpersonal community by creating the other motherhood and the other childhood, we tend to construct pathology from difference and see only what we have framed. As Walter Benjamin writes, "It is as if something that seemed inalienable to us, the securest among our possessions, were taken from us: the ability to exchange experiences."[26]

Other Western democracies have succeeded in alleviating the "social asphyxia" of poverty. There are workable models, plausible and practical proposals, that speak to mixed economies, to social democratic domestic structures, to full incorporation of one's citizenry as part of one's human entitlement—freedom from destitution and the right to a life of dignity. It is not too late to see another world as capable of being made. It is possible "for men and women both, to establish a place for freedom in the world of the given—and to do so in concern and with care, so what is indecent can be transformed and what is unendurable may be overcome."[27]

How to change the story is the question—the choosing in "plain clean-cut language," Tarrou tells us, between the pestilences and the victims, for "it is up to us, so far as possible, not to join forces with the pestilences."[28] The refusal to continue revisiting the old story, the old labels, the mystifications that dominate and conceal, will make possible a new telling. We need to reconstruct a language of existential entitlement that turns the mirror of sensibility, so that in seeing those others we construct ourselves, and the image opens not to a landscape of otherness but to a landscape of community.

It is time to write a new story.

AFTERWORD

Some Reflections
on the Future

THIS BOOK HAS NOT OFFERED easy solutions or quick fixes. At present, state after state continues to enact punitive and coercive legislation against single mothers and their children. The drastic cuts in benefits, the bribing of mothers on welfare to marry or use the contraceptive Norplant, the reduction of welfare grants when mothers or their children fail to attend school, the denial of benefits for additional children, the funding cuts for child care, for community agencies, for referral services, for teen-parent centers—all these measures become part of the "savage inequalities"[1] that scar the social and educational landscape. Yet in confronting the constructed disenfranchisement and the continuing squalor to which we have brought millions of fellow citizens, it is necessary to also think beyond—to reframe the poverty discourse that needs to take place in this country.

We cannot continue to enjoy unlimited privileges and still attack poverty. Redistribution of public and private income, an equitable tax structure, the making of an educational democracy, the restructuring of health care and child care, affordable and subsidized housing, and workplace reforms cannot be made as part of leftover policy for the poor. Redistribution in a land of plenty means that those of us with plenty may receive a little less, and will need to share a little more, so that others can survive with decency as part of our human community. Other people's children deserve entitlements to a future as much as our own children do; for their childhoods matter too.

1. Universal Health Care

The stories of the women in this book, and of countless others, dramatically illustrate the urgent need for universal health insurance. Increasingly the calls for health care reform are rapidly becoming a mainstream political agenda. In 1991, 35.7 million Americans, of which 9.8 million are estimated to be children, lacked health insurance.[2] The number is higher than at any time since Medicare and Medicaid were enacted in 1965. The youngest and poorest of our citizens, and the poorest of our mothers, will suffer the visible consequences well into the coming century. Health care is a civic entitlement, not a benefit, if we value the health of our citizenry. Pregnant mothers and their young children should not be forced onto welfare in order to receive Medicaid. Teenagers should have access to supportive teen clinics that supply contraception, education, and counseling to help them make responsible and informed choices. Abortion should be available as a choice for all, not only for those who can afford to make such a choice.

The expansion and large-scale funding of school-based clinics, nutrition programs for women and infants (WIC), maternal and child block grants, a national health corps, expansion of community and migrant health centers—all are among the recommendations of the latest Carnegie Commission Report, "Ready to Learn," in which the authors state that "good health and good schooling are inextricably interlocked."[3] But providing children with health care is more than an educational matter—it is a vital unmet crisis that currently causes nothing less than the destruction of infants and young children. In New York City, the Mobile Medical and Dental Van reports treating large numbers of three- and four-year-olds who cannot hear from recurrent ear infections, who suffer constant pain from untreated dental cavities, who have blurred vision, or who are chronically malnourished (New York Times, December 29, 1991). There are reports of a nationwide increase in destitute babies dying from water intoxication because of insufficient canned formula.[4] These diseases of scarcity and underdevelopment do not belong in a First World country. Lack of health care is a violation of human rights; when extended to children it is an abuse of human life. Neither resources nor lack of expertise stand in the way; rather it is power and mind sets. Both must be confronted through education and political action; for health care is a cornerstone of a viable democracy. There presently do exist community-based teen clinics, school clinics, mobile prenatal and child clinics, neighborhood immunization clinics, and preschool health screenings. All have demonstrated significant health improvements for poor children.[5] These, however, are all pocket successes; eligibility and access depend on where you live, on quotas, on state locale, on sustained funding, on committed volunteers. In short, what works, works sporadically. A national entitlement program is necessary.

2. Affordable Housing

Homelessness is another violation of democracy. The responsibility of government to provide housing for its citizens has been assumed in all of the Western democracies discussed in this book. Until the federal government underwrites social investment and sees housing as a basic human right, not a marketable commodity, the plight of families now spending up to 70 percent of their income on housing is unlikely to be ameliorated. Responsible social and physical planning and price controls must play a role if affordable housing is to become a reality. There is certainly no dearth of ideas, as Greg Barak points out: there are linkage laws requiring developers to fund public works, including affordable housing and job training; plans involving private and public sector collaboration that involve restructuring economic and social environments; the Institute for Policy Studies' Progressive Housing Program for America, proposed in Congress in 1989, which recognizes housing as a right, not as a commodity, and promotes nonprofit production and ownership of housing units; and the Schwartz plan, which, among other proposals, calls for a halt to the eviction of families.[6] Barak argues that the right to shelter should be seen as part of a larger entitlement—the right to human dignity. The disenfranchisement of the homeless at the present time means "the fundamental rights of liberty and property as expressed in the Bill of Rights are not going to be extended to homeless people in this century."[7] Many mothers flee unsafe apartments; 21 percent of the women in shelters are women who have fled abusive spouses or partners;[8] the million and a half children who are homeless on any given night cannot thread their lives together in an emergency shelter. A sustained policy commitment to viable housing as the right of all citizens is the solution.

3. Child Allowances and Maternity/Parental Leave

To address the chronic childhood poverty in this country, a universal child allowance must be instituted as a statutory family benefit. Such a benefit will address the unique vulnerability of the female-headed family. A universal child allowance removes a mother's extreme dependency on an irresponsible father and public assistance and therefore relieves her children from the constant threat of destitution; it also enables her children to begin their lives with a reasonable support system in place, which does not relegate them to hunger and homelessness. Such an allowance would thus help avert the crisis of sustained welfare poverty in the United States. Lessons from our international neighbors about family policies have been ignored, with bitter consequences.

The most recent and progressive policy recommendations for this country fall far short of what is really needed to halt the devastation of families that is currently taking place. The Report of the National Commission on Children recommends a $1000 child allowance as a tax credit;[9] yet for a family in poverty this is far too low a level to make a significant breakthrough. The Carnegie Foundation similarly endorses only unpaid parental leave,[10] but why? Every other major Western democracy offers its working mothers *at least* twelve to fourteen weeks' paid maternity leave as well as job protection.

Because women bear the burden of both economic and nurturing responsibility for their children, workplace reforms are essential. As long as women earn lower salaries than men and are relegated to pink-collar jobs, they will continue to be at the mercy of state and corporate patriarchies—both of which fail to recognize their unique position as citizen mothers and citizen workers. Low-wage employees cannot survive in our present economy; the minimum wage is a constructed injustice which condemns all employees, male and female, to poverty and contingency. For single mothers this become a double outrage.

4. A National Child Care System

Working mothers cannot have equal access to the labor market until the child care crisis is resolved.[11] The major early intervention programs for poor children have failed to address the unique situation of poor single mothers. Head Start's emphasis on parent education and involvement is premised on a 1950s ideal of female domesticity, not on the image of an economically independent working mother. The 1990 Head Start Silver Ribbon Panel Report recommends policies that recognize current life circumstances of individual families[12] and encourages the provision of full-day services for those families in need. Yet the panel falls far short of assuming an advocacy position on behalf of single mothers and young children, who at present form a significant constituency of Head Start families. A national child care system has been estimated by Zigler to cost $100 billion a year, while the combined current amount spent annually by the federal government to date has been about $6 billion.[13] Even with the reauthorization of funds by the 1990 Congress for $7 million by 1994 to serve eligible three-

and four-year-olds in Head Start,[14] it is clear there is an enormous disparity between what is and what should be.

The issue of early intervention raises another critical question: Why continue to perpetuate a two-tiered, race- and class-segregated child care system? Middle-income families also need affordable, high-quality child care. A national, public, early childhood education system, accredited by the NAEYC (National Association for the Education of Young Children), would guarantee access to all children. We have recognized public schooling as an entitlement. Why not public early education and child care? My advocacy of a national child care system is *not* a call for extending traditional, rigidified forms of schooling downward, but rather it is a call to create the space for early education structures to be developed in accordance with developmentally and culturally appropriate, flexible classroom practices. The NAEYC guidelines are a good start. Most public preschools, whether Head Start- or state-funded, promote segregation because access is classified and limited. Head Start has been a lifeline for millions of families for a quarter of a century; but it needs to change and become part of a larger, integrated child care system. In order to support the large number of mothers who are part of the labor force, and to assist those women who cannot take paid employment because of child care responsibilities, a national, subsidized child care system, which offers both part- and full-time care for young children and incorporates the supportive services of Head Start, should be implemented.

5. A Pedagogy of Equity

A pedagogy of equity must address the critical needs of poor children in public schools. Vast disparities in funding between rich and poor school districts have created school environments such as those in East St. Louis, which Jonathon Kozol describes as mired in "the hopelessness, the clouds of smoke and sense of degradation all around them."[15] Cast-away children in cast-away school districts need immediate attention and funding interventions. The national educational crisis has a great deal to do with fundamental inequities of available resources.

The conventional wisdom underlying Chapter I Compensatory Education Programs needs to be reexamined. Adverse consequences for children in pull-out programs have been documented ad infinitum. Yet these practices continue. The needs of children in poverty can be addressed by opening, rather than closing down, the spaces for empowerment and autonomy within classrooms. Poor children need a sense of themselves as active agents within autonomy-promoting landscapes; they need flexible agendas, a child-centered, hands-on, activity-based curriculum that promotes active learning, cooperative assignments, and integrative social relationships—a classroom ethos that values children's talk, that truly respects "prior experiences," so that the student comes to school as a person who matters.

Teacher training institutions must seriously address the diverse worlds of poor children and actively promote an anti-bias curriculum as a key component of a multicultural education. A pedagogy of equity, above all, requires an ethic of caring—a change of heart and a change in our ways of seeing.

Many of the social and educational entitlements I have advocated are already present in the various discourses about eradicating poverty and inequity; the ideas are here but legislative support and public sensibilities are not. One of the problems with the recommendations discussed, is that they lack widespread grass-roots involvement. The unique successes of the large-scale poor people's movements that followed the civil rights movement of the 1960s, such as the National Welfare Rights Organization and ACORN,[16] are important historical precedents as we approach the twenty-first century. Francis Fox Piven points out that women hold the majority of social service jobs in the government sector; by 1980, fully 70 percent of such jobs were held by women.[17] What if women were to strike, crippling the bureaucracy? What if squatting became an effective strategy for homeless people, as it was done in the Netherlands during the 1970s? What if poor women organized to take over buildings from abusive and neglectful landlords—refused to be evicted for inability to pay rent? What if evictions were resisted in the same way that segregated lunch counters once were? What if Head Start Teachers earning only $11,000 a year went on strike? What if poor, uninsured mothers marched on doctors' offices and clinics and hospitals that denied them services—just as black South Africans marched on white hospitals, forcing them to open their doors to all patients in 1990? All of these nonviolent strategies have been used as part of protest movements pushing for change against intractable judicial and legislative machinery. Such strategies, nevertheless, do create ominous risks, particularly for women with children. But the voices of the disenfranchised must be taken account of, and they must be heard. Their stories need to be told so that they are given voice and space to become actors. More attention must be paid to the linkages between those who suffer and those who care, so that caring becomes a committed advocacy, so that a concrete praxis may emerge. Empowerment of the poor hits at the heart of this failing democracy. It is time for the unmaking of poverty, and the unmaking of the Other America.

April 1992

Some Notes on Method

"Small facts speak to large issues"—Clifford Geertz

I N PRESENTING THE STORIES of single mothers, and in constructing the portraits of classrooms and children, I have used (1) an interpretive ethnographic approach, which follows in the tradition of the Utrecht School of Lifeworld Phenomenology developed by Marthinus Langeveld and Ton Beekman,[1] (2) the ethnographic qualtitative perspectives developed by anthropologists Jules Henry and Clifford Geertz, social psychiatrist Robert Coles, and educators Patricia Carini and Sara Lightfoot Lawrence[2] and (3) my own earlier ethnographic work in early childhood centers.[3] My methods were simple but time-consuming and labor-intensive—listening, watching, and writing.

Mothers' Stories

The stories in chapter 4 of the six teenage mothers and in chapter 5 of the five mothers were constructed from oral interviews which took place in Michigan between 1989 and 1991. The interviews were open-ended conversations in which the mothers were asked to talk about their experiences and struggles living in poverty with their children. Most of the interviews involved several meetings, with each informant, and all were tape-recorded and transcribed. Although eleven stories are told in this book, fifteen women were interviewed initially before more detailed interviews took place. In order to protect privacy, all the informants' names and identifying characteristics have been changed, and in certain cases a composite portrait has been used to further protect anonymity. The women were selected because of their willingness to tell their stories and their interest in the topic. The choice of informants was not random, but purposeful: I have chosen to tell the stories of resilient women, of the survivors and the fighters, because in their struggle are many lessons to be learned, many myths unveiled.

The Classrooms and the Children

The portraits in chapters 6 and 7 of the five classrooms and of individual children were gathered from observations in selected public schools and preschools over a two-and-one-half-year period in different school districts in Michigan. Over twenty classrooms were visited initially. After specific ones had been selected for further observation as "exemplaric" slices of life of children's school experiences, between five and ten further visits were made to each. As noted earlier, neither the best nor the worst of worlds is presented, but rather typical daily routines that pattern young children's experiences. As an educator, I chose these rooms with purpose and with prior knowledge, because in my experience of fifteen years of child watching in classrooms, I had seen their like before in other buildings, at other times. I have seen worse, I have seen better. Since my intention was to capture "dailiness," the classrooms I chose documented stories that usually are neither seen nor told. Once again, all efforts to protect anonymity of both children and schools have been made. In certain cases, a composite portrait has been drawn to ensure confidentiality. As my interest was in showing what school is like for poor young children, my observations trace the experiences of those children and not of others. Storytelling, as Walter Benjamin reminds us, is the art of weaving and spinning; "it does not aim to convey the pure essence of the thing like information or a report. It sinks the thing into the life of the storyteller, in order to bring it out of him again. Thus traces of the storyteller cling to the story the way the handprints of the potter cling to the clay vessel."[4] The stories told to me by single mothers have sunk into me, the worlds of their children are imprinted portraits in memory, and as the storyteller of their lives, I have attempted to recreate their voices in the larger landscapes of history and social policy.

NOTES

Introduction

1. The use of the terms *other* and *otherness* throughout this book follows in the tradition of existential and poststructuralist writers—Jean-Paul Sartre and his use of the *en-soi pour soi* modes of consciousness; Martin Buber; Simone de Beauvoir; Albert Camus; Paulo Freire; and Michel Foucault. Michael Harrington, *The Other America* (New York: Penguin Books, 1963), and Michael Katz, *The Undeserving Poor* (New York: Pantheon, 1989), in their writings about the meaning and construction of poverty in America, have also used the terms *other* and *otherness*. The interpersonal distance and the alienation of self from other selves, the distancing of the individual from the human community, are underlying themes embodied in otherness. Otherness symbolizes the objectification-through-language and policy of those who are consigned to the margins of society.

2. Katz, *The Undeserving Poor,* p. 7.

3. Fyodor Dostoyevsky, *The Brothers Karamazov* (1880; New York: Vintage Books, 1955), p. 344.

4. Children's Defense Fund, *The State of America's Children 1991* (Washington, 1991).

5. Toni Morrison, *The Bluest Eye* (New York: Washington Square Press/ Pocket Books, 1970), p. 9.

Chapter 1

1. Dostoyevsky, *The Brothers Karamazov,* p. 291.

2. Michel Foucault, in *Discipline and Punish: The Birth of the Prison* (New York: Vintage/Random House, 1979), discusses the intersection of power, knowledge, and the body in modern society. He identifies the body as a specific site through which the rituals of power take place, and this technology of the body he terms "biopower." See also Herbert L. Dreyfus and Paul Rabinow, Michel Foucault, *Beyond Structuralism and Hermeneutics,* 2d ed. (Chicago: University of Chicago Press, 1983).

3. Lloyd DeMause, "The Evolution of Childhood," in *The History of Childhood,* ed. Lloyd DeMause (New York: The Psychohistory Press, 1974), p. 1.

4. John Boswell, *The Kindness of Strangers* (New York: Pantheon, 1988); see, in particular, Boswell's discussion of "Continuities and Unintended Tragedy" in part 4, chapter 11. See also the proceedings of the International Colloquium on Abandoned Childhood and European Society held in 1987 in Rome, published in

1991 as *Enfance Abandonnée et Société en Europe XIV–XX Siècle* (Rome: Ecole Française de Rome).

5. Philippe Ariès, *Centuries of Childhood: A Social History of Family Life* (New York: Knopf, 1962). Ariès's thesis is disputed by many childhood and family historians; it is argued that both the Middle Ages and modern times have been far more differentiated and locally diverse. See, for example, Emmanuel LeRoy Ladurie, *Montaillou: Cathars and Catholics in a French Village, 1294–1324* (London: Scolar Press, 1978); Linda A. Pollock, *Forgotten Children: Parent-Child Relations from 1500 to 1900* (London: Cambridge University Press, 1983); and Philip Gavit, *Charity and Children in Renaissance Florence: The Ospedale degli Innocenti, 1410–1536* (Ann Arbor: University of Michigan Press, 1990).

6. J. H. Plumb, *In the Light of History* (London: Penguin Press, 1972); see, in particular, his essay "Children, the Victims of Time" in the same volume.

7. I am influenced by the work of Ton Beekman, a Dutch phenomenologist from the University of Utrecht, who has pointed out how the meanings of public and private space differed in the premodern world in terms of both social *and* interpersonal experience. (Personal communication.)

8. See the Dutch text on a social and cultural history of daily life by M. Boone, H. Gaus, and others, *Dagelijks Leven: Sociaal-culturele omstandigheden vroeger en nu.* (Deurne/Omnen, 1982).

9. Ariès, *Centuries of Childhood*, p. 395.

10. Robert Darnton, *The Great Cat Massacre* (New York: Vintage, 1984), p. 29.

11. Martine Segalen, *Historical Anthropology of the Family* (London: Cambridge University Press, 1986), part 1.

12. David Herlihy, *Medieval Households* (Cambridge, Mass: Harvard University Press, 1985).

13. Quoted in Herlihy, ibid., p. 27.

14. Quoted in Elizabeth Badinter, *The Myth of Motherhood: An Historical View of the Maternal Instinct* (London: Souvenir Press, 1981), p. 30. Originally published as *L'Amour en plus* (Paris: Flammarion, 1980).

15. Alice Miller, *For Your Own Good: Hidden Cruelty in Child-rearing and the Roots of Violence* (New York: Farrar, Straus & Giroux, 1984). Originally published as *Am Anfang war Erziehung* (Frankfurt am Main: Suhrkamp Verlag, 1980).

16. Foucault, *Discipline and Punish*, part 3.

17. Quoted in Miller, *For Your Own Good*, p. 13.

18. Quoted in John and Elizabeth Newson, "Cultural Aspects of Childrearing

in the English-speaking World," in *The Integration of a Child into a Social World,* ed. Martin Richards (London: Cambridge University Press, 1974), p. 56.

19. Ibid.

20. See Foucault, *Discipline and Punish.* Linda Pollock is one of the childhood historians who strongly disputes the brutality and violence thesis of childhood history and disputes the inferences that there was no appreciation of the special needs and vulnerabilities of children in past centuries, or that children were systematically mistreated by their parents or the state. Her evidence is drawn mainly from diary and autobiographical accounts, principally from the educated and the bourgeoisie. See Pollock, *Forgotten Children.* I am skeptical of her arguments and remain persuaded by the convincing historical and contemporary evidence of "concealment."

21. Dostoyevsky, *The Brothers Karamazov,* pp. 286–87.

22. DeMause, "The Evolution of Childhood."

23. These data, now widely quoted in the media, are drawn from a *Los Angeles Times* poll in 1985, quoted in John Crewdson, *By Silence Betrayed: Sexual Abuse of Children in America* (Boston: Little Brown, 1988), pp. 24–28.

24. Philip Greven, *Spare the Child: The Religious Roots of Punishment and the Psychological Impact of Physical Abuse* (New York: Alfred A. Knopf, 1991), p. 4.

25. Quoted in Robert E. Fathman, "Child Abuse in Our Schools," *Mothering,* Winter 1991, p. 94.

26. Dylan Thomas, "Fern Hill," in the *Collected Poems of Dylan Thomas 1934–1952* (New York: New Directions, 1957), p. 178.

27. M. Merleau-Ponty, *The Phenomenology of Perception* (London: Routledge and Kegan Paul, 1962), p. 407.

28. Friedrich Engels, *The Condition of the Working Class in England* (Oxford: Basil Blackwell, 1971), p. 235. Originally published in German in 1845.

29. Parliamentary Papers, "Reports of the Inspectors of Factories," quoted in Clark Nardinelli, *Child Labor and the Industrial Revolution* (Bloomington and Indianapolis: Indiana University Press, 1990), chap. 1.

30. Paul Mantoux, *The Industrial Revolution in the Eighteenth Century,* rev. ed. (London, Jonathan Cape, 1961), p. 411.

31. Ibid., pp. 410, 413.

32. See Philip Bean and Joy Melville, *Lost Children of the Empire: The Untold Story of Britain's Child Migrants* (London: Unwin Hyman, 1989).

33. Ibid., p. 29.

34. Ibid., chap. 4.

35. *Children and Youth in America: A Documentary History,* vol I; 1600–1865, ed. Robert H. Bremmer (Cambridge, MA: Harvard University Press, 1970), chap. 2 and pp. 148, 149.

36. Ibid., p. 154.

37. Alan Kulikoff, "The Beginnings of the Afro-American Family in Maryland," and Herbert Gutman, "Persistent Myths About the Afro-American Family," in *The American Family in Social-Historical Perspective,* 2d ed., ed. Michael Gordon (New York: St. Martin's Press, 1978).

38. The story, told by William Wells Brown, is reprinted in *Children and Youth in America,* p. 380.

39. Rachel Fuchs, *Abandoned Children* (Albany: State University of New York Press, 1984), p. 277.

40. Ibid., p. xiii.

41. Quoted in ibid., p. 35.

42. Ibid., pp. 17–19, 47.

43. Ibid., p. 23.

44. Bandinter, *The Myth of Motherhood,* pp. xix, 94.

45. Ibid., chap. 3 and p. 95.

46. Gavit's study of the Ospedale degli Innocenti in Renaissance Florence paints a far more benevolent view of the care of abandoned infants through an institutionalized charity structure in which, he argues, Florentine society placed children at the center of family life. Yet destitute women were still the ones who served as wetnurses. Many were sold as slaves or bound over for several years to the hospital, and many of their infants were accordingly fostered out to even more destitute mothers. What does differ significantly between the foundling hospitals of the fifteenth century, in particular the Ospedale degli Innocenti, and those of the eighteenth century is the markedly lower mortality rates during earlier times, which in part reflected lower proportions of abandoned children. See *Charity and Children in Renaissance Florence.*

47. See the discussion in Fuchs, *Abandoned Children,* pp. 276–81.

Chapter 2

1. Jean-François Lyotard, in *The Postmodern Condition: A Report on Knowledge* (Minneapolis: University of Minnesota Press, 1984), defines the postmodern perspective as an "incredulity toward metanarratives." A metanarrative refers to a grand overarching narrative—a transcending validity that is part of a "metadiscourse."

2. Steven Mintz and Susan Kellogg, *Domestic Revolutions: A Social History of American Family Life* (New York: The Free Press, 1988), p. xiv.

3. Peter Laslett, foreword to Michael Mitterauer and Reinhard Sieder, *The European Family* (Chicago: University of Chicago Press, 1982). Originally published as *Vom Patriarchat zur Partnerschaft: Zum Strukturwandel der Familie* (Munich: Oscar Beck, 1977), p. ix.

4. Mitterauer and Sieder, in *The European Family,* point out that the German *Familie,* based on the French *famille,* derives in turn from the Latin *familia.* The term refers to house/hearth, which incorporates the total number of household members, blood relatives, servants, slaves, and children that are all connected as a domestic community, where ties of kin play a secondary role to the household functions performed by the domestic unit.

5. See the summary review in Mintz and Kellogg, *Domestic Revolutions,* chap. 1.

6. John Demos, *A Little Commonwealth: Family Life in Plymouth Colony* (New York: Oxford University Press, 1970).

7. Mintz and Kellogg, *Domestic Revolutions,* pp. 11, 7, 12.

8. The Diary of Puritan preacher Cotton Mather, is cited in Demos, *Past, Present and Personal: The Family and the Life Course in American History* (New York: Oxford University Press, 1986); and Demos, *A Little Commonwealth.*

9. See Mintz and Kellogg, *Domestic Revolutions,* chap. 2, for an informative discussion of life in the Chesapeake Colonies (Maryland and Virginia). The authors describe how these colonies were devastated by epidemics, with consequent high mortality rates, and, owing to the indentured service of young men late marriages were common. During the seventeenth century, the rate of immigration to these colonies was seven times as high as to New England.

10. African-Americans began to serve as a critical labor pool and key capital in the plantation colonies. Almost all blacks in Maryland and Virginia before 1780 were slaves. While masters circumscribed the outer boundaries of formal families, Africans and their first-generation American children constructed domestic groups who shared eating and sleeping arrangements as families identified by blood and kinship. While young slave children were sometimes reared by their mothers, due to the masters' practice of selling women and "their issue" together, the two-parent family structure became a norm on large plantations, where slave families had a better likelihood of staying together. See Kulikoff, "The Beginnings of the Afro-American Family in Maryland," in M. Gordon, ed., *The American Family in Social-Historical Perspective.* Kulikoff, by reconstructing charts of slave household composition based on slave registers, probate inventories, and diaries, draws an illuminating picture of slave families' domestic lives. Both Gutman (see "Persistent Myths about the Afro-American Family," also in Gordon) and Kulikoff argue, in strong refutation of Frazier's matriarchy thesis, that despite the brutality of slavery and the forcible sales and relocations of family members, the nuclear-extended unit formed a distinctive family form and, under such conditions, dem-

onstrated a remarkable durability. African-American family life mirrored neither the Puritan colonies of new England nor the farm and plantation family structure emerging in the South, but recreated in new form the African kinship traditions. Also see Mintz and Kellogg, *Domestic Revolutions.*

11. See Mintz and Kellogg, *Domestic Revolutions,* chaps. 2 and 4, for an extremely useful account that speaks to further expansion of the monolithic image of family. While enormous differences in language and culture existed, all Native American tribes were organized on the basis of kinship. Family ties were based on marriage or bloodlines, but family forms differed from tribe to tribe, as did male/female roles—from a woman's right to initiate divorce, to premarital sexuality, to polygamy, to communal housing arrangements. Mothers from all tribes generally nursed their own babies for two years.

12. Demos, "Images of the Family, Then and Now" in *Past, Present, and Personal.*

13. Badinter, *The Myth of Motherhood,* p. 71.

14. Ibid., chap. 3, "Maternal Indifference."

15. Ibid., p. 189.

16. Jean-Jacques Rousseau, "The Education of Girls," in *Emile,* book 5, part 1, in *Emile, Julie, and Other Writings,* ed. R. L. Woodbury (New York: Barrons, 1964), p. 218.

17. Jacques Donzelot, *The Policing of Families* (New York: Pantheon, 1979), originally published as *La police des familles* (Paris: Les Editions de Minuit, 1977).

18. Badinter, *The Myth of Motherhood,* p. 181. In the following decades, mothers assumed an increasingly responsible role in rearing their children for the state. See, for example, Napoleon's Civil Code, mandating the submission of women to their husbands' authority in Article 212. Addressing the issue of women's education, Napoleon is reported to have asked Mme. Campan, newly appointed director of a school for girls in Ecouen: "'The old systems of education are worthless. What is there that prevents young people in France from being well brought up?' 'Mothers,' answered Mme. Campan. 'Well then,' he said, 'there you have it. A whole educational system. You must, Madame, make mothers capable of raising their children.'" Badinter, *The Myth of Motherhood,* p. 213.

19. Donzelot, *The Policing of Families,* p. 16. Donzelot would presumably ascribe the same philanthropy of regulation to the Ospedale degli Innocenti during the Renaissance. See Gavit, *Charity and Children in Renaissance Florence.*

20. Quoted in Donzelot, *The Policing of Families,* p. 32.

21. Linda Gordon, *Heroes of Their Own Lives: The Politics and History of Family Violence* (New York: Penguin Books, 1988).

22. I have borrowed this term from Badinter, *The Myth of Motherhood.*

23. Catharine E. Beecher, *A Treatise on Domestic Economy for the Use of Young Ladies at Home and at School,* rev. ed. (Boston: Thomas H. Webb & Co., 1842), pp. 25–26, 38. See also Catharine Beecher and Harriet B. Stowe, *The American Woman's Home, or Principles of Domestic Science* (New York: J. B. Ford and Co., 1869).

24. Barbara Welter, "The Cult of True Womanhood, 1820–1826," in M. Gordon, ed., *The American Family in Social Historical Perspective,* p. 313.

25. Dr. William Acton, in the widely read *Functions and Disorders of the Reproductive Organs* (1857), quoted in Carl N. Degler, "What Ought to Be and What Was: Women's Sexuality in the Nineteenth Century," in M. Gordon, ed., *The American Family in Social Historical Perspective,* p. 411.

26. J. H. Pestalozzi, *Leonard and Gertrude,* translated and abridged by Eva Channing (Boston: D. C. Heath and Co., 1906).

27. Friedrich Froebel, *The Education of Man* (New York: D. Appleton and Company, 1900), p. 64.

28. Beecher urged productive female labor for all classes of women and extolled the vocation of teaching, where working-class women would leave the factories and go out west as missionary teachers. Upper-class women would contribute to the proper education of all children, while the well-to-do would act in a supervisory role; thereby all would elevate the teaching profession into a "true and noble" one, making it the special profession of women. For a full discussion of Catharine Beecher's educational philosophy and mission, see the biography by Kathryn Kish Sklar, *Catharine Beecher: A Study in American Domesticity* (New Haven: Yale University Press, 1973).

29. Mary Ellen West, *Childhood: Its Care and Culture* (Chicago: Women's Temperance Publishing Association, 1892), pp. 73–75.

30. Jules Michelet, *La Femme* (1859), quoted in Badinter, *The Myth of Motherhood,* p. 215.

31. See Linda Gordon's discussion of Child Protection Agencies in *Heroes of their Own Lives,* chap. 1.

32. Ibid., p. 84.

33. Isabel Simarel, quoted in Ruby Takanishi, "Childhood as a Social Issue: Historical Roots of Contemporary Child Advocacy Movements," *Journal of Social Issues* 34, no. 2 (1978): p. 12.

34. See Takanishi, ibid., for a further discussion of the child advocacy movements.

35. However, there were notable exceptions among progressive urban reformers, who displayed a different set of sensibilities. During the first decade of this century, reform projects dealing with the redesign of urban living for poor and immigrant families received impetus from reformers such as Ellen Swallow Rich-

ards, who taught sanitary chemistry at the Massachusetts Institute of Technology, and Jane Addams, a reformer who founded Hull House in Chicago. Both pioneered settlement work to deal with the vast problems of the urban slums. By uniting the new techniques of domestic and social science, with pragmatic services for poor women and their children, these reformers addressed sanitary improvements of tenement conditions, cooperative living arrangements, public kitchens, and child care, all of which were vital to poor women's lives.

36. Charlotte Perkins Gilman, "The Passing of Matrimony," *Harper's Bazaar* 40 (June 1906), p. 496.

37. The material for this discussion is drawn from Dolores Hayden, *The Grand Domestic Revolution: A History of Feminist Designs for American Homes, Neighborhoods, and Cities* (Cambridge, MA: MIT Press, 1981).

38. Melusina Fay Peirce, quoted in Hayden, *The Grand Domestic Revolution,* p. 67. Indeed Peirce, while arguing for cooperative housing and payment for housework, also advocated a female suffrage. As she envisioned it, women would take political control of their own affairs, for, as she argued in 1880, "no despotism of man over man that was ever recorded was at once so absolute as the despotism—the dominion of men over women." Ibid. p. 84.

39. Marie Howland, quoted in Hayden, *The Grand Domestic Revolution,* p. 105. During this period many utopian ideals were experimented with by progressive urban planners who began to design collective urban residential spaces in several cities. "Kitchenless houses" with socialized domestic work and collectivized child care were incorporated into apartment blocks designed for the middle classes, and into model housing for the poor.

40. Gilman, *Women and Economics: A Study of the Economic Relations between Men and Women as a Factor in Social Evolution* (1898; New York: Harper Torchbooks, 1966). In her fiction, Perkins Gilman celebrated cooperative domestic work, and in the utopian novel *Herland* (1915; New York Pantheon Books, 1979), she depicted economically independent autonomous women in a society without men.

41. Catharine Beecher, *Treatise on Domestic Economy,* p. 26.

42. John and Elizabeth Newson, "Cultural Aspects of Children in the English Speaking World," in *Integration of a Child into a Social World,* ed. Richards.

43. Freud describes the "peculiar painfulness" which appears to characterize separation from a love object, and focuses on "the one situation which we believe we understand—the situation of the infant when he is presented with a stranger instead of his mother. He will exhibit the anxiety which we have attributed to the danger of loss of object." Sigmund Freud, *Inhibitions, Symptoms and Anxiety,* International Psycho-Analytical Library no. 28, ed. Ernest Jones (London: Hogarth Press, 1936), pp. 166–67.

44. See René A. Spitz, "Hospitalism: An Inquiry into the Genesis of Psychiatric Conditions in Early Childhood" (1945), reprinted in *Influences on Human Development*, ed. Urie Bronfenbrenner and Maureen A. Mahoney (Hinsdale, IL: Dryden Press, 1975); Anna Freud, *Infants without Families, and Reports on the Hampstead Nurseries 1939–1945*, International Psycho-Analytical Library no. 96, ed. M. Masud R. Khan (London: Hogarth Press, 1974); John Bowlby, *Attachment and Loss*, vol. 1 (London: Hogarth Press, 1969), and *Maternal Care and Mental Health* (Geneva: World Health Organization, 1952).

45. Jeffrey Moussaieff Masson, *The Assault on Truth* (New York: Farrar, Straus & Giroux, 1984). Masson created a stir in the psychoanalytic establishment when as director of the Freud archives he brought to light the controversial Freud-Fliess letters, which document Freud's reversal of a key theory—the seduction theory that Freud developed in 1895. This theory proposed that the root cause of hysteria was sexual abuse in infancy and early childhood. Masson, however, claimed that Freud dropped this explosive theory because of threats of isolation and peer rejection, formulating instead the cornerstone of psychoanalytic theory—infantile sexuality and the Oedipal complex. It was thus fantasy, not abuse, that characterized a child's earliest experiences.

46. See Crewdson, *By Silence Betrayed*, pp. 28–30. The Bagley survey in Canada reported that 22 percent of female respondents and 9 percent of male respondents had been molested under the age of eighteen. See *Who Speaks for the Children*, ed. Jack C. Westman (Sarasota, FL: Professional Resources Exchange, Inc.), pp. 223–25.

47. Larry Wolff, *Postcards from the End of the World* (New York: Atheneum, 1988), p. 4.

48. Helene Deutsch, *The Psychology of Women*, vol. 2: *Motherhood* (New York: Grune & Stratton, 1944), pp. 1, 19.

49. Deutsch explains: "Usually such a woman has spent her affectivity on other values (eroticism, art, or masculine aspirations) or this affectivity was too poor or ambivalent originally and cannot stand a new emotional burden . . . [and she] feels restricted and impoverished." Ibid., p. 55.

50. Catharine Beecher, *Treatise on Domestic Economy*.

51. Erik H. Erikson, *Childhood and Society* (New York: W. W. Norton & Company, 1950, 2d ed., 1963).

52. Bowlby, *Maternal Care and Mental Health*, p. 67.

53. Ibid. Such claims assume particular irony when we consider the alarming statistics on child physical and sexual abuse cited earlier, which document that the majority of such cases occur within families.

54. M. Ainsworth and S. Bell, "Attachment, Exploration and Separation: Il-

lustrated by the Behavior of One-year-olds in a Strange Situation," *Child Development* 41 (1970): 467–70.

55. Nancy Chodorow, *The Reproduction of Mothering* (Berkeley: University of California Press, 1978), p. 7.

56. Alice Kessler-Harris, *Out to Work: A History of Wage-earning Women in the United States* (New York: Oxford University Press, 1982).

57. Sylvia Hewlett, *A Lesser Life: The Myth of Women's Liberation in America* (New York: Warner, 1987).

58. See Miller, *For Your Own Good,* for a decoding of our myths about child-rearing in families. Miller argues that a "poisonous pedagogy" vengefully reflects our own childhoods of abuse and violence.

59. L. Gordon, *Heroes of Their Own Lives.*

60. Linda Gordon, "Family Violence, Feminism, and Social Control," in *Women, the State, and Welfare,* ed. Linda Gordon (Madison: University of Wisconsin Press, 1990) discusses one of the complex ironies of family violence: that while women and children historically have been victims of male violence, children too have been victims of female violence. It was the early feminist movements in the 1870s that were most influential in working for the prevention of cruelty to children. They originally focused on child abuse, but through those interventions were drawn into other forms of violence, such as wife beating. Child abuse as an issue was discovered in the late eighteen hundreds, but went into a period of quiescence after the Progressive era until its rediscovery in 1962 with the publication of Helfer and Kempe's landmark *The Battered Child,* 4th ed., rev. and exp. (Chicago: University of Chicago Press, 1987). In the 1970s and 1980s feminist contributions to scholarship about childrens' rights have been negligible. Linda Gordon writes: "This silence is the more striking in contrast to the legacy of the first wave of feminism, particularly in the period 1880 to 1930, in which the women's rights movement was tightly connected to child welfare reform campaigns. By contrast, the second wave of feminism, a movement heavily influenced by younger and childless women, has spent relatively little energy on children's issues" (p. 183). It is as if, she remarks, we fear the loss of a deserving-victim status to women if we begin to confront the issue of women as aggressors; and it is clear that "these complexities are at their greatest in the situation of mothers because they are simultaneously victims and victimizers, dependent and depended on, weak and powerful. "Family Violence, Feminism, and Social Control," p. 182.

61. See L. Gordon, *Heroes of Their Own Lives,* Donzelot, *The Policing of Families,* and W. Norton Grubb and Marvin Lazerson, *Broken Promises,* 2d ed. (Chicago: University of Chicago Press, 1988), for a further discussion of the role of state intervention in families.

Chapter 3

1. See Katz, *The Undeserving Poor.* In formulating my discussion of poverty discourse, I have benefited from Katz's discussion in both the Introduction and Epilogue.

2. Michel Foucault, "Practices and Discourses in Foucault's Early Writings," in Hubert L. Dreyfus and Paul Rabinow, *Michel Foucault: Beyond Structuralism and Hermeneutics,* 2d ed. (Chicago: University of Chicago Press, 1983).

3. Katz, *The Undeserving Poor,* p. 7.

4. Nancy Fraser, "Struggle over Needs: Outline of a Socialist-Feminist Critical Theory of Late-Capitalist Political Culture," in L. Gordon, ed., *Women, the State, and Welfare.*

5. Orshansky, quoted in Katz, *The Undeserving Poor,* p. 116. For further discussion of the poverty line see also Grubb and Lazerson, *Broken Promises;* and Mary Jo Bane and Daniel T. Ellwood, "One-fifth of the Nation's Children: Why Are They Poor?" *Science,* September 8, 1989.

6. Katz, *The Undeserving Poor,* p. 117.

7. See Children's Defense Fund, *The State of America's Children, 1991,* pp. 22, 151.

8. Grubb and Lazerson, *Broken Promises,* p. 187.

9. The Reverend Charles Burroughs, addressing the chapel of the New Alms-House in Portsmouth, 1834. Quoted in Katz, *The Undeserving Poor,* p. 13.

10. Walter Channing, "An Address on the Prevention of Pauperism," quoted in Katz, ibid., p. 14.

11. George F. Will, a Washington columnist, writing on "A Moral Environment for the Poor," *The Washington Post,* May 30, 1991.

12. Grubb and Lazerson, *Broken Promises,* p. 197.

13. *Parens patriae,* an English legal doctrine, gave the state parental powers to intervene on the behalf of children in families judged defective by the state. See chapter 2 of *Broken Promises* for a discussion of the term.

14. *Broken Promises,* p. 44.

15. John R. Berrueta-Clement, Lawrence J. Schweinhart, W. Steven Barnett, Ann S. Epstein, and David P. Weikart, *Changed Lives* (Ypsilanti, MI: High Scope Press, 1984).

16. Grubb and Lazerson, *Broken Promises,* p. 56.

17. See William Ryan, *Blaming the Victim* (New York: Vintage, 1976).

18. Helen Campbell profiles the experiences of poor working women in the garment industry in New York in *Prisoners of Poverty,* originally a series of papers

for the Sunday edition of the *New York Tribune.* The case of Rose Haggerty forms chapter 2 of the book *Prisoners of Poverty: Women Wage-Workers, Their Trades and Their Lives, 1887* (New York: Garrett Press, 1970).

19. Marina Warner, *Into the Dangerous World* (London: Chatto & Windus, 1989), p. 53.

20. Hawthorne, *The Scarlet Letter,* p. 67.

21. Ibid., p. 89.

22. L. Gordon, *Heroes of Their Own Lives,* p. 83.

23. Ibid., p. 84.

24. Ibid., pp. 86, 15.

25. Virginia Shapiro, "The Gender Basis of American Social Policy," in *Women, the State, and Welfare,* ed. L. Gordon. The quoted passage is from p. 51.

26. See L. Gordon's discussion in "The New Feminist Scholarship on the Welfare State," in L. Gordon (ed.), *Women, the State, and Welfare.*

27. For a detailed discussion and interesting comparative analysis see Jane Jensen, "Representations of Gender: Policies to 'protect' Women Workers and Infants in France and the United States," in L. Gordon (ed.), *Women, the State, and Welfare.*

28. Ibid., p. 157.

29. Ibid., p. 171.

30. Grubb and Lazerson, *Broken Promises,* pp. 20–21.

31. See Barbara Nelson, "The Origins of the Two-Channel Welfare State: Workmen's Compensation and Mothers' Aid," in L. Gordon (ed.), *Women, the State, and Welfare,* p. 132.

32. For an informative discussion of mothers' pensions see Irwin Garfinkel and Sara S. McLanahan, *Single Mothers and Their Children* (Washington, D.C.: Urban Institute Press, 1986), chap. 4.

33. See L. Gordon, *Heroes of Their Own Lives,* chap. 4.

34. Garfinkel and McLanahan, *Single Mothers and Their Children,* chap. 4.

35. The material for this discussion is drawn from Nelson, "The Origins of the Two-Channel Welfare State."

36. Ibid., p. 124.

37. Quoted in Garfinkel and McLanahan, pp. 101–2.

38. Ibid., p. 102.

39. Ibid., pp. 110–11.

40. Teresa L. Amott, "Black Women and AFDC: Making Entitlement out of Necessity," in L. Gordon (ed.), *Women, the State, and Welfare.*

41. Grubb and Lazerson, *Broken Promises,* chap. 7; and Shapiro, "The Gender Basis of American Social Policy," in L. Gordon (ed.), *Women, the State, and Welfare.*

42. Carol Stack, *All Our Kin: Strategies for Survival in a Black Community* (New York: Harper & Row, 1974), p. 108.

43. See Frances Fox Piven and Richard A. Cloward, *Regulating the Poor: The Functions of Public Welfare* (New York: Pantheon, 1971), p. xvii.

44. Quoted in Amott, "Black Women and AFDC," p. 289.

45. Ibid., pp. 289–90.

46. Deborah K. Zinn and Rosemary C. Sarri, "Turning Back the Clock on Public Welfare," in *Women and Poverty,* edited by Barbara C. Gelphi and others (Chicago: University of Chicago Press, 1983), pp. 25–40.

47. Walter Channing, quoted in Katz, *The Undeserving Poor,* p. 14. Former President Reagan, quoted in Amott, "Black Women and AFDC," p. 290.

48. Diana Pearce, "Welfare Is Not *for* Women: Why the War on Poverty Cannot Conquer the Feminization of Poverty," in L. Gordon (ed.), *Women, the State, and Welfare.* See also Pearce, "The Feminization of Poverty," *Urban and Social Change Review* 11, no. 1 (February 1978), pp. 28–36.

49. CDF, *The State of America's Children 1991,* pp. 24–25, 27. For the most recent update on child poverty, see *CDF Reports* (13) 2, November 1991, which documents a further increase over the preceding year's 19.6 percent.

50. Ibid., pp. 21–35, esp. 26–27.

51. For further discussion of the Family Support Act see Children's Defense Fund, *The State of America's Children, 1991;* Amott, "Black Women and AFDC"; and L. Gordon, "The New Feminist Scholarship on the Welfare State."

52. L. Gordon, ibid., p. 28.

53. Pearce, "Welfare is not *for* Women."

54. Ibid.

55. The U.S. Bureau of the Census, Current Population Reports Series P-60, No. 168, *Money Income and Poverty Status in the United States 1989* (Advance Data from the March 1990 Current Population Survey) U.S. Government Printing Office, Washington, D.C.: 1990.

56. The material for this discussion is drawn from Pearce, "Welfare Is Not *for* Women," pp. 270–73.

57. Ibid., p. 271.

Chapter 4

1. Children's Defense Fund, *The State of America's Children 1991*, pp. 97–98.

2. Ibid., p. 93.

3. Lisebeth B. Schorr, *Within Our Reach: Breaking the Cycle of Disadvantage* (New York: Anchor Press/Doubleday, 1988).

Chapter 5

1. Morrison, *The Bluest Eye*, p. 18.

2. Public Act 357 of 1990 reduced AFDC Benefits in Michigan by 17 percent, effective May 1, 1991. But some AFDC grants were partially restored after budget negotiations between Governor Engler and the Legislature, reducing the cuts to 8.7 percent, effective July 1, 1991. See Joan M. Abbey, Analisa Vestevich, and Ira M. Schwartz, "Michigan's Children Went Missing," a Prepublication Report, University of Michigan Center for the Study of Youth Policy, August 1991. Effective November 1, 1991 the cuts were restored to the previous 1988 levels (personal communication with Margaret Anzinger, Public Affairs Director, Department of Social Services, Wayne County, Michigan).

3. Morrison, *The Bluest Eye*, p. 18.

4. Jonathon Kozol, "The Homeless and their Children, Part II," *The New Yorker*, February 1, 1988, pp. 50–51.

5. See Charles Murray, "Helping the Poor: A Few Modest Proposals," *Commentary*, May 1985, p. 31.

6. Charles Murray, *Losing Ground* (New York: Basic Books, 1984), p. 117.

7. Children's Defense Fund, *The State of America's Children 1991*. See particularly "Housing and Homelessness," pp. 107–19.

8. *Housing and Homelessness: A Teaching Guide* (Washington, D.C.: Housing NOW Publication, 1989), p. 17.

9. William Apgar, cited in *Housing and Homelessness*, p. 17.

Chapter 6

1. Cited in Schorr, *Within Our Reach*, p. 196.

2. Ibid.

3. Grubb and Lazerson, *Broken Promises*, pp. 55–56.

4. Cited in Margaret O'Brien Steinfels, *Who's Minding the Children? The History and Politics of Daycare in America* (New York: Simon and Schuster, 1973), p. 38.

5. See the classic educational study of the self-fulfilling prophecy, conducted by Robert Rosenthal and Lenore Jacobson, in *Pygmalion in the Classroom: Teacher Expectations and Pupils' Intellectual Development* (New York: Holt Rinehart and Winston, 1968).

6. Schorr, *Within Our Reach,* p. 195.

7. Cited in Steinfels, *Who's Minding the Children?* p. 45.

8. Ibid., p. 61.

9. Edward Zigler, "Using Research to Inform Policy: The Case of Early Intervention," in Sharon Lynn Kagan, ed., *The Care and Education of America's Young Children: Obstacles and Opportunities,* Ninetieth Yearbook of the National Society for the Study of Education, part 1 (Chicago: University of Chicago Press, 1991), pp. 154–72. Urie Bronfenbrenner used the term ecological in relation to child development and a focus on the whole child within his/her family, community and cultural milieu.

10. Polly Greenberg, "Before the Beginning: A Participant's View," *Young Children,* September 1990.

11. "NAEYC Position Statement on Standardized Testing of Young Children 3 Through 8 Years of Age," *Young Children,* March 1988; see also "Guidelines for Appropriate Curriculum Content and Assessment in Programs Serving Children Ages 3 Through 8," *Young Children,* March 1991 (NAEYC Reprint no. 725).

12. Herbert Ginsburg, *The Myth of the Deprived Child* (Englewood Cliffs, NJ: Prentice-Hall, 1972), pp. 20–21.

13. A survey of the conventional psychometric research on early childhood intervention programs yields positive results when the programs are viewed from a measurable-outcomes perspective. A 1985 review of over two hundred Head Start evaluations indicated that the intervention programs had immediate positive effects on children's cognitive development as measured by IQ gains, but these advantages apparently disappeared after about two years. When these same programs were evaluated from a broader perspective, however, other gains emerged such as improved motivation, greater self-esteem, better health, and parent involvement. See Zigler, "Using Research to Inform Policy."

14. Piaget distinguishes between figurative/static and operative/transformative knowledge. "Figurative" generally refers to recall of the static *given* aspects of reality; "operative/transformative" refers to the active constructing and transforming of reality into a developing structure of knowledge. See Jean Piaget, *The Construction of Reality in The Child* (New York: Basic Books, 1954); *The Grasp of Consciousness: Action and Concept in the Young Child* (Cambridge, MA: Harvard University Press, 1976); and, with B. Inhelder, *Memory and Intelligence* (London: Routledge & Kegan Paul, 1971). Piaget's pedagogical philosophy is best summed up by his statement, "The goal in education is not to increase the amount of

knowledge, but to create the possibilities for a child to invent and discover . . . Learning will be deformed, as is all learning that is not the result of the subject's own activity." Quoted by Eleanor Duckworth in "Piaget Rediscovered: A Report of the Conference on Cognitive Studies and Curriculum Development," in *Piaget Rediscovered,* ed. R. E. Ripple and V. N. Rockcastle (Ithaca, NY: Cornell University Press, 1964).

15. See *Recommendations for a Head Start Program,* chair Dr. Robert Cooke, John Hopkins University (Washington, DC: U.S. Dept. of Health, Education and Welfare, Office of Child Development, 1972).

16. Shirley Brice Heath, *Ways with Words* (Cambridge, UK: Cambridge University Press, 1983).

17. Barbara Bowman, "Educating Language Minority Children: Challenges and Opportunities," in Kagan, ed., *The Care and Education of America's Young Children.*

18. See Ginsburg, *The Myth of the Deprived Child,* chap. 4, for a full discussion of the Klaus and Gray Early Childhood Training Project. See also R. Klaus and S. Gray, "The Early Training Project for Disadvantaged Children: A Report after Five Years," *Monographs for the Society for Research in Child Development,* 1968.

19. Ginsburg, *The Myth of the Deprived Child,* p. 99.

20. Beth Blue Swadener proposes viewing all children as "at promise" in her article, "Children and Families 'At-Risk': Etiology, Critique and Alternative Paradigms," *Educational Foundations,* Fall 1990.

21. For a description of the methods used to gather the observational material in the classrooms, readers are referred to the Appendix.

22. Millie C. Almy and Celia Genishi, *Ways of Studying Children: An Observation Manual for Early Childhood Teachers,* rev. ed. (New York: Teacher's College Press, 1979), p. 74.

23. The erosion of play and the bureaucratization of experience is documented in Valerie Polakow, *The Erosion of Childhood* (Chicago: University of Chicago Press, 1982; new ed., 1992).

24. For a description of the High/Scope Curriculum, see M. Hohman, B. Banet, and D. Weikart, *Young Children in Action: A Manual for Preschool Educators* (Ypsilanti, MI: High/Scope Press, 1979); and David P. Weikart, "Quality in Early Childhood Education," in *A Resource Guide to Public School Early Childhood Programs,* ed. Cynthia Warger (Alexandria, VA: Association for Supervision and Curriculum Development, 1988).

25. Joan Lombardi's article "Head Start: The Nation's Pride, a Nation's Challenge" summarizes the recommendations of the Silver Ribbon Panel, sponsored

by the National Head Start Association. In *Young Children,* September 1990: 23–24.

26. Ibid., p. 29.

27. See Children's Defense Fund, *The State of America's Children 1991,* p. 44.

28. See *Beyond Rhetoric: A New American Agenda for Children and Families: Final Report of the National Commission on Children* (Washington, D.C., 1991), pp. 190–93.

29. The purpose of Chapter I is to provide special educational services for educationally disadvantaged children, in areas of high concentrations of low-income families and local institutions for neglected or delinquent children, so that they achieve at a level appropriate for their age. Chapter 1 has four specific goals for these children: success in the regular instructional program, attainment of grade-level proficiency, improvement in basic skills, and improvement in more advanced skills. Chapter 1 also provides assistance to educationally disadvantaged native American students. Annual federal appropriations are allocated among the states based on a formula that includes the state's per-pupil expenditures for education and the incidence of children from low-income families.

services subject to withdraw al annually

30. The Perry preschool project, generally considered the most successful preschool intervention program, demonstrated in a longitudinal study that at the age of nineteen there were significant differences between program participants and control-group children: fewer were classified as mentally retarded (15% vs. 35%), more graduated from high school (67% vs. 49%), more attended college or received training (38% vs. 21%), more held jobs (50% vs. 32%), their arrest rate was lower (31% vs. 51%), and fewer were on public assistance (18% vs. 32%)— leading researchers to claim that, over a lifetime, such a program yielded a 1–7 rate of return. See John Berrueta-Clement, Lawrence J. Schweinhart, and others, *Changed Lives* (Ypsilanti, MI: High/Scope Press, 1984); and Weikart, "Quality in Early Childhood Education." For a discussion of the Cornell Consortium Data, see Richard Darlington and others, "Preschool Programs and Later Competence of Children from Low-Income Families," *Science* 208 (April 1980): 202–4; for a discussion of the Department of Health and Human Services Studies, see Carol E. Copple and others, *Path to the Future: Long Term Effects of Head Start in the Philadelphia School District* (Washington, DC: U.S. Dept. of Health and Human Services, 1987).

31. See Sue Bredekamp, ed., *Developmentally Appropriate Practice in Early Childhood Programs Serving Children from Birth through Age 8,* expanded edition (Washington, DC: National Association for the Education of Young Children, 1991); and Louise Derman-Sparks, *Anti-Bias Curriculum: Tools For Empowering Young Children* (Washington, D.C.: National Association for the Education of Young Children, 1989).

32. See Children's Defense Fund, *The State of America's Children 1991*, p. 37.

33. Sharon Lynn Kagan, "Excellence in Early Childhood Education: Defining Characteristics and Next-Decade Strategies," in Kagan, ed., *The Care and Education of America's Young Children*, p. 245.

Chapter 7

1. Tyrone and the other children portrayed in this chapter were all identified as "at-risk." They were selected because they were singled out for special treatment in their classrooms.

2. See Samuel Meisels, "High Stakes Testing," *Educational Leadership,* April 1989; Lorrie Shepard and M. L. Smith, "Escalating Academic Demand in Kindergarten: Some Non-solutions," *Elementary School Journal* 89 (2); Sue Bredekamp and Lorrie Shepard, "How Best to Protect Children from Inappropriate School Expectations, Practices, and Policies," *Young Children,* March 1989; and "NAEYC Position Statement on Standardized Testing," *Young Children,* March, 1988.

3. The McKinney Homeless Assistance Act of 1987 encompassed twenty separate programs, including educational protection for homeless children. In 1990, Congress amended the McKinney Act's Education for Homeless Children and Youth Program, removing not only residency barriers but also regulations regarding guardianship, transportation, immunization, and school records; and state funds were authorized for remedial education and transportation. See Children's Defense Fund, *The State of America's Children 1991*, pp. 114–15. In practice, however, these barriers remain in place in many of the school districts in which homeless children attend school. It is currently estimated that one in four homeless children nationwide is not attending school.

4. Grubb and Lazerson, *Broken Promises*, p. 207.

5. Albert Camus, *The Plague* (New York: Vintage, 1972), p. 110. Originally published as *La Peste* (Paris: Librairie Gallimard, 1947).

Chapter 8

1. Jeannie Oakes, *Keeping Track* (New Haven: Yale University Press, 1985), p. xiv.

2. Kenneth Clark, foreword, in R. C. Smith and Carol A. Lincoln, *America's Shame, America's Hope: Twelve Million Youth at Risk* (Charles Stewart Mott Foundation, 1988), p. iv.

3. Michael S. Knapp and Brenda Turnbull, eds., *Better Schooling for the Children of Poverty: Alternatives to Conventional Wisdom,* vol. 1 (Washington,

DC: U.S. Dept. of Education, Office of Planning, Budget & Evaluation, 1990), p. 1.

4. Richard L. Allington, "Effective Literacy Instruction for At-Risk Children," in Knapp and Turnbull, eds., *Better Schooling for the Children of Poverty*, pp. I–3 to I–19.

5. Ibid., p. I–3.

6. Jere Brophy and Thomas L. Good, "Teacher Behavior and Student Achievement," in *Handbook of Research on Teaching*, ed. M. C. Wittrock (New York: Macmillan, 1986), p. 365.

7. Chester Finn, quoted in Michelle Fine, "Of Kitsch and Caring: The Illusion of Students at Risk," *The School Administrator* September, 1988: 18.

8. John J. Goodlad, *A Place Called School* (New York: McGraw-Hill Book Company, 1984), p. 229.

9. Key figures in compensatory education research on young children were: R. Klaus and S. Gray, "The Early Training Project for Disadvantaged Children"; and C. Bereiter and S. Engelman, *Teaching Disadvantaged Children in the Preschool* (Englewood Cliffs, NJ: Prentice-Hall, 1966). Bereiter and Engelman are best known for their controversial DISTAR Program. (A programmed direct teaching instructional approach).

10. See the discussion by Luis Moll in "Social and Instructional Issues in Educating Disadvantaged Students," in Knapp and Turnbull, eds., *Better Schooling for the Children of Poverty*.

11. Jean Anyon, "Elementary Schooling and Distinctions of Social Class," *Interchange* 12, 1981.

12. Oakes, *Keeping Track*, pp. 86–89.

13. Jack Frymier and Bruce Gardner, "The Phi Delta Kappa Study of Students at Risk," *Phi Delta Kappan*, October 1989: 142.

14. Elizabeth Blue Swadener, "Children and Families 'At-Risk': Etiology, Critique and Alternative Paradigms," *Educational Foundations*, Fall 1990: 18.

15. Quoted in Larry Cuban, "The 'At-Risk' Label and the Problem of Urban School Reform," *Phi Delta Kappan*, June 1989: 780.

16. Ibid., pp. 781–82.

17. William Labov and others, "A Study of the Non-Standard English of Negro and Puerto Rican Speakers in New York City Final Report, Cooperative Research Project No. 3288, mimeographed, U.S. Office of Education, 2 vols. (New York: Columbia University, 1968).

18. Ginsburg, *The Myth of the Deprived Child*, p. 16.

19. *Child Care in the Public Schools: Incubator for Inequality: A Report* (Washington, DC: National Black Child Development Institute), 1985.

20. Published in *Revised Administrative Rules for Special Education*, (Lansing, MI: Michigan State Board of Education, Special Education Services, January 1991), p. 8.

21. Swadener, "Children and Families At-Risk," p. 22.

22. Susan Bailey, director of the Resource Center on Educational Equity, Council of Chief State School Offices, quoted in "Child Care in the Public Schools: Incubator for Inequality," p. 22.

23. Lewis Carroll, *The Annotated Alice: Alice's Adventures in Wonderland and Through the Looking Glass* (New York: Bramhall House, 1960), p. 269.

24. See Paulo Freire, *Pedagogy of the Oppressed* (New York: Seabury Press, 1970); and Roland S. Barth, "On Sheep and Goats and School Reform," *Phi Delta Kappan*, December 1986.

25. Albert Camus, *The Plague*, pp. 3–4.

26. Jean Piaget, quoted by Eleanor Duckworth in "Piaget Rediscovered," in *Piaget Rediscovered*, ed. Richard E. Ripple and Verne N. Rockcastle (a Report of the Conference on Cognitive Studies and Cornell University, Curriculum Development, 1964), p. 3.

27. Michel Foucault, *Discipline and Punish: The Birth of the Prison.* (New York: Vintage, 1979), pp. 135–169.

28. Herman Melville, *Moby Dick* (1851; Berkeley: University of California Press, 1981), p. 216.

29. Dostoyevsky, *The Brothers Karamazov*, p. 273.

30. Maxine Greene, "Wide-Awakeness and the Moral Life," in *Landscapes of Learning* (New York: Teacher's College Press, 1978).

31. Maxine Greene, *The Dialectic of Freedom* (New York: Teacher's College Press, 1988), p. 3.

32. Ludwig Wittgenstein, *Philosophical Investigations 1953*, trans. G. E. M. Anscombe (New York: Macmillan, 1968).

33. Urie Bronfenbrenner, "Reality and Research in the Ecology of Human Development," *Proceedings of the American Philosophical Society* 119 (1973): 439–69.

34. John Dewey, "My Pedagogic Creed," in *John Dewey on Education: Selected Writings*, ed. Reginald D. Archambault (Chicago: University of Chicago Press, 1964), p. 431.

35. Abraham Maslow, *Toward a Psychology of Being*, 2d. ed. (New York: Von Nostrand, 1968).

36. Greene, *The Dialectic of Freedom*, p. 5.

37. Sylvia Ashton-Warner, *Teacher* (New York: Simon and Schuster/Bantam, 1963), p. 30.

38. Herbert Kohl, *Thirty-six Children* (New York: New American Library, 1967).

39. Patricia Carini. *The Art of Seeing and the Visibility of the Person* (Grand Forks, ND: University of North Dakota Press, 1979).

40. Patricia Carini. *The School Lives of Seven Children: A Five Year Study* (Grand Forks, ND: University of North Dakota Press, 1982).

41. Patricia Carini, "Building from Children's Strengths," in *The Landscape of Childhood and the Politics of Care,* ed. Valerie Polakow, *Journal of Education* 168 (3), (1986): 17.

42. Shirley Brice Heath, *Ways with Words* (New York: Cambridge University Press, 1983).

43. Sara Lawrence Lightfoot, *Worlds Apart* (New York: Basic Books, 1978), p. 5.

44. Derman-Sparks, *Anti-Bias Curriculum.*

45. James Banks and others, *Curriculum Guidelines for Multi-Ethnic Education* (Washington, DC: National Council for the Social Studies, 1976).

46. Asa Hilliard, *NEA Today,* January 1989: 68.

47. Hilliard, "Equity Access and Segregation," in Kagan, ed., *The Care and Education of America's Young Children,* p. 208.

48. See the Carnegie Foundation data cited in Jacqueline Jordan Irvine's *Black Students and School Failure: Policies, Practices, and Prescriptions* (New York: Greenwood Press, 1990), p. 16.

49. The suspension rate for Hispanic students is also far higher than for whites—100 per 1,000 students in Michigan. See the report by Charles B. Vergon, *Disciplinary Actions in Michigan Public Schools: Nature, Prevalence, and Impact, 1978–1986* (Ann Arbor, MI: University of Michigan School of Education, 1990).

50. For further discussion of multicultural perspectives, see Barbara Bowman, "Educating Language Minority Children: Challenges and Opportunities," in Kagan, ed., *The Care and Education of America's Young Children;* Janice Hale-Benson, *Black Children, Their Roots, Culture, and Learning Styles,* rev. ed., (Baltimore, MD: The John Hopkins University Press, 1982); and Lisa Delpit, "The Silenced Dialogue: Power and Pedagogy in Educating Other People's Children," *Harvard Educational Review* 58 (3) (1988).

51. James A. Banks, "Citizenship Education for a Pluralistic Democratic Society," *Social Studies,* September/October 1990: 211.

52. Foucault, *Discipline and Punish,* p. 136.

53. Greene, *The Dialectic of Freedom,* p. 130.

Chapter 9

1. *The State of America's Children 1991,* pp. 60, 59, 63, 93. It is significant that findings from the study on teenage pregnancy in industrialized countries sponsored by the Alan Guttemacher Institute indicate that the United States is the only one of six countries (Canada, England and Wales, France, Netherlands, Sweden) in which the incidence of pregnancy has increased over time. U.S. birthrates are higher at every age for teenagers (particularly the youngest) and by a considerable margin. The Netherlands, described as the "perfect contraceptive population," has the lowest rates of birth, abortion, and pregnancy among teenagers—achieved in little more than three decades through intensive public educational/public health services with both contraception and abortion widely available. Sweden has the next lowest rates. Elise F. Jones and others, *Teenage Pregnancy in Industrialized Countries* (New Haven and London: Yale University Press, 1986).

2. See *The State of America's Children 1991,* pp. 110–11. The poverty statistics cited in this chapter and elsewhere in the book are the most accurate available as of January 1992.

3. The figures are controversial. The National Coalition for the Homeless disputes the estimates of the U.S. Government Accounting Office, which places the number of children homeless on a nightly basis at 68,000. The National Academy of Sciences places the number at 100,000. Cited in *The State of America's Children 1991,* pp. 109–10.

4. Paulo Freire discusses "praxis" as the embodiment of both critical reflection and action in order to transform the structures of oppression and domination. See his *Pedagogy of the Oppressed,* chap. 4.

5. Harrington, *The Other America,* p. 17.

6. Pearce, "Welfare Is Not *for* Women.

7. William Julius Wilson, *The Truly Disadvantaged: The Inner City, the Underclass, and Public Policy* (Chicago: University of Chicago Press, 1987).

8. See Pearce, "Welfare Is Not *for* Women," and L. Gordon, "The New Feminist Scholarship on the Welfare State," both in L. Gordon, ed., *Women, the State, and Welfare.*

9. Sheila Kamerman, "Maternity, Paternity, and Parenting Policies," in Sylvia A. Hewlett, Alice S. Ilchman, and John J. Sweeney, eds., *Family and Work: Bridging the Gap* (Cambridge, MA: Ballinger Publishing Co., 1986), pp. 60–62.

10. Ibid.

11. Children's Defense Fund, *The State of America's Children 1991,* p. 15.

12. Ibid., pp. 39–40.

13. See the articles in *Early Schooling: The National Debate,* ed. Sharon L. Kagan and Edward F. Zigler; *Developmentally Appropriate Practice in Early*

Childhood Programs Serving Children From Birth Through Age 8 (expanded edition), ed. Sue Bredekamp (Washington: NAEYC, 1991).

14. Children's Defense Fund, *The State of America's Children 1991*, pp. 39–41.

15. Ibid., pp. 42–43.

16. See the report on childhood poverty in Michigan by Joan M. Abbey, Analisa Vestevich, and Ira M. Schwartz, *Michigan's Children Went Missing* (University of Michigan, Prepublication Copy, August 1991), pp. 18–19.

17. *Family Policy Panel of the Economic Policy Council (EPC) of UN/USA Work and Family in the United States: A Policy Initiative* (New York: United Nations Association, 1985). See also David Orsini, "Family Day Care in Denmark: A Model for the United States," *Young Children*, July 1991.

18. See Sheila Kamerman, "Women, Children, and Poverty: Public Policies and Female-Headed Families in Industrialized Countries," in *Women and Poverty*, ed. Barbara C. Gelphi and Nancy M. Hartsock, and others (Chicago: University of Chicago Press, 1986), pp. 41–63. See also Sheila Kamerman and Alfred J. Kahn, *Child Care, Family Benefits, and Working Parents* (New York: Columbia University Press, 1981).

19. Ibid.

20. For a full discussion of the commission's recommendations, see *Beyond Rhetoric: A New American Agenda for Children and Families*, Final report of the National Commission on Children (Washington, 1991). See particularly chap. 5.

21. Unpublished data obtained from personal communication with Jill Foley, Research Analyst, Employee Benefit Research Institute, Washington, December 1991. These data are based on the March 1991 *Current Population Survey* of the Census Bureau.

22. Quoted in the article "Federal Panel Proposes Tax Credit of $1000 for each Child in the U.S.," *New York Times*, June 25, 1991.

23. See Joan M. Abbey and others, *Michigan's Children Went Missing* pp. 2, 13–15; and Children's Defense Fund, *State and City Child Poverty Data from the 1990 Census* (Washington, 1992).

24. See the op-ed article "War on Poverty, War on Women," *New York Times*, August 3, 1991.

25. Jean-Paul Sartre, *Search for a Method* (New York: Vintage Books, 1968), p. 18.

26. See Walter Benjamin, "The Storyteller," in *Illuminations*, ed. Hannah Arendt (New York: Schocken Books, 1969), p. 83.

27. Greene, *The Dialectic of Freedom*, p. 86.

28. Albert Camus, *The Plague*, p. 236.

Afterword

1. Jonathan Kozol, *Savage Inequalities: Children in America's Schools* (New York: Crown, 1991).

2. Unpublished data obtained from personal communication with Jill Foley, Research Analyst, Employee Benefit Research Institute, Washington, DC, December 1991. These data are based on the March 1991 *Current Population Survey* of the Census Bureau.

3. See the Carnegie Foundation Report, *Ready to Learn: A Mandate for the Nation* (Princeton, NJ: Princeton University Press, Embargoed for Release Dec. 8, 1991), p. 160.

4. *American Journal of Diseases in Children*, September 1990.

5. See Lisebeth Schorr, *Within Our Reach*, and the Carnegie Foundation Report, *Ready to Learn*, for a discussion of programs that have been successful in different communities.

6. For a full discussion of affordable housing policy alternatives, see Greg Barak, *Gimme Shelter: A Social History of Homelessness in Contemporary America* (New York: Praeger, 1991), chap. 8.

7. Ibid., p. 153.

8. See the op-ed article, "Cost-effective Compassion," *New York Times*, December 28, 1991.

9. See *Beyond Rhetoric: A New American Agenda*.

10. See Carnegie, *Ready to Learn*.

11. For a discussion of corporate involvement in child care and the mere 1,200 employers nationwide (including 200 corporations) who provide on- or near-site child care, see Ellen Galinsky, "The Private Sector as a Partner in Early Care and Education," in S. L. Kagan, *The Care and Education of America's Young Children*.

12. Lombardi, "Head Start: The Nation's Pride," p. 26.

13. See the discussion in Gwen Morgan, "Regulating Early Childhood Programs: Five Policy Issues," in S. L. Kagan, *The Care and Education of America's Young Children*.

14. *Beyond Rhetoric: A New American Agenda*.

15. Kozol, *Savage Inequalities*, p. 41.

16. See Francis Fox Piven and Richard A. Cloward, *Poor People's Movements: How They Succeed and Why They Fail* (New Orleans: Pantheon, 1977).

17. Francis Fox Piven, "Ideology and the State: Women, Power and the Welfare State," in L. Gordon, ed., *Women, the State, and Welfare*.

Appendix

1. Ton Beekman, "Human Science as Dialogue with Children," *Phenomenology and Pedagogy* 1983 (1); Ton Beekman and Karel Mulderij, *Beleving and Ervaring* (Amsterdam: Boom, Meppel, 1978).

2. Jules Henry, *Pathways to Madness* (New York: Vintage, 1973); Clifford Geertz, *The Interpretation of Cultures* (New York: Basic Books, 1973) and *Local Knowledge* (New York: Basic Books, 1983); Robert Coles, *Women of Crisis I: Lives of Struggle and Hope* (with Jane Coles) (New York: Delta Seymour L. Lawrence, 1978); Patricia Carini, *The School Lives of Seven Children: A Five Year Study* (Grand Fords, ND: University of North Dakota Press, 1982); Sara Lightfoot Lawrence, *The Good High School* (New York: Basic Books, 1983).

3. Valerie Polakow, *The Erosion of Childhood* (Chicago: University of Chicago Press, 1982; new ed., 1992).

4. Walter Benjamin, *Illuminations*, ed. Hannah Arendt (New York: Schocken, 1969).